ABOUT THIS BOOK

Health service delivery is being restructured in many different ways in both the industrialised and developing countries. As the public health scholars and policy makers in this volume show, this process is set to accelerate worldwide as a result of diverse factors including fiscal pressure on welfare provision, privatisation of infrastructure, and the impending renegotiation of the WTO General Agreement on Trade in Services (GATS). The key policy issues that arise concern the implications of these changes for access and equity in public health provision, both of which look likely to be negatively affected.

The research in this volume, which has been supported by the European Commission, reviews the rapidly changing context in which financing health care and its relationship to globalization and privatisation are taking place. It examines the specific mechanisms and institutional processes involved. And it explores the contrasting experiences in four very different regions. These include:

- The USA where the creed of market competition and managed care in the health sector is most advanced and where, despite soaring costs, reduced public provision and popular disillusion with HMOs, major reform in the interests of access and affordability remains blocked.
- Western Europe where social health insurance reforms aimed at market competition and freedom of choice are taking place at the expense of deteriorating quality, equity and universality of provision.
- Developing countries where a varying mix of pressures arising out of structural adjustment policies, among other factors, is dramatically reducing the role of the state in healthcare delivery.
- Cuba where the remarkable gains of a generation of socialist health care delivery have come under pressure since 1989, but which shows what continuing political commitment to public health can achieve even when resources available are falling.

The up-to-date policy-relevant analysis and empirical investigation in this volume, including the UK's National Health Service, ought to be of great use to scholars, postgraduate students and policy makers.

ABOUT THE AUTHOR

Dr Kasturi Sen was born in Calcutta, India, but moved to the UK during her teens in 1971. She is currently at the Institute of Public Health, Department of Public Health, University of Cambridge. She has been involved in international public health research and teaching for the past twenty years. Her particular interests are in comparative health systems research with a focus on health policy and planning. She has coordinated several multi-centre studies for the European Commission, in the Middle East and in South Asia. She lives in Oxford with her son.

Restructuring Health Services

Changing contexts and comparative perspectives

EDITED BY KASTURI SEN

Zed Books

LONDON · NEW YORK

Funded by the European Commission,
DG Research, International Co-operation,
Research for Development

Restructuring Health Services: Changing contexts and comparative perspectives was first published by Zed Books Ltd, 7 Cynthia Street, London N1 9JF, UK and Room 400, 175 Fifth Avenue, New York, NY 10010, USA in 2003, in association with the European Commission, DG Research, International Co-operation, Research for Development.

www.zedbooks.demon.co.uk

Cover designed by Andrew Corbett
Set in Monotype Fournier by Ewan Smith, London
Printed and bound in the United Kingdom
by Biddles Ltd, www.biddles.co.uk

Distributed in the USA exclusively by Palgrave, a division of
St Martin's Press, LLC, 175 Fifth Avenue, New York, NY 10010

A catalogue record for this book is available from the British Library.

US CIP data is available from the Library of Congress.

ISBN 1 84277 288 0 cased
ISBN 1 84277 289 9 limp

362.1
Res

Contents

Tables

Acknowledgements

The meeting on 'The Restructuring of Health Services' and its follow-up in the form of this book happened with the support of the INCO–DEV Programme of the European Commission. The Commission has in recent years played an important role in bringing together practitioners and scholars of public health from both developing and developed countries and in many different forums for exchanging information and ideas about changes taking place in public health systems throughout the world. I am thankful for their support, in particular that of their Scientific Officer, Dr Anna Karaoglou, whose enthusiasm for this project has been a great source of encouragement. Professor Hans Maarse of the University of Maastricht's Faculty of Health Sciences has been a willing and supportive partner despite the additional demands upon his time through this collaboration.

The Research Grants Division of the University of Cambridge provided help with the management of funds. On technical matters, I would like to thank Brenda McWilliams for copy-editing and Indira Chakravarti for providing invaluable editorial assistance and moral support throughout the months of editing and preparing the text. I would also like to thank Andi Reiss for the cover design and most of all I would like to thank all the participants for so willingly relinquishing valuable time to participate at the meeting and also for their efforts in producing chapters for this book. Thanks also to Zed Books, in particular Robert Molteno and the editorial team, for support and encouragement. However despite support from this large group of people, any errors in the volume are entirely my responsibility and cannot be attributed to any other party involved and the views expressed are those of the authors and the editor alone.

Kasturi Sen, Cambridge

Acronyms and Abbreviations

AIDS	acquired immune deficiency syndrome
AIHS	Academy of International Health Studies
APHM	Association of Private Hospitals of Malaysia
APLA	Andhra Pradesh Legislative Assembly
AP	Andhra Pradesh
CAT	computerised axial tomography
CESS	Centre for Economic and Social Studies
CPS	Centre for Public Services
CSMBS	Civil Servant Medical Benefit Scheme
DALE	Disability-Adjusted Life Expectancy
DBFO	design, build, finance and operate
DOTS	Directly Observed Therapy – Short Course
DRG	diagnostic related group
DTI	Department of Trade and Industry
ECJ	European Court of Justice
ECUs	Euro
EFPIA	European Federation of Pharmaceutical Industry Associations
EHCMA	European Health Care Management Association
ESF	European Services Forum
EMU	European Monetary Union
ESIS	Employees' State Insurance Scheme
EU	European Union
EWC	European Works Council
FADSP	Federación de Asociaciones para la Defensa de la Sanidad Pública
FFI	Fairness in Financial Contribution
FIOCRUZ	Fundación Institucional Oswaldo Cruz
FMRAI	Federation of Medical Representatives Association of India
GATS	General Agreement on Trade in Services
GDP	gross domestic product
GHO	Galician Health Ordination Bill
GOI	Government of India

HIAA	Health Insurance Association of America
HMOs	health maintenance organisations
IAHP	International Association of Health Policy
ICSSR	Indian Council for Social Science Research
ICMR	Indian Council for Medical Research
IFC	International Finance Corporation
IIPS	International Institute of Population Studies
IMF	International Monetary Fund
IRAP	Imposta Regionale sulle attività produttive
IRPEF	Imposta Regionale sulle persone fisiche
ISP	Internal Stability Pact
LEA	Livelli Essenziali di Assistenza
LOTIS	liberalisation of trade in services
MIGA	Multilateral Investment Guarantee Agency
MNCs	multi-national companies
MEDTEC	Galician Institute for Technical Medicine
MOPH	Ministry of Public Health
MRI	magnetic resonance imaging
MSA	medical savings account
MUFACE	Mutualidad General de Funcionarios Civiles del Estado
NAFTA	North Atlantic Free Trade Agreement
NCHS	National Commission on Health Security
NESDB	National Economic and Social Development Board
NFHS	National Family Health Research
NHFA	National Health Financing Authority
NHIA	National Health Insurance Act
NGOs	non-governmental organisations
NHF	National Health Care Fund
NHS	National Health Service
NSO	National Statistical Office
OECD	Organisation for Economic Co-operation and Development
PAHO	Pan American Health Organisation
PFI	Private Finance Initiative
PHC	Primary Health Care
PLI	Iniciativa Legislativa Popular
PNHSD	Plataformas para la Defensa y Mejora de la Sanidad Pública
PPPs	public–private partnerships
PSI	Public Services International

PSIRU	Public Services International Research Unit
SAPs	structural adjustment programmes
SDP	state domestic product
SERGAS	Galician Health Service
SSN	Servizio Sanitario Nazionale
SSS	Social Security Scheme
TNCs	trans-national corporations
TRIPs	Trade-Related Intellectual Property Rights
UNICEF	United Nations Children's Fund
UNDP	United Nations Development Programme
USCSI	United States Coalition of Service Industries
USTR	United States Trade Representative
VHAI	Voluntary Health Association of India
VHCS	Voluntary Health Card Scheme
WDR	World Development Report
WHO	World Health Organisation
WHR	World Health Report
WTO	World Trade Organisation
WCS	Workmen's Compensation Scheme

Preface

The European Commission funded a meeting in Maastricht, The Netherlands, in July 2001, to evaluate experiences of the restructuring of health services world-wide. The aim of the meeting was to bring together scholars and practitioners working in the field of healthcare to compare and contrast experiences of restructuring in different regions. The meeting was intended to explore the comparative dimensions of the restructuring of health services in south Asia and Europe, taking into account the socio-economic, political and historical contexts. We aimed at assessing the explanatory models that have acted as the ideological rationale for the current shifts in the reorganisation and financing of healthcare. Examples of health service reforms in the USA and Cuba were also included for their relevance and pertinence.

For Europe and south Asia we aimed to explore the impact of reforms upon policy-making at national level to changes in the health sector, in particular the restructuring of health services and the privatisation of health services provision. We wanted especially to consider the implications for equity and access to changes in public health provision.

Finally we wanted also to explore also the possibilities of creating a network of scientists among and between the regions represented at the meeting, to continue to share and exchange ideas about the globalisation of public health policy and practice in the twenty-first century.

This collection is therefore the combined experiences of public health scholars, physicians, researchers and policy-makers from different regions of the world affected by the reorganisation of health services on a global scale. It shows how varied historical and socio-political circumstances are brought together by very similar mechanisms and processes of changes, as with the finance, organisation and delivery of healthcare. This collection is unique since few previous attempts have been made to assess the effects of two decades of privatisation on the ability to deliver health care through a public provider and the implications for citizenship.

Kasturi Sen, Cambridge

CHAPTER I

Introduction: Restructuring Health Services – Public Subsidy of Private Provision

KASTURI SEN

GLOBALISATION AND TRANSFORMATIONS IN THE HEALTH SECTOR

In the aftermath of the Second World War the general consensus in Europe as well as in the newly independent states of Africa and Asia was in favour of a planned economic transition to development with what may be described as a liberal welfarist approach (Qadeer et al. 2001). In the health sector of developing countries, the aim was to create universal provision by supporting and extending primary healthcare, especially in the rural areas, where the majority of the population continued to reside. However, this vision was to be short-lived in much of the developing world and, more recently, has been subject to re-organisation and restructuring in the western world.

The energy crisis of the 1970s set in motion reforms of the economy and society that overturned the planned expansion of welfare and in its stead brought restrictive monetary policies. The falling prices of goods and the subsequent reductions in export taxes and revenues sounded the death-knell of public provision as well as any planned expansion in many of these economies, already historically vulnerable with high levels of poverty and unemployment. Rising interest rates on the world market brought economic havoc and set the stage for economic reforms in the form of loans from the International Monetary Fund. However, the loans were conditional upon cuts to public expenditure and a total overhaul of public sector provision. Different countries were affected at different periods and with varied measures, but most were forced to restructure the finance of public provision. Debates about the consequences of such reforms continue among policy-makers and researchers, while the real costs are experienced by the populace at large.

The first region to be affected by the new economic policies was Latin America in the late 1970s; it was followed by the African economies and, during the late 1980s and early 1990s, much of Asia. All experienced policies of structural adjustment which were to transform the health and social sectors. Similarly, during the 1980s, the OECD countries also reassessed their commitment to public sector provision as part of an ideological shift from welfare to markets. This was reflected in stringent fiscal policies, the creation of internal markets within the health sector and other services, and plans also to decentralise government and overall service provision. The declared rationale behind these policies was an economic one but it was also claimed that markets would provide more consumer choice. The reality, as will be revealed in several chapters in this book, has been rather different. Within a decade, certainly in the health sector, the picture is one of spiralling costs and reduced quality of provision (Sen and Koivusalo 1998).

In Europe, most governments had opened up their services to market competition by the early 1980s. These included telecommunications, utilities (water, gas and electricity), transport (buses, railways) and housing (new build) as well as elements of public services such as street lighting and hospital security, portering, laundry and catering. The country with the earliest and most advanced privatisation programmes in Western Europe was the United Kingdom. According to some observers, the UK took the lead in this process because it had the closest association with multinationals and deregulation was well advanced in the years of Conservative rule (1979–97). The UK also has a particularly close political, economic and cultural relationship with the United States, whose ideological role in promoting markets over state should not be underestimated.

Thus, the rapid transformation of state over markets at the global level has been linked to a decline in profits from manufacturing industries and a parallel search for profits from other sectors of the economy. This led to the targeting of the services sector for privatisation and more rapid global integration than at any other time. The process was facilitated by advances in information technology as well as in the nature of the accumulation process. Drache and Sullivan (1999) suggest that, even up to the 1980s, the notion that a publicly financed healthcare system would be competing with the private sector was largely unthinkable. By the early 1990s, governments everywhere were rapidly redrawing the boundaries between public and private in order to offload from the public purse the financial responsibility for providing services, in favour of market-led polices and provision. However, such transformations, in our view, are not simply premised upon a shortage of funds or an overstretching of the public purse, although this has been the proclaimed rationale.

The current process of globalisation through privatisation and expansion of corporate entities and market-led activities has been accelerating over the past decade. Globalisation in this mode may be described as a form of internationalisation that is responding to the specific needs of the expansion of capital in seeking new forms of investment for profit in the public sector.

Thus, international healthcare reforms are integral in a wider global agenda that is opening trade and creating markets in public services. Some have described it as a new era of privatisation that has witnessed, in some cases, the dismantling of nationalised industries (as in the UK) and the part-privatisation of others, leaving open to transformation the core of welfare provision. This would include health, education and social services, which have been under pressure for the past two decades due to the emergence of a new form of capital accumulation that depends to a large degree upon international investments and transfers, thereby creating major distortion/discrepancies in national income and revenues, premised upon personal taxation, and the main source of income for the nation-state.

In Western Europe, retrenchment within the public sector has been compounded by demographic changes, wherein steady increases in life expectancy, paralleled by a stable and in some cases falling fertility rate, has added to the growth of an ageing population. There is thus an additional discrepancy between the numbers of those actively employed and those in retirement, so increasing dependency ratios. The ageing of the population in Western Europe at large is also having an important impact upon the cost of health and social services because healthcare costs increase exponentially with age (Sen 1996; Poulder et al. 2002)

The dependency ratio has been compounded by the technological revolution that has inflated the numbers of unemployed people among the adult working population, thus reducing income-generating capacity which, in turn, has had an impact upon profit levels. This demographic and economic context has been worsened by the restructuring of economies through neo-liberal policy measures first implemented in the late 1970s; these have reduced levels of personal taxation and promoted minimalist state intervention. Their long-term effects may be seriously damaging for the welfarist tradition in Europe, since some authors argue that the political and cultural repercussions of denting the traditions of social solidarity, particularly among health professionals, are difficult to repair (Mackintosh 1995).

Thus, the globalisation of commerce, investment and finance has reduced the income-generating potential of the nation-state to appropriate surplus from labour, and has shifted the basis of capital accumulation from a national to an international arena. As a result, the power of national governments to make decisions about their economies based upon national interests is substantially undermined, and trans-national corporations play an increasing role in governance and economic strategy. For example, European nations have had planned welfare provision for the past several decades, based upon principles of universality and solidarity, and underpinned by risk-pooling and risk-sharing; their ability to implement these long-established principles as policy measures is premised upon not treating public services as commodities whose existence depends entirely upon the rate of profit. However, legislation emerging out of the World Trade Organisation (WTO), and in particular the General Agreement on Trade in Services (GATS), has meant that, unless otherwise specified, the majority of public services must be prepared for tender, or must be organised in such a manner as to be least trade restrictive (Price et al. 1999).

In the developing world, the situation is more critical since the nascent welfare states that emerged in the 1950s and 1960s appear to be retreating into a state of neo-colonial dependency. This is illustrated by the way in which countries succumb through neo-liberal policies to the needs of multinational corporations (MNCs); some suggest that this is due to the fact that the budgets of the latter often far exceed the national incomes of many countries in the developing world (Renaud 1998). There may be a trade-off and, inevitably, an impact upon policy-making at the national level (when lobbying is effective), which determines the rules that govern policy and practice in trade and in the service sectors in individual countries.

While most countries, whether in the developing world or not, are prone to MNC pressures, the former are especially vulnerable owing to the fragility of political institutions and regulatory frameworks. In addition, low-cost labour makes much of the developing world vulnerable to predatory investment, which in turn is protected by multinational regulations. The establishment of the World Trade Organisation with its legally binding arrangements, most notably the GATS, is also testimony to this process.

The globalisation of commerce, investments and finance has thus become a major force behind the setting of public policies including, and especially, in the health sector. The most significant means of such consolidation has been the establishment of the World Trade Organisation in 1995. This organisation acts as the main platform from which national governments as well as trans-national corporations (TNCs) can trade in the newly established markets of the service sector. The General Agreement on Trade in Services is an integral part of the WTO arrangements and to date covers some 160 services, including health, education, public utilities (gas, electricity, water), social welfare, financial services and transport. GATS encourages trade across borders and requires countries signed up to the WTO to treat all countries and traders in the same way.

Hence the liberalisation of trade in this mode is premised upon two main principles: first, the most favoured nations, whereby countries are allowed the same treatment; and, second, the national treatment factor whereby foreign companies must be treated in the same way as national firms. In effect, this rules out protection or the provision of subsidies to national entities (import substitution) undertaken in the post-war period by the newly independent and mainly developing countries in order to iron out some of their disadvantages and encourage the process of national capital accumulation.

According to Whitfield (2001) and others (Corner House 2001), the emergence of GATS poses the greatest threat to public provision in recent times, not only because services under these criteria have a broad remit but also because GATS can specifically target those with any privatised elements (Whitfield 2001). Since most public services in both the developing and the developed world do have some element of privatisation (owing to the preceding decades of liberalisation), then most of these are vulnerable to being taken over, possibly by more 'advanced' foreign firms.

Following two decades of intervention in public services under structural adjustment programmes (SAPs), and as part and parcel of the need to expand the profit-making base for capital, there are major consequences for populations worldwide, but most notably in the developing world. Here the ruling elites in tandem with international capital have benefited greatly from the new opportunities opening in the public sector (Qadeer et al. 2001), but there has also been a concomitant rise in inequalities in both the health and social sectors. In some cases this has had an impact upon the infant mortality rate, which rose in the

1990s for the first time in over a decade in parts of Africa; in India and China a steady decline has been halted. Overall reports from Africa, Asia and Latin America warn of negative consequences of SAPs for the population at large (Sen and Koivusalo 1998; Hsiao 1995; Navarro 1998; Renaud 1998).

The rise in social inequality over the past two decades is one effect of the monetary polices advocated by SAPs and it applies to both developing and developed countries. The rise may be attributable to three main factors. First and foremost it is evident that since the late 1970s there has been an unprecedented growth in wealth and incomes derived from capital rather than from labour. Second, this has led to a major polarisation of wages and consequent wage dispersion. Third, the most serious factor has been the diminishing role of the state and especially of the welfare state where it existed as an agency for the redistribution of risks and resources. This has been compounded by the dismantling of public infrastructure, notably in the least developed countries (Navarro 1998; Whitfield 2001).

This book has arrived at an opportune moment; allowing scholars from different regions of the world – most notably south Asia and Europe – to compare and contrast their experiences of globalisation in the health sector. In particular, they are concerned with the restructuring of services and the effects upon finance of public provision. There are two major contributions to this book in which the contradictions contained within the cost-effectiveness approach are highlighted. The first is in relation to the United States (Woolhandler, Chapter 12) where health services are dominated by health maintenance organisations and private providers. Not only are the administrative costs high but also choices are limited and quality is not assured since health need is determined by cost and profit margins for shareholders. In Cuba on the other hand, the per capita costs are much lower and, although the choices for the type of care available are limited, the system delivers universal coverage with among the best health indicators in the world (Sansó-Soberats, Chapter 13). The implications of the US system of managed care, particularly upon access to healthcare and to health outcomes, is a core element of comparison in this book, since the US model (of private providers in healthcare) is the one advocated by major donor agencies supporting the process of restructuring.

This book thus reflects the cumulative experiences of scholars and public health practitioners from different regions of the world in dealing with the restructuring of health services; it also looks at the financial mechanisms involved in transforming those services. There are fifteen chapters in all, divided into three sections. The first section is concerned with concepts and the legislative background to the transformation in the social sector; the second is concerned with the process of change which evaluates methods and their outcomes; and the third and final section provides the reader with country case studies of globalisation and restructuring of the health sector, mainly from south Asia and Europe as well as the United States and Cuba.

PART ONE: CONCEPTUAL AND LEGISLATIVE FRAMEWORK

Part One is concerned with the conceptual and legislative framework and opens with a global review of reforms of the health sector by the editor. This chapter discusses the changes in the health sector in both developed and developing countries from a historical perspective. It examines the role of the state as a provider in different regions: universal coverage continues to be provided in some parts of Western Europe, while only fledgling welfare provision exists in the majority of the developing world. It explores how, under the reform programme, coverage is being rapidly transformed in both regions.

The key element is the difference between the two regions. For example, whereas in Europe the restructuring of services has involved the privatisation of parts of provision, overall the state has maintained responsibility as the provider. In developing countries, on the other hand, the restructuring process has been much more dramatic. Here public services are being replaced by the private sector, including the entry of TNCs and MNCs, with the state often maintaining a cursory role as provider (see Chapter 14 by Chee Khoon and Chapter 16 by Narayana).

One of the major concerns, one which applies to both regions, is the emergence of a new phenomenon integral to the process of restructuring; this involves the active intervention of the state to facilitate the process of privatisation and restructuring through the provision of tax benefits and concessions to the private sector. In effect, this provides a subsidy from public to private sectors for the takeover of public provision. Numerous examples are provided in this volume to show that the corporatisation of public health provision is in effect a major subsidy from public to private sector. This undermines to a large degree the rationale of the transition (from public to private) as a bid to improve the efficiency and competitiveness of public services. It also reinforces the argument that without such gains and subsidies the process of accumulation would not be so attractive, and public services would not be so profitable for corporate entities.

The outcome is that all-powerful corporate monopolies are created which, in some cases in the developing world in particular, can exceed many of the political and legislative powers traditionally held by the nation-state. Chapter 2 provides an overview of the whole reform process and sets the scene for the remainder of the book

Chapter 3 by Sarah Sexton, 'Trading Healthcare Away', provides a detailed explanation of the General Agreement on Trade in Services (GATS) which has been established under the aegis of the WTO in order to increase international trade in services. It outlines the main provision of GATS, its legal constituents and its power to overrule any national legislation to provide national services. Sexton suggests that while for some countries it may be necessary to have the security of regulations governing trade between corporations and national govern-ments, it is difficult to maintain a balance between national and global entities. For example, some of the legislation on procurement remains ambiguous and could be interpreted in favour of the most powerful entity, given the inequality in the distribution of power and resources.

The most important point made in this chapter and one that is relevant to the whole book is the fact that GATS makes irreversible the provision of public services by a private provider once the transition has taken place and that service has entered the global arena. Sexton shows that the first steps of this process are changes made to the accounting system of a particular service, described as the process of coporatisation or devolved financial management. Thus a revised GATS could give the for-profit sector the power to make privatisation irreversible.

Chapter 4 in this section is authored by Imrana Qadeer. It examines the transformation in concepts of healthcare over the past two decades, which, according to the author, appear to have undermined the funda-mental ethics of medical care. The chapter considers four dimensions of medical care that have been traditionally influenced by values and ethics: first, the issue of access to medical care for the relief of individual suffering; second, medical care as an instrument of disease control; third, the volume of medical care; and fourth, the sources of healthcare financing. Within each of these sections the author examines the im-plications for access and equity and the right to health. Drawing upon the experience of India, Qadeer suggests that in the drive to expand medical markets there has been a conscious effort among donors and health planners to retain so-called ethical guidelines as slogans only, while some of the fundamental principles of universal provision are overturned. This is being undertaken through the creation of markets and the packaging of health services as a commodity for customers, as opposed to their development premised upon patient need. Qadeer argues that the validity of this assumption and the actions that have been derived from it need to be recognised and acted upon before it is too late to save most of the historical gains in public health and development from dismemberment.

PART TWO: THE PROCESS OF CHANGE

The second section of the book focuses on the process of change. In the opening chapter, Claudia Travassos, who works in a leading Brazilian public health research institute, considers the methodological issues involved in the collection of evidence to make policy, particularly global health policy. It involves a critique of the methods contained within the *World Health Report 2000* (WHR 2000) which was directed at measuring the performance of health systems of member states (of the WHO) and was intended to be applied annually.

The WHR 2000 is a seminal document since its focus on summary measures and the composite index is intended as a formula for supplying quality essential services, defined mainly by cost-effectiveness criteria, to the population as a whole. Composite measures such as these and composite indices have been advocated by the World Bank since the early 1990s when the concept of 'Disease Burden' was introduced (World Bank 1993). Despite the controversy, which focused on the unreliability of data and the flawed nature of the concept in terms of cross-cultural validity among other factors (Sen and Bonita 2000), the World Health Organisation appears to have fallen prey to the strong arm of the World Bank in undertaking a similar task in 2000.

Travassos is part of a Brazilian team (FIOCRUZ) which has undertaken the task of systematically dismantling the concepts enshrined in the report to show that its underlying ideas are flawed and will therefore not be able to assess the effectiveness of healthcare policies. This includes primary healthcare, and the Alma Ata Declaration of 1978. The WHR 2000 is a sustained attack on the principles of risk-pooling and redistribution and attempts to substitute them with market-oriented healthcare systems. While the chapter calls for a wide-ranging critique of the methodology of the WHR 2000, it is evident that composite indices do not and cannot capture the meaning of health, ill-health or well-being.

The issue of terms and conditions of employment and their effects upon the workforce is the focus of the next chapter. David Hall's chapter on privatisation, globalisation and health workers shows that globalisation and the growth of multinationals over the past decade have induced workers in all sectors to develop international links in order to deal with a common employer in the form of multinational or transnational corporations. Hall argues that public service workers face the contradictory task of domestically challenging the process of privatisation and at the same time being forced to utilise the tools of globalisation to forge links with those workers who are also trying to cope with the process of trans-nationalisation. Hall suggests that the introduction of privatisation is instigated primarily at the national level, despite the international pressures, financial and economic crises. He reiterates that it is essential to be mindful of the complexities of the linkages and dynamics between the national and the global, and of their effects not only upon terms and conditions of work but also upon the health and well-being of workers. In the ongoing debates over globalisation, this chapter is one of few which illustrate the ad hoc rather than systematic nature of global takeovers and mergers, as well as their inherent weaknesses. It shows through careful documentation that the accumulation of capital is beset by irrationality and instability.

In Chapter 7, Meri Koivusalo explores the effects of privatisation and globalisation upon the principles of solidarity and universal coverage which have been distinctive goals in the organisation and functioning of European welfare systems. Koivusalo argues that these values are increasingly under threat as a result of the linear quest for 'effectiveness' and competition embodied within the new economic policies of European Community law. This chapter highlights dilemmas over the principles of subsidiarity; it also provides evidence of an absence of coherence in European policy-making as a result of a lack of integration in the policy-making process and considers the detrimental effect this has on health policy-making primarily in the European Union but equally important at the level of the nation-state. In particular, this chapter highlights the contradiction between national decision-making processes over health and social policy-making and the legitimacy of legal principles at the level of the European Community.

PART THREE: CASE STUDIES OF RESTRUCTURING –
COMPARATIVE PERSPECTIVES

Belgium, the Netherlands, Switzerland, Germany There are nine
chapters in this section, drawing out comparisons in the process of
restructuring in different socio-economic and socio-political contexts.
The opening chapter by Hans Maarse and Aggie Paulus, on the impact
of social health insurance reform upon solidarity, considers the reforms
of social health insurance in Belgium, Germany, Switzerland and the
Netherlands. Empirical research in these countries found varying degrees
of restructuring of health insurance schemes under the aegis of healthcare reform. However, in each, the role of statutory insurance cover has
remained the dominant mode of healthcare financing. Changes which
had been introduced in the 1990s through reform included changes to
benefit packages, priority setting, increasing of private payments as well
as changes in the relationship between insurer and provider.

The authors make a distinction between risk solidarity and income
solidarity: while the former has an emphasis on redistribution, the latter
places greater emphasis upon ability to pay. Moreover, the degree to
which each dimension experiences changes has varied between countries.
Their distinguishing feature is that most changes taking place have done
so under regulation by the state. In this context, the results appear to
suggest that health insurance reforms have not in these cases increased
the burden of payments from rich to poor. The tentative conclusions
suggest that reforms are determined by context (the degree and type of
interventions made) and cannot always be described as negative for the
process of equity. However, the authors claim that while to date there
has been no major dent upon the principles of solidarity and risk distribution, this may not hold for the future due to increasing pressures
for more drastic changes towards privatisation. They suggest that the
situation is likely to be compounded by demographic transition in
Europe, as well as advances in genetic medicine which will push further
in the direction of risk individuation.

Italy The second case study (Chapter 9) on the restructuring of health
services in Italy considers the paradox of devolution. Francesco Taroni
explores the strategies of devolution contained within the reform process
and argues that the decentralisation of health services, ranging from the
simple delegation of administrative responsibilities to the wholesale
devolution of political and fiscal responsibilities, has been the focus of

health sector reforms in Italy, and that these changes are proving to be fundamentally iniquitous. This contrasts sharply with the perception of devolution as being politically appropriate for bringing services to the people (through localisation), as offering greater efficiency (local management of resources) as well as increased accountability in the functioning of public systems.

With evidence from a devolved region in Italy, Taroni assesses some of the contradictions involved and argues that while devolution is generally considered to be a qualitatively different as well as socially beneficial process, the outcomes are not dissimilar to those arising out of market-oriented reforms taking place elsewhere in the world. Inherent in the process of globalisation are incentives for privatisation that have negative long-term consequences for public provision and in particular for equity and for access.

UK   The third case study (Chapter 10) looks at the United Kingdom. Jean Shaoul explains the rise of neo-liberal policies in the context of globalisation, providing a succinct analysis of the UK reforms and their constituents, such as the introduction of financial targets in the public sector, quasi markets, creeping privatisation, public–private partnerships and the outsourcing of non-core services among others. Shaoul argues that big business needs public services to be cut back so as to reduce costs and remain internationally competitive in an era in which services have become a trade priority. This case study sets the local context within a global framework. It suggests that globalisation and the policy shifts that have accompanied it have already produced deep-seated social polarisation and inequality, which Shaoul claims is most glaringly visible in the UK. The core issue in this chapter is the question of whether all economic life should be run in the interests of the few seeking ever higher profits, instead of meeting the social and public needs of future generations.

Spain   M. Sanchez Bayle and Hixinio Beiras are physicians working in Galicia. Their chapter (11) provides us with a historical overview of reforms within the health sector in Spain and, more significantly, of the resistance to the reforms that has emerged from the successful struggles of health workers across the professional divide. The Spanish health system with its universal coverage has produced among the best health indicators in Western Europe. However, despite this evidence, the pressures of globalisation and the need to make the health service profitable have brought about major changes. These have involved the creation of hospital trusts, an increase in the outsourcing of a substantial component of public health services, encouraging the uptake of private insurance and placing restrictions on the purchase of some essential drugs and medicines. Bayle and Beiras show that current policies in Spain undermine the redistributive elements contained within the Spanish national health service and ultimately penalise sections of the population, such as elderly people, who are most vulnerable. As in other cases of reforms worldwide, the Spanish case reveals that public subsidy appears to be intrinsic to the current phase of corporate privatisation.

The authors show that there is growing and widespread opposition channelled through the People's Legislative Initiative, which has successfully managed to publicise and raise awareness of the implications of privatising public provision in Galicia. The authors argue that the wider public, and most notably workers within the health sector, actively opposed the current dismantling of public provision. On the basis of the success of public opposition in Galicia, they claim that the privatisation of public provision is not inevitable.

The United States Chapter 12 is an important case study of the US healthcare system. The predominance of the market model makes it of considerable interest to the rest of the world. The US model of healthcare provision serves as a linchpin of laissez-faire zealotry for improving the efficiency of the public sector. Under the current reform programmes worldwide, however, there has been little discussion of what this might mean for access and for the quality of care, or whether in advocating efficiency it is reasonable to compare the two sectors operating under very different criteria (public versus private). In order to improve the functioning of public provision, does it really need to be replaced with such a radical alternative? Steffie Woolhandler's chapter lays bare the arguments in relation to the economic supremacy of the market model. It shows clearly that the predominance of the market in health services is a costly alternative that is likely to reduce access, undermine risk distribution and will not always deliver the quality of care that its proponents claim.

The statistics from this chapter speak for themselves and act as a vivid reminder to those advocating market-led healthcare for the developing world, in particular where inequality in relation to the distribution of risks and resources remains endemic and safety-nets are few and far between. This chapter also shows that making profits integral to the delivery of care undermines wholly the principle of universality. It shows that just across the border in Canada, universal provision has been feasible without costing the earth and that economic arguments against this remain largely spurious since they are driven, as Woolhandler suggests, entirely by a 'greed is good for business' ethic.

Cuba   In the next case study in this section (Chapter 13), Félix J. Sansó Soberats reveals a very different picture of reforms of the health system in Cuba. The significance of this chapter lies in the fact that Cuba has not been indebted to international donors, and the production and distribution of goods and services are controlled by the socialist state and are therefore beyond the realm of the global capitalist system and the dictates of neo-liberal reforms. The state in Cuba advocates primary healthcare and prevention, and is committed to universal provision. This chapter highlights the significance of a historical approach to understanding the health system as well as the struggles undertaken by the Cuban population to ensure basic health services, universally. The political dimension of the Cuban health system has served as an integral feature of its reform process.

For example, the main reforms undertaken are those intended to eradicate social and health inequalities together with changing lack of access and poor-quality healthcare left over from the pre-socialist era. The overall aim of reform in Cuba has been to establish instead a national health service accessible to all. A strong emphasis upon primary care and prevention, together with strengthening of the primary healthcare infrastructure, has enabled the state to achieve high life expectancy and low rates of infant mortality (Cuban Ministry of Public Health 2000).

While Cuba made progress through its political and social commitments to universalism, Soberats points out that most of its achievements were made despite the USA's harsh economic blockade. At times the blockade threatened to overturn the whole system and undermine basic health infrastructure. Despite such aggressive interference, this chapter shows how much progress may be achieved without the market-led paradigm in health services. It serves also to highlight the wastefulness and poor quality of market-led health services by comparison, especially with the USA.

Malaysia   The following case study (Chapter 14) assesses the political economy of healthcare reforms in Malaysia. Chan Chee Khoon underlines the impact of global transformation in welfare provision upon the health sector. He highlights the current global trend towards trade in services and relates this to over-capacity in production and under-consumption throughout the global economy. The decline of manufacturing industry worldwide leads capital to search endlessly for markets to ensure competitive advantage. This transformation at the global level links directly to the retrenchment of the welfare state with rising levels of unemployment compensation and demand for welfare. This is the context in which the Malaysian state is transforming its health sector.

For Chee Khoon, privatisation, most notably of public hospitals in Malaysia, signals the emergence of an indigenous bourgeoisie with continued and favoured access to state assets and privileges. This particular class is also increasingly associated with international business and the trans-national health industry, providing a valuable comparison with the dynamics of the Indian health sector.

Thailand The authors of Chapter 15 – Sanguann Nitayarumphong and Supasit Pannarunothai – are policy-makers from Thailand who provide us with a historical backdrop to the reforms of the health sector in Thailand over the past decade. This chapter offers interesting insights into attempts by developing country policy-makers to generate an autonomous path in the strategy for reform, in order to improve access and the quality of provision. Unlike other countries in the same region, Thailand appears to have attempted a monetarist strategy with the introduction of fee-paying market mechanisms into its health sector, but within a decade it was apparent that key performance indicators relating to access and quality had not altered. In some regions they had worsened with a concentration of resources (hospitals, doctors, beds), while in others there was little of worth.

The health sector in Thailand has also been a costly one since 'consumer choice' has meant the provision of costly hi-tech care that is accessible only to a small segment of the population. It is against this backdrop (that of the failure of the first round of reforms of the 1980s) that we have a fresh new approach which seeks to prioritise as well as raise the profile of the health sector and the changes to be undertaken from within.

The authors suggest that the east Asian economic crisis of 1999 provided the opportunity for the government to reassess its commitments and prioritise issues of access and equity in health service provision. Hence this chapter focuses on the technical dimensions of reforms such as mechanisms of payment and criteria for selection based upon comparable experiences elsewhere, in countries at similar levels of development.

India K.V. Narayana's study of the corporatisation of the health sector in Andhra Pradesh (AP) in India (Chapter 16) reveals the acceleration of private provision in healthcare. The chapter focuses in particular on the role of the state in facilitating this process. The analysis is based on a combination of data from national sample surveys as well as primary data collected by the author. The findings of the study are outlined and highlight the core theme of this book, that of the restructuring of the health sector whereby privatisation is helped by the public provider. The state of Andhra Pradesh was selected as a model by the World Bank for an experiment into the process of changing the status of public providers into private entities. While India has a legacy of private providers and high levels of out-of-pocket expenditure for healthcare, the experience of AP shows that this is now taking place at an accelerated rate. There are important considerations for access as well as the effect upon existing private provision which has consisted of small-scale providers such as general practitioner-led nursing homes. These are no longer able to compete with trans-national providers. Not surprisingly, among the consequences are rising costs, the use of unnecessary and expensive technology, and a quality of care that is not reliable due to an almost complete absence of monitoring and quality control.

The experience of AP highlights the current dilemma faced by public providers. In the search for greater profits, and aided by legislative changes at the global level (WTO, GATS), the march to restructure the health sector is a rapid one. But it is often undertaken with little regard for efficiency or effectiveness, which leads us to conclude that the primary motive is profit rather than need. We hope that this book will provide information to public health researchers, policy-makers, health-care workers, as well as to the population of users, about the real meaning of the restructuring of the health sector. It indicates a crisis of accumulation on a world scale rather than a drive to improve the efficiency of the public sector.

REFERENCES

Corner House (2001) *Trading Healthcare Away? GATS, Public Services and Privatisation* (Corner House Briefings 23: Trade and Health Care), Dorset, UK: Corner House.

Cuban Ministry of Public Health (2000) *Statistical Annual 2000*, Havana: Ministry of Public Health.

Drache, D. and Sullivan, T. (eds) (1999) *Health Reforms: Public Success, Private Failure*, London: Routledge.

Hsiao, W. (1995) 'The Chinese health care system: lessons for other nations', *Social Science and Medicine*, 41 (8), 1047–55.

Mackintosh, M. (1995) 'Competition and contracting in selective social provisioning', *European Journal of Development Research*, 7, 26–52.

Navarro, V. (1998) 'Health and equity in the world in the era of globalisation', *Proceedings, International Association of Health Policy*, Perugia, Italy (September), 23–8.

Poulder, J., Bonneux, L., Meerding, P. and Van de Maas, P. (2002) 'Age specific increases in health care costs', *European Journal of Public Health*, 12, 57–62.

Price, D., Pollock, A. M. and Shaoul, J. (1999) 'How the World Trade Organisation is shaping domestic policies in health care', *The Lancet*, 354, 1889–92.

Qadeer, I., Sen, K. and Nayar, K. R. (eds) (2001) *Public Health and the Poverty of Reforms – the South Asian Predicament*, New Delhi: Sage.

Renaud, M. (1998) 'IAHP 23 years after its foundation' (Opening Address) *Proceedings, International Association of Health Policy*, Perugia, Italy (September 1998) 1–4.

Sen, K. (1996) 'Health sector reforms and the implications for later life from a comparative perspective', *Health Care in Later Life*, 1 (2), 73–85.

Sen, K. and Bonita, R. (2000) 'Global health status: two steps forward, one step back', *The Lancet*, 356, 577–82.

Sen, K. and Koivusalo, M. (1998) 'Health care reforms and developing countries – a critical overview', *International Journal of Health Planning and Management*, 13, 199–215.

Whitfield, D. (2001) *Public Services or Corporate Welfare: Rethinking the Nation State in the Global Economy*, London: Pluto Press.

WHO (2000) *The World Health Report, Health Systems: Improving Performance*, Geneva: WHO.

World Bank (1993) *World Development Report*, New York: Oxford University Press.

PART ONE

Conceptual and Legislative Framework

Restructuring Health Services and Policies of Privatisation – an Overview of Experience

KASTURI SEN

REFORMS OF THE HEALTH SECTOR

During the 1990s, international debates in health policy appear to have converged towards an approach that calls for targeting provision of health and social care for vulnerable groups in both developed and developing countries (World Bank 1993; Baru 1995; Koivusalo and Ollila 1997; Drache and Sullivan 1999). This approach has been an integral feature of reforms of the health sector, particularly in the developing world, where poverty is endemic and economic and socially vulnerable groups form a substantial share of the overall population.

In the Western European region, the nature and implementation of reforms have varied from one country to another. However, since the mid-1980s a number of mechanisms have been used to set the pace of change towards the privatisation of elements of public provision. These included the contracting out or privatisation of components of health and social care, increasing co-payments by particular patients, rationing parts of the service for the chronically sick and increasing the role of private insurance schemes in healthcare across the board.

While the privatisation of health services has proceeded at a steady pace in Western Europe, this experience differed from that in the developing world by the fact that essential safety-nets remained in place across the region. Health services continued to be funded mainly through the public purse, despite the privatisation of various elements. New methods of autonomous management were implemented in a number of countries, including the more recent introduction of private financing schemes (such as PFI) in places such as the UK (Gaffney et al. 1999).

It is a cause of concern that public debates on equitable and sustainable funding schemes are increasingly thin on the ground, while the political push for changing the economic base of the funding of services (as in PFI UK) increases steadily. A number of researchers and public health scholars have argued that the proposed changes to funding, through the introduction of charges and a reorganisation of finance mechanisms, are not only regressive but are also being undertaken despite lack of evidence that they might improve 'efficiency' or decrease the costs of providing the service (Gaffney et al. 1999).

While the funding of health and social services in European countries is varied in source and dispensation, most commonly it has been raised through general taxation and social insurance schemes. Over the past two decades, however, a number of countries have encouraged the growth of private health insurance and out-of-pocket payment schemes (i.e. the Netherlands and Belgium), while others such as the UK or Italy have not as yet transformed their predominantly public funding base. The indications that they will do so remain. Overall, in nearly all the countries of Western Europe, the largest share of funding for health services has remained under the aegis of the public sector (Koivusalo 2000; Maarse in this volume).

In developing countries on the other hand, the degree to which the state has been involved in the provision of health services has varied somewhat, but the support for universal coverage has been high on the popular agenda. This is related to the fact that in some countries of south Asia (Sri Lanka and India) the initial years of independence witnessed health services taking a large share of planned outlays for investment in development. This, though, was to be a short-lived experience, for post-independence rhetoric was often not matched by sustained support for public services when private interests superseded public claims. This was less the case in Sri Lanka than in India and has since been reflected in the differences in population health status, among other developmental indicators, between the two countries.

When the structural adjustment programme measures (SAPs) arrived in south Asia from the late 1980s onwards, the public sector was not in a position to negotiate. The process of shifting the balance of power from public to private providers appeared almost inevitable, especially in a country such as India, due to the already established strength of private medicine and the support it received from a vocal middle-class lobby. This political economy created an easier transition. Moreover, at a global level, during this period the role of the state was being transformed quite rapidly from that of a 'Provider to that of an Enabler' of service provision. It was becoming increasingly clear that with a little help from donor agencies, these were more often 'private for profit' services.

In a country such as India, the increasing emphasis on expanding the private sector is premised upon the desire to maintain low-cost public healthcare for the poor, and to enable the private marketing of services for others (Qadeer and Sen 1998). There is growing concern, however, that skeleton public provision in most regions of the country at primary, secondary and tertiary levels has been unable to keep up with the expansion of the private sector in the context of the changing profile of health needs (Green 1995; Sen 1996; Yang 1997; Qadeer 2000). However, there are some fundamental differences in the European approaches to reforms of the health sector and those advocated for the developing world, which require further exploration.

Research from countries as politically varied as India and China has recently begun to question the value of exporting policies of organisational and structural change to regions where the public sector has always played a dominant role in health services. The process of corporatisation, for example, is a case in point since this has led to the acceleration of 'privatisation' through transforming the management of secondary facilities. This is part and parcel of the World Bank's (1993) package of reforms to health systems whereby public hospitals gain much greater autonomy and attain semi-private sector status. Significantly, they also enjoy substantial public subsidy (see Narayana in this volume). They are able to make decisions on the introduction of charges for patients or in relation to contracting out of hospital services. However, these changes also have consequences for access to healthcare by the very groups that are being targeted for support under the overall reforms. These are the vulnerable groups technically being targeted by the major donor agencies and national governments. Impoverishment and loss of access to services among this very group has raised much concern among public health researchers with regard to the validity of the schemes (Sauerborn et al. 1994; Bloom and Xingyuan 1997; Tang et al. 1997; Swaminathan 2000).

Some of the reforms in the organisation and management of health services in India are also in direct conflict with the stated intentions of the current five-year plan (9th Plan, Government of India 1997 to 2001) which has made a clear commitment to ongoing support for primary healthcare and to upgrading rural health services to provide for the poor. But the focus for investment in India and elsewhere appears to be on large hospitals in urban areas, since they are potentially the most profitable entities despite national commitments to primary healthcare provision.

The changes being implemented in the overall division of services (away from rural areas) and increasing financial autonomy not only have implications for access and equity of provision, but also have consequences for actual health especially among the most needy (the elderly, young children, younger women and so on). Some observers suggest that this is due to the fact that inherent in the policy is an assumption, hardly debated, that the so-called 'vulnerable groups', such as the elderly, will need access only to 'basic' healthcare at the level of primary provision, rather than also needing access to secondary-level care which may be purchased. So the assumption that targeting essential health services at this level will ensure a more efficient allocation of resources is not borne out by evidence on current patterns of utilisation, which are high among these vulnerable groups for both communicable and non-communicable diseases (Sen 1996).

In China, substantial changes to the organisation and financing of healthcare have led to significant increases in the cost of health services, which are no longer able to rely upon a public subsidy. The Chinese government is now grappling with the health and social costs of changing the financial base of a well-established public sector, within a short space of time. This is owing to the profound implications for access to and population coverage of healthcare. For example, as a result of the changes to finance mechanisms, some 800 million people lost their health insurance protection when user fees grew in importance from 24 to only 36 per cent of healthcare finance during the late 1980s (Hsiao 1995).

In Malaysia, there is evidence of a growing phenomenon of the corporatisation of public hospitals, whereby previously state-owned hospitals emerge as freestanding corporate entities with considerable operational and financial autonomy. In effect, these evolve into publicly subsidised private corporations. In parallel, there has been an increasing tendency to privatise health insurance from its public sector base in a number of countries. There is concern among public health scholars that these may be the first steps towards the wholesale privatisation of public provision, which could lead to a segmented provision of health services for the population (Chan 2000). Under this scenario, those who are able to pay would utilise the corporate sector (incorporating primary, secondary and acute care) and those who are unable to pay would continue to have access to a poorly resourced public system as more of its resources are transferred to subsidise the emerging corporate structures.

There is increasing evidence that organisational structures that work well in advanced market economies, reflecting a mix of public and private provision, are not necessarily appropriate for low- and middle-income countries. This is the case where administrative and regulatory mechanisms under the public sector are already weak, coupled with historically low levels of investment in public health provision. While the latter example may not apply to all low- and middle-income countries, it is certainly the case for a substantial majority of them in terms of the historical background to public health provision and development (Nitayarumphong 1997; Bhat 1997; Yang 1997).

Emerging views suggest that unless such issues are taken into account in the economic reforms of the health and social sectors, the consequences for services are likely to be negative and disruptive in terms of access and equity (Bloom and Xingyuan 1997; Koivusalo 2000). The implication of this unresolved debate is that policy-makers need more information on how health sectors have functioned (public–private mix for example, over and above health needs identified) in different regions from a historical perspective. This needs to account for socio-economic, demographic and epidemiological realities, prior to the implementation of shifts in policies towards the finance and organisation of health service provision.

Typically, there is much debate in Europe over the efficiency of the public–private mix in healthcare. However, there are few conclusions on the most appropriate balance, whether in the structure or the financing mechanisms, that will have a positive effect upon health outcomes. There is a broad consensus, however, that the privatisation of any element of a health service, particularly at the point of service provision, will increase costs (such as in the USA, see Woolhandler's chapter in this volume) and that the role of the state as a gatekeeper for maintaining the quality of provision will always be an important one (Propper and Green 1999; Saltman and Figuerras 1997). There is some evidence also from the Netherlands that ad hoc changes to funding of provision without careful monitoring can lead also to an escalation of costs for the public purse (Maarse 2001). There is little cumulative evidence, however, that supports the changes to the funding and organisation of care, from a global perspective, without taking into account particular circumstances. This places the least developed countries at the greatest disadvantage.

GLOBALISATION AND REFORMS OF THE HEALTHECTOR

The current process of globalisation through expansion of corporate entities has been taking place at a rapid pace over the past decade. Globalisation, apart from the ongoing debates about whether it is a new phenomenon or a long-standing one (Whitfield 2001), may be defined in the health sector as a form of 'internationalisation' that responds to specific financial and economic interests, which is articulated in the class relations of each society (Navarro 1998).

The globalisation of commerce, investments and finance has become a major force influencing public policies, including health policies as described in the preceding section. According to Renaud (1998), the power of national governments has been reduced by an increasingly competitive international economy, where the interests of multinational corporations take precedence and determine the rules that govern policy and practice in individual countries and across trade and service sectors. The rapid expansion of the WTO and its gamut of legally binding arrangements, most notably the GATS, are also testimony to this (Whitfield 2001; Sexton in this volume).

There continues to be an illusion, often perpetuated by policy-minders from donor agencies such as the IMF and the World Bank, that inherent in the process of globalisation is equality of opportunity. In this author's view, this could not be further from the truth, since many developing countries, and in particular the poorest countries among them, join the process at a considerable disadvantage in terms of their earning capacity as well as in low levels of human development (life expectancy, levels of literacy and so on). Their competitive role is often restricted to the provision of cheap labour and low running costs for capital accumulation and to a lesser extent as consumers of globalised services such as healthcare, but only so among the elite.

CURRENT DEBATES OVER GLOBALISATION AND THE RESTRUCTURING OF HEALTH SERVICES

According to the advocates of the restructuring of services, the benefits include the actual process facilitating globalisation since this is viewed positively as supporting much needed economic growth, expansion, competition and investment. All these conditions are viewed as necessary for progress (Renaud 1998). It is claimed that this transformatory process will ultimately minimise costs, including the social and human costs, of economic growth, that it will also optimise its benefits through the reduction in prices of all commodities, that it will promote the internationalisation of the division of labour, international cooperation and scientific development. Most of these aspects are viewed by the advocates of globalisation and privatisation as its major benefits.

However, advocates such as Lincoln Chen also recognise some of the negative consequences of globalisation (Chen 1998). These include inequality and exclusion, but they are viewed as short-term shocks and hence only as short-term problems. However, contrary to this picture, the evidence on the process of globalisation is now beginning to highlight some of its actual and real effects throughout the world. These include a decline in average wages, a decline in real incomes together with an unprecedented growth in inequalities, as wealth becomes more concentrated when the basic structures of employment are fundamentally changed.

In addition, this situation is compounded by a slowing down of past improvements in health in several regions in both the developed and developing world (Qadeer et al. 2001; Sen and Bonita 2000). The negative effect on health status is made worse by growing economic disparities within and between nations. For example, in 1999 UNDP reported that 20 per cent of the population living in high-income countries accounted for 86 per cent of private consumption, while 28 per cent of the world's population consumed 1.3 per cent. There is further evidence, also from UNDP, showing that the combined income of a few hundred (n: 358) of the richest people in the globe is equivalent to that of the poorest 45 per cent – some 2.3 billion people. According to Navarro (1998), these inequalities are growing unchecked and at an unprecedented rate owing to the ongoing advocacy of 'growth' at all cost (Renaud 1998).

There is evidence from several countries of Latin America, sub-Saharan Africa and south Asia that the SAPs adopted during the past two decades have worsened income distribution; this issue remains unaddressed by the new economic policies which have continued to increase the concentration of income among rich households (Renaud 1998). In parts of south Asia, most notably India, the infant mortality rate has begun to rise for the first time since the 1980s.

Such inequalities are also reflected at the national and regional levels, reinforcing the point that the negative consequences of global changes are not simply about inclusion or exclusion or for that matter about improving democracy and human rights, but rather about the power relations that are sustained by this mechanism and articulated by the process at international, national and local levels.

In the many parts of the world, according to some observers, the dismantling of public provision, coupled with policies that support selective access (as in insurance schemes and increasingly to healthcare provision in particular), have led to a growing social crisis reflected in increased violence in the community, the family and on the streets. In some Latin American countries violence, for example, is the first or second cause of death.

IMPACT UPON HEALTH SERVICES AND THE HEALTH SECTOR

The liberalisation of trade and the economic sectors has facilitated the rapid expansion of commercial health insurance into healthcare provision in the majority of developing countries over the past decade. This has substantially weakened the ability and role of the state to manage or direct healthcare systems effectively or to guide health policies. Managed care systems, which originated in the United States, have been shown long before their expansion to be costly as well as unsustainable (Woolhandler in this volume). Utilising this mode of managed care for service delivery inevitably leads to exclusion from the basic human right of access to healthcare of those people who cannot afford to pay.

This model of healthcare provision also has its critics in the USA. For example, a nationwide poll undertaken by the AHA (American Hospital Association) in 1996 showed that a substantial majority of the population believe that the healthcare they receive is neither a planned system nor a consumer-oriented service, but rather a service that exists for the sake of maximising profit from ill-health and misery, blocking access, reducing quality and limiting spending. The poll concluded that the majority of Americans believe that their health insurance companies have too much influence and exert too much control over their healthcare ('The state of American opinion on the medical care of the population 1996', cited in Renaud 1998). This view is reinforced in this volume by Chapter 12 on the USA (Woolhandler). Renaud (1998), in his critique of market-led healthcare, suggests that it is essential to continue to undertake research that provides evidence of the effects of globalisation through the policies of economic adjustment and reforms of public provision. It is important to document cumulatively the process and outcomes of care and ascertain the potential consequences in terms of the health of vulnerable populations, of changes to the structure and provision of healthcare as it accelerates its activities throughout the globe.

It has been well established through research based upon assessment of current public health status as well as from historical records, that the nature and quality of socio-economic environments has an enormous impact upon people's health, on their longevity and upon their quality of life. This is reiterated in numerous national and multinational studies which show beyond reasonable doubt that the higher one is in the social hierarchy the better off one is in terms of health. Differences in the rate and pace of health are also shown by these studies, which repeat an essential fact: the better the distribution of social and economic resources in a particular society, the better the performance in the overall state of life expectancy.

There is also considerable evidence to show the broad socio-economic determinants of health, which include the provision of clean water, sanitation, minimum nutrition, housing, educational opportunities and, most crucially, employment. Many countries neglect this long-standing evidence that medical care alone is only one (though important) parameter in the promotion of good health.

There is also increasing evidence to show that neo-liberal economic and social policies have seriously undermined the capacity of the state to undertake the basic and essential functions of improving opportunities and redistributing risks and resources. Instead, economic and social policies have promoted and supported the supremacy of markets. This, despite the fact that we have sufficient evidence by now to show that the market is associated with inequity, inefficiency, high costs and an overall undermining of population-based strategies.

EROSION OF SOLIDARITY

Most critics of the reform process have argued that the provision of care in accordance with the ability to pay is having important and negative consequences for social solidarity and for the advancement of civil society. According to Renaud (1998) in Canada, for example, US policies of reform have had a negative effect. The established system of community-based care has been largely replaced by managed care under autonomous hospitals and there is real danger of this turning the system into a two-tiered one, in part a replica of the multitiered system which exists in the USA. It is well known that the public health system in the USA is highly regressive and excludes a substantial majority of its population from access to health services. There is little room for appraisal and for change under the stranglehold of market forces.

In different regions of the world (including and especially so in countries of Western Europe), there is gradual erosion of the popular right to criticize and appraise public services (Roy Hattersley in the *Guardian*, 22 May 2002). This, despite the fact that globally and regionally there are policy measures being introduced across the board that support segmented care which reduces access, and despite the voluminous evidence of the cost and often poor efficiency of multitiered, segmented rather than universal healthcare. At another level there is growing concern that current shifts towards corporate service provision will inevitably weaken solidarity and lead to the destruction of truly public policies and of public space. It would encourage also the loss of programmes of social security and social support which have historically been premised upon values of citizenship and solidarity.

To conclude on a more optimistic note, there is growing evidence that large sections of the population in both developed and developing countries are not willing to concede to the unchecked rise of corporate power and the forms of corporate care which have emerged. New types of challenges are emerging that are based upon the rights of citizens and of access to health and social care as a human right, despite being diametrically opposed to the process of accumulation of capital through the sale of the social sector.

REFERENCES

Baru, R. (1995) 'Structure and utilisation of health services: an inter-state analysis', *Social Scientist*, 256–9 (Sept.–Dec.), Tulika, New Delhi, 245–59.

Bhat, R. (1997) 'The private–public mix in health care in India', *Health Policy and Planning*, 8 (1).

Bloom, G. and Xingyuan, G. (1997) 'Introduction to health sector reform in China', in G. Bloom and A. Wilkes (eds), 'Health in transition: reforming China's rural health services', *IDS Bulletin*, 28(1).

Chan, C. K. (2000) *The Citizens' Health Initiative – Policy Analysis with Health Care Activism*, Report, Kuala Lumpur: Citizens' Health Initiative Action Group.

Chen, L. (1998) 'Globalisation: health equity or social exclusion', in *Proceedings, International Association of Health Policy*, Perugia, Italy (September), 13–15.

Drache, D. and Sullivan, T. (eds) (1999) *Health Reforms: Public Success, Private Failure*, London: Routledge.

Green, A. (1995) 'The state of health planning in the 90s', *Health Policy and Planning*, 10, 22–9.

Hsiao, W. (1995) 'The Chinese health care system: lessons for other nations', *Social Science and Medicine*, 41 (8), 1047–55.

Koivusalo, M. (2000) 'Trends in global health policies and implications for health systems development', in J. Le Roy and K. Sen (eds), *Health Systems and Social Development: An Alternative Paradigm in Health Systems Research* (Proceedings of a Meeting in Brussels: European Commission, RIAGG, Maastricht, the Netherlands, September 2000), 7–16.

Koivusalo, M. and Ollila, E. (1997) *Making a Healthy World. Agencies, Actors and Policies in International Health*, London: Zed Books.

Maarse, H. (2001) *Creeping Privatisation in Dutch Health Care*, unpublished MS.

Navarro, V. (1998) 'Health and equity in the world in the era of globalisation', *Proceedings, International Association of Health Policy*, Perugia, Italy (September), 23–8.

Nitayarumphong, S. (ed.) (1997) *Health Care Reform: At the Frontiers of Research and Policy Decisions*, Thailand: Ministry of Public Health, Office of Health Care Reforms.

Gaffney, D., Pollock, A. M., Price, D. and Shaoul, J. (1999) 'How the World Trade Organisation is shaping domestic policies in health care', *The Lancet*, 454, 1889–92.

Propper, C. and Green, K. (1999) 'A larger role for the private sector in health care: a review of the arguments' (Working Paper No. 99/009), Centre for Market and Public Organisations, University of Bristol.

Qadeer, I. (2000) 'Health care systems in transition III. Part I: The Indian experience', *Journal of Public Health Medicine*, 22 (1), 25–32.

Qadeer, I. and Sen, K. (1998) 'The crisis in welfarism – public health debate in South Asia', *Journal of Public Health*, 21 (3), 93–6.

Qadeer, I., Sen, K. and Nayar, K. R. (eds) (2001) *Public Health and the Poverty of Reforms – the South Asian Predicament*, New Delhi: Sage.

Renaud, M. (1998) 'IAHP 23 years after its foundation' (Opening Address) *Proceedings, International Association of Health Policy*, Perugia, Italy (September), 1–4.

Saltman, R. B. and Figuerras, J. (1997) 'Analysing the evidence on European health care reforms', *Health Affairs*, 17 (2), 85–108.

Sauerborn, R., Nougtara, A. and Latimer, E. (1994) 'The elasticity of demand for healthcare in Burkina Faso: differences across age and income groups', *Health Policy and Planning*, 2, 185–92.

Sen, K. (1996) 'Health sector reforms and the implications for later life from a comparative perspective', *Health Care in Later Life*, 1 (2), 73–85.

Sen, K. and Bonita, R. (2000) 'Global health status: two steps forward, one step back', *The Lancet*, 356, 577–82.

Swaminathan, M. (2000) *Weakening Welfare – The Public Distribution of Food in India*, New Delhi: Leftword Books.

Tang, S., Xueshan, F. and Lucas, H. (1997) 'Introduction to the three country study', in G. Bloom and A. Wilkes (eds), 'Health in transition: reforming China's rural health services', *IDS Bulletin*, 28 (1).

Whitfield, D. (2001) *Public Services or Corporate Welfare: Rethinking the Nation State in the Global Economy*, London: Pluto Press.

World Bank (1993) *World Development Report*, New York: Oxford University Press.

Yang, Bon Min (1997) 'The role of health insurance in the growth of the private health sector in Korea', in W. NewBrander (ed.), *Private Health Sector Growth in Asia: Issues and Implications*, Chichester: John Wiley.

CHAPTER 3

Trading Healthcare Away: The WTO's General Agreement on Trade in Services (GATS)

SARAH SEXTON

OVERVIEW

Services are now a significant part of the economies of industrialised countries and are governed by complex domestic regulations. These countries are now trying to revise the World Trade Organisation's General Agreement on Trade in Services (GATS) so as to increase international trade in services. If they are successful, GATS could be used to overturn almost any legislation governing services, from national to local level. Particularly under threat from GATS are public services – healthcare, education, energy, water and sanitation, for instance. A revised GATS could give the for-profit sector further access to the public sector and could make existing privatisation effectively irreversible. This chapter outlines the main provisions of GATS, proposed revisions to it, and key corporate aims. It explores the potential for private companies to capture the most profitable components of publicly provided and funded healthcare services, leaving a reduced public sector to cope with the elderly, chronically sick and the poor who most need healthcare and who can least afford it. The result will be a decline in accessibility to healthcare worldwide.

Heart surgery and electricity transmission, education and childcare, water purification and pesticide application, sewerage and sports centres, road construction and film-making, toxic waste disposal and mobile telephone communication – all are services, not tangible commodities. Some are luxuries, others are essential. Services have become an important part of the economies of many countries in recent years, in some places overtaking manufactured goods in significance. Providing services (excluding public services) now represents over 60 per cent of the GDP of industrialised countries – an estimated 80 per cent in the USA (Vastine 1999; PSI 1999a: 5).

Most services are provided and consumed in one and the same country, but international trade in services, particularly between the United States and Europe, is growing. In 1999, such trade was worth US $1.35 trillion – about one-quarter of the global trade in goods – up from some $400 billion in 1985 (PSI 1999a: 5).[1] This trade is firmly in the grip of the industrialised countries, which exported nearly 71 per cent of services traded internationally in 1997 and imported 67 per cent. The EU regards itself as the biggest services exporter in the world (ESF 1999), while more than one-third of US economic growth over the past five years has been due to exports of services (USTR 1998, quoted in Price et al. 1999). The single largest US export industry is entertainment, in particular, films and television programmes (UNDP 1999: 3). Developing countries import and export less than one-third of the services traded internationally (Balasubramaniam 2000). Because of vast differences in the ability of developed and developing countries to supply services, it is major traders in the industrialised world who have most to gain from increased access to services markets. The US Coalition of Service Industries is confident that any increase in the consumption of services anywhere in the world effectively means an increase in consumption of US services (Vastine 1999).

THE GENERAL AGREEMENT ON TRADE IN SERVICES (GATS)

In the mid-1980s, many western governments, faced with worldwide recession, inflation and unemployment, decided that removing obstacles to international trade in services, particularly national regulations, could increase the momentum to export services. One way of doing this was to bring services under the rules of the international trading system, which, until then, had covered only goods.

The ambitious and ambiguous General Agreement on Trade in Services (GATS) came into effect at the beginning of 1995, at the same time as the World Trade Organisation (WTO). It sets out rules governing international trade in practically all services, and makes no distinction between public (or voluntary) services and those provided on a for-profit basis.[2]

GATS encourages trade across national borders in services by requiring a WTO member country to treat all countries the same (most-favoured nation principle), to treat foreign companies just as they do domestic ones (national treatment principle), and to allow foreign companies into a country (market access principle). However, some GATS rules and requirements apply only to those services which a country has indicated it is prepared to open up to foreign competition, which is unusual for a WTO agreement. The USA tried to get all the rules governing trade in goods simply transposed into services as a whole (although financial services were of prime interest), but encountered substantial resistance. Many developing countries reluctantly agreed to GATS only if they could choose which of their services it covered. A government thus provides the WTO with a 'schedule of specific commitments', listing which services, and which of four different ways of supplying that service – cross-border supply; consumers going abroad; companies setting up in other countries; and employees going abroad – it is prepared to open up to competition under GATS.

The power of GATS, as with all WTO agreements, is that its rules can be enforced by trade sanctions. To avoid even the threat of being taken by another WTO member to a WTO dispute panel, many governments may not institute legislation or public policy objectives that might be interpreted as being against WTO rules. GATS does allow countries to protect human, animal and plant life or health through measures which might otherwise contravene the agreement, but its preamble, according to the US Alliance for Democracy, 'has a caveat large enough to drive a truck through' (Caplan n.d.). WTO dispute panels have so far interpreted exemptions and exclusions narrowly and forcefully in favour of trade.[3] These rulings 'show that GATS can be used to challenge an almost unlimited range of government regulatory measures that, even indirectly or unintentionally, affect the conditions of competition of international service suppliers' (Sinclair 2000: 1).[4] In essence, the aim of GATS is to regulate governments, not corporations. Compared to markets in goods, markets in services and access to them are much more constrained by government interventions. Once a government has committed itself under GATS to opening a service sector to foreign competition, service exporters, importers and investors in that sector in the country have almost guaranteed financial conditions.

GATS RENEGOTIATIONS

The GATS agreement is innovative, complex and without legal precedent. Few of its provisions have been tested or clarified by challenges brought to the WTO dispute panel. Little information exists so far on the impact of GATS in facilitating trade in services, or on the economic benefits that have accrued to countries from services liberalisation, let alone their social and environmental effects. There are few baseline data upon which to make comparisons. Nevertheless, WTO representatives have begun to negotiate to extend the scope of GATS.

When the agreement was signed in 1995, some countries considered it to be incomplete. A clause was therefore included mandating 'successive rounds of negotiations ... aimed at achieving a progressively higher level of liberalization' – in practice, privatisation and deregulation. It specifies that the first 'successive round' of negotiation should begin within five years of GATS coming into effect, that is, by the year 2000. Talks on renegotiation opened on 25 February 2000 in Geneva, home to WTO headquarters, and are scheduled to be completed by 2005.[5] Much of the negotiation is taking place between government representatives behind closed doors, but in close consultation with international corporate lobbyists.[6]

The USA, European Union, Japan and Canada (known as the Quadrilateral or 'Quad' governments) are thus seeking more access to southern markets, to each other's public services, and further deregulation of services already in private hands but publicly regulated, such as media, publishing, telecommunications, energy, transport, financial and postal services. To gain such access, these countries are pushing hard to:

- increase the services and ways of supplying services that WTO member countries agree to open up to foreign competition (market access)
- reclassify services to get around some countries' reluctance to open them up to foreign competition[7]
- insert new rules and restrictions that apply to all members, services, sectors of services and ways in which services are supplied, irrespective of whether countries have agreed to open such services to competition
- place new constraints on domestic regulation

These revisions, if they are agreed upon, could mean that the supposed voluntary nature of GATS – under which a country decides which services to list as open to foreign competition – would in effect be meaningless. Guarantees, such as those from the UK's Department of Trade and Industry, that 'the UK government has no intention whatsoever of offering to privatise public healthcare or education under the GATS 2000 negotiations', would have little force (DTI 1999).

TURNING PUBLIC INTO PRIVATE

Although GATS encompasses all services, many civil servants and government ministers believe that it makes an exception for public services – those 'supplied in the exercise of governmental authority' – such as healthcare, education or utilities. But GATS defines government services so narrowly – 'any service which is supplied neither on a commercial basis, nor in competition with one or more service suppliers' – that the exception could be almost meaningless if one country were to challenge another country's public services at the WTO dispute panel as contravening GATS. The WTO's Council for Trade in Services has said that exceptions need to be 'interpreted narrowly' when applied to health services. Council minutes are used by dispute panels to interpret WTO agreements (see Government of British Colombia 2001; Krajewski 2001).

To establish a trade in services, as GATS aims to do, there has to be a market in services – services have to be bought and sold. Until recently, however, many countries have not had markets in healthcare, education, water and sewerage, or energy. By and large, all have been provided by government or non-profit organisations. The state has set up schools and paid the teachers, built the hospitals and trained the nurses and doctors.

Markets are now being created, by enabling entities other than the state to provide services. Governments the world over have been de-regulating and privatising both the funding and the provision of public services, sometimes on their own initiative, sometimes as a condition of IMF structural adjustment programmes (SAPs) and sometimes on World Bank advice (see Martin 1993; Hildyard 1998). In some cases, governments have simply sold off public entities. For instance, in Britain, the railways, telephones, and electricity, gas and water utilities have been transferred to the for-profit sector. Governments are transforming other public services, particularly those which it might be politically unacceptable to privatise outright, by requiring the public body to contract services out to for-profit companies or to institute a process of compulsory competitive tendering (private provision). They have separated infrastructure such as buildings from service provision, and privatised the infrastructure by means of an array of public–private 'partnerships' that retain an ostensible public dimension and thus appear more politically acceptable. They have privatised the financing of public services (by charging users of the service, using private capital and encouraging private health insurance). Governments have also introduced internal markets, that is, divided purchasers from providers within a public service sector (PSI 1999b: 9; Whitfield 2001; CPS 2001). Management from the private sector has been introduced to infuse the public service sector with market-oriented methods and principles. As pointed out by D. Hall of the Public Services International Research Unit: 'The corporatisation of public service organizations ... usually involves the introduction of business accounting ... and may be a change as significant as that to private ownership itself' (Hall 2001a: 17).

Healthcare services have not generally been explicitly privatised. Instead, there has been an incremental process of government retrenchment accompanied by private sector enlargement as the services have been commercialised. Markets – and thus the potential for trade – have crept in through the back door. As far as GATS is concerned, if a government contracts out any part of its public services, such as cleaning or catering, or if private (either for-profit or voluntary) companies supply services also provided by the government (for instance, if private schools exist alongside state ones, or if there is a mixture of public and private funding), then those services could be judged by a WTO dispute panel as not being a government service. Thus they will be subject to GATS rather than exempt from it, that is, subject to competition from operators from abroad.[8]

As a result of existing deregulation and privatisation, national – and, increasingly, trans-national – companies have sprung up and made inroads into a wide range of public services in many countries, particularly utilities (water, energy, telecommunications, transport), refuse collection, prisons, housing, social services and support services (cleaning, catering, information technology) (PSI 1998: 3). Via GATS, they could gain access to many more. Private companies could also prise open for themselves public funding for services. The EU and USA spend a substantial amount of public money on public services. In the countries of the OECD (Organisation for Economic Co-operation and Development), public expenditure on health services and education accounts for more than 13 per cent of gross domestic product (Pollock and Price 2000a: 1996). Much of this spending now goes to public or voluntary bodies but could end up being channelled to for-profit groups. Nearly 50 per cent of UK tax revenue now goes to profit-making companies.[9]

The bulwarks of public health – air quality, safe drinking water, food safety, road safety, drainage and sanitation – have been under threat because of privatisation for some time now; under GATS, they could be permanently dismantled. The consequences were evident not only in nineteenth-century Europe, but are visible today in many poorer countries, namely high mortality rates, especially high maternal death rates, a proliferation of contagious diseases, and high levels of poverty and homelessness (PSI 1999b: 4).

TURNING HEALTHCARE INTO HEALTH MARKETS

Healthcare is just one example of a public service threatened by GATS. Commercial interests now provide some of the health services in many countries, sometimes in competition (albeit limited and regulated) with public providers.[10] In the UK, for instance, for-profit nursing homes and privately financed hospital buildings provide health services in competition with public ones (Pollock and Price 2000a: 1996).[11] This dual system gives the WTO a useful rationale for encouraging further competition and privatisation through GATS:

> The hospital sector in many countries ... is made up of government-owned and privately-owned entities which both operate on a commercial basis, charging the patient or his [sic] insurance for the treatment provided ... It seems unrealistic in such cases to argue for continued application of Article 1.3 (that the service is a government service) and/or to maintain that no competitive relationship exists between the two groups of suppliers of services. (WTO 1998)

The stakes are huge: expenditure on health in OECD countries is estimated at more than US $3 trillion annually (WTO 1998).[12] To date, however, GATS has not been instrumental in privatising healthcare services and opening them up to foreign competition.[13]

Health and social services are 'trailing behind other sectors' in the rate they are being listed under GATS as open to competition. The WTO acknowledges that some governments do not want to commercialise their hospitals because they are part of their national heritage (WTO 1998).

As of 1998, fifty-nine countries had put one or more aspects of their professional (medical, dental, veterinary, nursing, midwifery, physiotherapy) services or health-related and social services (including hospitals) under GATS. Medical and dental services had the highest tally with forty-nine countries, while thirty-nine countries had agreed to open up hospital services to foreign suppliers. In the financial services sector, including health insurance, however, seventy-six countries have made commitments (WTO 1998; see http://gats-info.eu.int).[14] Poorer countries have made more commitments in the hope of attracting the services they lack. Sierra Leone is the only country to have included all eight health service categories under GATS, while the USA has included just hospital and health insurance services. Even if they have made such commitments, however, countries can still limit market access to foreign suppliers and specify which ways of supplying the service are open to competition. The highest number of restrictions in ways of supplying health services is in 'commercial presence'.

During GATS renegotiation talks, US negotiators have made health-care a special target: 'The United States is of the view that commercial opportunities exist along the entire spectrum of health and social care facilities, including hospitals, outpatient facilities, clinics, nursing homes, assisted living arrangements, and services provided in the home' (Kuttner 1999a). The US Coalition of Service Industries is calling for majority foreign ownership of all public health facilities to be allowed:

> We believe we can make much progress in the (GATS) negotiations to allow the opportunity for US businesses to expand into foreign health care markets … Historically, health care services in many foreign countries have largely been the responsibility of the public sector. This public ownership of health care has made it difficult for US private-sector health care providers to market in foreign countries.

The US private healthcare sector also wants to gain access to 'rapidly expanding health care expenditures in many developed countries' experiencing 'an increase in their aged population' (Gould 1999).

USING GATS TO PRIVATISE PUBLIC HEALTHCARE

GATS could facilitate further privatisation and competition in healthcare services if more countries are pressured during the GATS renegotiations to list healthcare services on their schedule of commitments in all ways of supplying the service.

In the longer term, challenges under GATS could be made in another way. For instance, the USA could take Britain to the WTO dispute panel if the British government or any other body refused a US multinational permission to buy a British public National Health Service hospital which had been financed through the Private Finance Initiative (PFI). Similarly, the Canadian province of Alberta plans to allow private, for-profit hospitals to provide services previously provided only by public hospitals. If any of these private entities are based outside Canada (and a US-based company could use the North American Free Trade Agreement, NAFTA, to gain access), Alberta could be obliged under GATS to extend the same rights to every other 'like' foreign provider.[15]

A third way by which GATS could facilitate privatisation and competition is if mechanisms and principles underpinning the design, funding and delivery of public services are in effect proscribed; for example, if a vague GATS requirement for 'domestic regulation' to be 'least burdensome' to trade is redefined as 'pro-competitive' (Pollock and Price 2000a). 'Universal risk pooling', for instance, is a key principle of public healthcare services which would be at risk because it is not 'pro-competitive'. It means that the different risks of people needing healthcare services are pooled together across society. Some people are healthy most of the time and need little healthcare; others are chronically ill for years on end and need more. It is also well established that vulnerable groups are at greatest risk of ill-health and hence need greater access to care. Access and entitlement to healthcare services are thus based on an individual's need for them, not on their ability to pay.

Also threatened is another widely used principle: 'cross-subsidisation'. Under this principle, areas or services that cost less subsidise areas and services that cost more. In many countries, profitable services such as international telephone calls have subsidised less profitable but socially beneficial telephone services in rural areas.

In transport, bus services or railway branch lines serving outlying areas are easily paid for by routes in busy, more congested areas.[16] Risk pooling and cross-subsidies between rich and poor, healthy and sick ensure that all get tolerably equal access to similar levels of care because the basis of public services aims to be redistribution.

Governments that currently use non-market mechanisms, such as risk pooling, social insurance funds, block contracts and cross-subsidising, to deliver public services to as much of their population as possible could find such practices challenged as anti-competitive under GATS. Moreover, this clause on domestic regulation could be interpreted as applying to all services, not just to those which a country has offered to liberalise. Getting rid of cross-subsidisation is an essential step in service privatisation. It allows corporations to divide up integrated healthcare services, extract the more profitable ones and the more profitable patients (usually those who least need healthcare) and leave behind a reduced public sector. Such break-ups threaten the principles of universal coverage and shared risk that tax-funded (as in Britain and Canada) or social-insurance-funded (as in France or Germany) healthcare systems generally uphold (Pollock and Price 2000a; Evans 1999).[17] The trend is towards something like the healthcare system of the United States, which has come to be dominated by for-profit organisations over the past decade. There, tacit cross-subsidies are being eliminated and hospitals treated more and more as businesses: 'Temporary losses are defensible only as investments in future profits, so cross-subsidy must be avoided … There is no place for uncompensated care, unprofitable admissions, research, education, or public health activities – all chronic money losers from a strictly business viewpoint' (Kuttner 1996).

Health systems researchers Pollock and Price have pointed out that the adoption of proposals to redefine domestic regulation 'would transform the WTO from a body combating protectionism to a global agent of privatisation' (Pollock and Price 2000a).

A revised GATS could not only reduce equitable access to healthcare services, but could also undermine mechanisms for containing the costs of public sector healthcare. It could override national regulations governing healthcare and affect the kind of services provided, thus restricting rather than enlarging people's choice of services and of the places in which they are provided.[18] With reduced public expenditure on health and social services, the unpaid task of nursing and caring for the sick and elderly who cannot find or afford healthcare would increasingly fall upon the women among their family and friends (Allaert and Forman 1999; Macdonald 2000; Zarilli and Kinnon 1997).

IMPLICATIONS OF PUBLIC VERSUS PRIVATE

The move towards for-profit providers undermines the public sector in several ways. Competition among providers leads to competition for patients – the private sector tends to take the healthier and wealthier, while the public sector is typically left to care for more vulnerable people, despite cutbacks in funding, because less money ends up flowing into the public system. The inevitable result is a loss of preventive services: the public sector has less money for these services, while the private sector is not interested in them. Private health providers do not aim to provide healthcare to society, but health products or surgical procedures to individuals. They will not supply inherently unprofitable care to anyone, least of all to those who are in no position to pay for it (PSI 1999b: 9). Moreover, healthcare cannot be planned on the basis of individuals or highly segmented medical practice; it is about populations and matching resources to known priorities.

Changes in healthcare provision in the United States and Latin America over the past two decades illustrate these trends clearly. In the early 1990s in the USA, a growing number of hospitals, health maintenance organisations (HMOs – insurer-type intermediaries between employers and hospitals), nursing homes, home-care services and hospices became for-profit companies, publicly traded on stock exchanges. HMOs, transformed from a social form of medicine into multibillion-dollar businesses depending on a mixture of public funding, private health insurance and user charges, acquired non-profit hospitals cheaply and gained effective control over US hospitals.

The pursuit of market share, the search for profitable admissions and relentless cost-cutting came to dominate all aspects of healthcare, even that provided by socially-oriented entities. By the late 1990s, pressure to protect profit margins had led to insurers and hospitals avoiding sick patients, the micro-management of physicians, worsening of staff-to-patient ratios, and the outright denial of care to many. Instead of exercising greater efficiency in the use of available resources and greater integration of preventive and treatment services, the industry merely tries to avoid costs (Kuttner 1996, 1998, 1999a, 1999b; *The Economist*, 24 June 2000, pp. 72–3). 'More than any other country,' concludes *The Economist*, 'America has turned healthcare into a business.' Healthcare is the largest sector of the US economy; over \$1 trillion is spent on it every year, 46 per cent coming from government insurance programmes.[19] Nevertheless, some 44 million US Americans – one in six people – do not have health insurance, while millions of others are underinsured.[20]

Meanwhile, Latin America (particularly Chile, Colombia, Peru, Argentina, Brazil, Mexico and Venezuela) has become a testing ground for the privatisation of healthcare in the name of 'reform', pushed by the World Bank, Inter-American Development Bank, US-trained national economists, and US healthcare providers and insurers. Private insurers tend to select the 'best risks', mainly young and healthy people. They reject those with chronic illnesses and leave behind those who cannot afford the insurance. Private companies tend not to operate in the countryside where health services have always been sparse (W. Hsiao, Director, Harvard School of Public Health, reported in the *New York Times*, 17 June 1999, cited in PSI 2000).

Yet private operators rely on the very state health and social services that they are undermining. They take trained and experienced staff from the state system, select patients whose needs the public services have already identified, offer only the (profitable) services they want to, and set up private facilities, ranging from laboratory analysis to residential care, which can be rented or contracted out to the public service. The WTO itself acknowledges that: 'Private health insurers competing for members may engage in some form of "cream skimming", leaving the basic public system, often funded through the general budget, with low-income and high-risk members. New private clinics may well be able to attract qualified staff from public hospitals without ... offering the same range of services to the same population groups' (WTO 1998).

In Brazil, the private sector can now offer 120,000 doctors for one-quarter of the population, while the public sector has fewer than 70,000 doctors for everyone else. As Public Services International concludes, such private healthcare 'is never cheaper or more comprehensive than state care' (PSI 1999b: 10). The USA is the most extreme example of this provision: it has, administratively, the most expensive health system in the world, covering the lowest percentage of the population (PSI 1999b: 10). In India, under the influence of World Bank reforms, medical care has been handed over to the private sector without mechanisms to ensure the quality and standards of treatment. Infectious disease control programmes run by the state have been disrupted because they have been deprived of funds (see Narayana in this volume). Similar results have occurred in sub-Saharan Africa (Price et al. 1999).

In other words, private provision is not an effective means to promote public health. Yet without good public health, the health of every individual is endangered (PSI 1999b: 16). As food policy analyst Tim Lang points out, many public health gains such as clean air, clean water and food safety were won once the affluent and the middle classes recognised that they could not escape the consequences of unhealthy conditions, and that it was in their interests to tackle the causes of ill-health together (Lang 2001). G. Rayner of the UK Public Health Association stresses that 'a market-based approach to health not only drives up the costs of healthcare, but it can also lead to disinterest in the factors that make people ill. A consumer society promises – falsely – that medical technology can fix diseased individuals, and that good health can be bought and sold in the marketplace rather than being something to promote or work for' (Rayner 2001).

WTO REFORM AND PUBLIC SERVICE EXCLUSION

By means of GATS, the WTO is stage-managing a new privatisation bonanza. Multinational and trans-national corporations, including pharmaceutical, insurance and healthcare companies, are lobbying hard to capture the chunks of gross domestic product that governments currently spend on public services such as health and education. Revisions to GATS are by and large being proposed by trade negotiators from countries bent on obtaining better market access to export markets for domestic industries. Officials in other government departments responsible for health, agriculture or the environment may not be aware of what is being negotiated, nor its implications. Publicly accountable services could be dismantled and the door effectively closed to ever reviving them.

A wide range of southern governments, unions and NGOs contend that a thorough assessment of the health, social, environmental and cultural impacts of existing service liberalisation (and indeed of all the WTO agreements) must be conducted, with special reference to the poorest and to women, before negotiations continue on GATS. Such an exercise should be independent of the WTO and associated bodies such as the World Bank or IMF. GATS itself mandates an assessment of trade in services, particularly of the impacts on developing countries, but the WTO Secretariat has so far done little towards this. Public sector unions are calling for public services to be modernised and improved, but based on principles of democratic accountability, effective delivery, adequate funding, equality of access and fairness and partnership at work (UNISON n.d.; Citizen 2002). The current 'exclusion' of public services from GATS should be made actual for services provided in the public interest.

Opposition to GATS, however, should go hand-in-hand with support for campaigns against privatisation more broadly and generally. It would be a hollow victory for GATS to be curtailed only for bilateral and multilateral arrangements with the same effects to increase or for the IMF's hold in the south to tighten. After all, many governments are already themselves restructuring public services; in several respects GATS is merely a mechanism for 'locking-in' existing commercial practices. In Ecuador and Brazil, various groupings and coalitions of physicians, public health activists, trade unions and community groups resisting the privatisation of healthcare services and supporting alternatives to strengthen public services are working along lines similar to those of GATS critics. So are activists in other countries who stress that the public sector can be cheaper, as efficient, more flexible, more transparent and accountable than privatisation or public–private partnerships (Hall 2001b).

International rules governing investment are certainly needed. The current set, however, and the way in which they are implemented, are invariably a charter for corporations to do as they please. Just because the World Trade Organisation, and indeed the World Bank and IMF, are doing the wrong job does not mean that international institutions are not needed to iron out the vast inequalities of the global economy or to prevent further meltdowns in financial markets. At issue is not whether to have rules governing international trade, but what kind of rules to have and how they should be implemented so that they do not have adverse health, social and environmental impacts or exacerbate inequities. As K. Watkins of Oxfam stresses: 'We desperately need a rules-based system of global governance that places people before corporate profit, and shares the benefits of globalisation more equitably' (Watkins 2000).

Health is a fundamental human right, recently defined under the UN Covenant on Economic, Social and Cultural Rights: 'All people have the right to the highest attainable standard of health … as a prerequisite for the full enjoyment of all other human rights.' Human rights and public health policies are indispensable. Trade policies, however, are negotiable.

NOTES

1. The estimates are calculated from WTO figures of national balance of payments records and thus represent cross-border trade only. The value of services provided in one country by companies based in another (commercial presence) could be at least as large as cross-border trade (see http://gats-info.eu.int).

2. The GATS text is available at www.wto.org/english/tratop_e/serv_e/gatsintr_e.htm (see also WTO 1999). For a range of articles and documents on GATS, see: www.xs4all.nl~ceo/gatswatch/gatswatch/html

3. For example, a WTO dispute panel decided in 1996 that a US ban of gasoline imports from Brazil and Venezuela on grounds that they did not meet its Clean Air Act standards contravened GATT rules. In September 2000, however, a WTO dispute panel upheld a French ban on imports of 'white' asbestos that was challenged by Canada. This was the first time that a trade-restrictive measure had been exempted from WTO rules on health grounds. In March 2001 the appeals body of the WTO ruled that a product's health risk was a legitimate factor in determining whether it was 'like' another product (see Waskow and Yu 2001).

4. GATS Article XIV exemption for measures 'necessary to protect human, animal or plant life or health' is borrowed from GATT (Article XX), but leaves out an additional GATT exemption for measures 'relating to the conservation of exhaustible natural resources', an omission which could be interpreted as intentional.

5. By the end of March 2001, members had agreed to guidelines and procedures as to how the renegotiations were to be carried out. Countries went on to the more detailed 'request-offer' phase: countries request each other to liberalise a particular service under GATS and respond with offers of their own. Southern countries will more often be the 'requestee' rather than the 'requester'. Bilateral trade-offs are then extended on a most-favoured nation basis to all WTO members. At the WTO ministerial meeting in Qatar in November 2001 (a meeting held every two years of all 141 WTO members), members agreed to a timetable for the negotiations: countries should submit initial requests by 30 June 2002 (as of November 2001, over 90 per cent of the proposals came from developed countries) and countries should respond with offers by 31 March 2003. The Qatar meeting linked GATS renegotiations to renegotiations on all other issues agreed at the meeting. This means that concessions on GATS can now be traded for concessions in other agreements. Many governments might prefer to make concessions in one agreement, for instance, the Agreement on Agriculture, in return for concessions in another agreement, such as GATS. Some fear that developing countries will be persuaded to give way in the services negotiations in order to get desperately wanted, and long argued for, gains on other issues such as tariff reductions, agriculture, textiles and intellectual property rights.

6. For example, representatives of financial services industries and UK civil servants meet regularly as the LOTIS (Liberalisation of Trade in Services) group. Minutes of this group suggest that documents not publicly available were released to the corporate lobbyists (see Wesselius 2001).

7. Negotiators aim to reclassify services by:

- narrowing the description of service subsectors in which governments have made the least number of commitments (such as health, education and social services) and broadening that of those in which members have made the greatest number
- disaggregating services to make it easier for countries to demand or to offer access to a particular subsector
- clustering related services together so that a country's specific commitment applies to the whole group rather than just one sector
- reclassifying new services so that they are encompassed by existing commitments

Hospital management, for instance, could be reclassified under business services and thereby hived off from health-related service sectors in which WTO members have not made many commitments. Or health information systems could be classified under 'computer and related services' instead of 'health-related and social services'. Or ancillary services such as catering, laundry and cleaning could be classified not under health services but elsewhere. The EC has proposed that water supply should be considered part of an environmental services 'cluster', while the USA has argued that all energy-related services should be treated as a cluster.

These reclassifications would affect the interpretation of existing commitments as well as future commitments. Canadian researcher Scott Sinclair regards service reclassification, a seemingly simple technical procedure, as a means 'to expand GATS coverage by stealth' (see Sinclair 2000: 67–71; Gould 2001).

8. Under the North American Free Trade Agreement (NAFTA), for instance, US for-profit hospitals argued that the user fees charged by the Canadian public health system to patients were commercial charges and that denying US companies entry to the Canadian health market was a denial of the right of US companies to profit from that market. Moreover, European trade officials have emphatically reassured WTO members that an exemption for governmental services in the European Treaty had offered no protection at all in practice (see Gould 2001).

9. Calculated by Allyson Pollock from 1999 data.

10. The multinational expansion of private healthcare companies has not been as coherent or extensive as that of other public service sectors such as water, waste management and energy. But companies active in insurance, hospitals, laboratories (clinical diagnosis, MRI scans and therapy such as dialysis) and support services (cleaning and catering) all have an impact on healthcare services. Support service multinationals with contracts in hospitals in many countries include ISS (Denmark), Sodexho (France), Rentokil/Initial (UK), Granada/Compass (UK) and EDS (USA). Some of the main multinational companies involved in health insurance include Aetna (Netherlands), Allianz (Germany), Aon (UAS), CIGNA (USA), United Health Care International (USA) and AIG (USA). In the UK, Bupa and PPP have 70 per cent of the health insurance market. Among the largest for-profit chains of hospitals are Hospital Corporation of America (HCA), Sun Health Care (USA), Tenet (USA), Humana (USA) and National Medical Enterprises (NME) (USA). Private healthcare companies, particularly US ones, are targeting countries which have a sufficiently affluent elite willing to pay for healthcare or which have an existing private health service base. Countries and regions of special interest are Latin America, South-East Asia, China and the Pacific Rim, the Middle East and, to some extent, south Asia (see Koivusalo 1999; Price et al. 1999; Hall 2001a).

11. Health-related services include not only professional and clinical services (hospitals and doctors) but also insurance, occupational, laboratory, infrastructure, support, nursing, community care and pensions services.

12. Hospital services represent between 40 and 50 per cent of this expenditure, pharmaceuticals between 30 and 40 per cent and outpatients the remainder. OECD countries account for about 90 per cent of worldwide healthcare expenditure. The public share of total health spending in the USA is 45 per cent, lower than any other industrial country. The OECD average is about 75 per cent.

13. GATS schedules list several categories of health services divided into three areas:

- professional services, encompassing medical, dental, veterinary, nursing and midwives, laboratory services
- health-related and social services, encompassing hospital, other human health, social, community care (including of the elderly) and other services
- health and pensions insurance

14. The WTO Secretariat points out that nineteen of the fifty-nine countries

that have made commitments on medical or hospital services have not made commitments on health insurance services, while thirty-five of the seventy-six members with commitments on health insurance have not made commitments on medical or hospital services.

15. This is despite the fact that Canada has not made any commitments under GATS to liberalise professional, health or social services (see Sanger 2001).

16. A cross-subsidy equivalent in the commercial world is 'loss leaders': selling something at less than cost price to draw in customers, but with the costs paid for by other higher-priced goods.

17. A general principle to ensure equity in healthcare has been to provide services according to need and to finance them according to ability to pay. A comparison of different finance mechanisms suggests that general taxation and public provision is the least regressive approach, while financing healthcare services through private insurance and patients' out-of-pocket payments is the most regressive. Universal social insurance, such as is common in continental Europe, falls somewhere in the middle. The privatisation in Britain of utilities (electricity, gas, water), transport and long-term care have adversely and disproportionately affected the poor, elderly, disabled and unemployed (see Koivusalo 1999; Pollock and Price 2000b).

18. GATS could also enable pharmaceutical companies to run hospitals. In the USA, the pharmaceutical industry, one of the most profitable and fastest-growing sectors of the world economy, is integrating vertically into managed care companies (those that act as an intermediary between doctor and patient) and other services. Merck, for example, has acquired Medco, the largest US prescription drugs provider. Zeneca, the world's second largest manufacturer of cancer drugs, has taken over the management of eleven cancer treatment centres in the USA. Meanwhile, the confidentiality of medical records could be undermined. For instance, a country may not have opened up its health services to competition under GATS, but may have opened up data-processing or database services. Would national measures relating to the confidentiality of health records be classified under health services or under database services? (See Sinclair 2000: 36–7; Sanger 2001.)

19. The USA spends more than any other country on healthcare in absolute terms and as a proportion of GDP. It accounts for 3–4 per cent of the world's population, yet spends 35–40 per cent of the world's spending on healthcare. Despite its high expenditure on healthcare, however, the USA has some of the worst health indices of OECD countries. Increased spending does not mean increased health or healthcare; one-fifth of the spending is on administration. Those who need healthcare do not receive or have access to it; the spending is driven by a technological model of health and medical consumerism; and the underlying causes of sickness are increasing. 'The irrationality of the system extends even to the rich,' points out Richard Levins , 'who are over-treated. Nearly 200,000 people in the US die each year through improper medical interventions, while many more die from misuse of heavily advertised prescription drugs, over-the-counter remedies and other preparations' (see Levins 2000).

20. The US healthcare system is financed by insurance, although programmes and companies vary from state to state. For nearly two out of three Americans, this

health insurance is paid for by their employers. Publicly funded national insurance schemes, paid for out of national and state budgets, were introduced in 1965, modelled on private health insurance schemes and based on the needs of doctors and hospitals rather than patients. Medicare pays for hospital and doctor treatment (but not drugs outside hospitals) for some 39 million people over the age of sixty-five, while Medicaid pays for some 34 million people on low incomes or with disabilities. But today, the vast majority of the 44 million uninsured are employed. More than one-third of Hispanics and one-fifth of blacks do not have regular insurance, compared with 12 per cent of white Americans. Despite state-sponsored insurance programmes, America's poor have little access to medical care of any sort. Moreover, the number of people who are underinsured is growing as employers cut back on their costs. Like the uninsured, they pay for care themselves or forgo it. Medicare and Medicaid have insufficient resources to check that treatment is necessary or that bills are accurate. The US Department of Health estimates that it overpays private hospitals $23 billion a year. Medicare and Medicaid together underwrite about three-quarters of the costs of the $86 billion long-term care industry.

REFERENCES

Allaert, B. and Forman, N. (1999) *Gender, Trade and Rights: Moving Forward* (WIDE Bulletin, May), Brussels: WIDE.

Balasubramaniam, K. (2000) 'Globalisation and liberalisation of healthcare services: WTO and the General Agreement on Trade in Services', paper prepared for People's Health Assembly, Dhaka, December 2000; website: www.pha2000.org

Caplan, R. (n.d.) *GATS Handbook*, Waltham, MA: Alliance for Democracy; website: www.thealliancefordemocracy.org

Centre for Public Services (CPS) (2001) 'What future for public services? Private finance initiative and public private partnerships'; website: www.centre.public.org.uk/briefings

Citizen (2002) 'Stop the GATS attack, international statement'; website: www.citizen.org/trade/wto/gats/Sign.on/articles.cfm?ID=1584

Department of Trade and Industry (DTI) (1999) 'GATS 2000, health and education services', briefing note (2 December 1999), cited in Pollock and Price 2000a, p. 1996. See also website: www.dti.gov.uk/worldtrade/service.htm.

EU-GATS (n.d.) 'Opening world markets for services: a guide to the GATS: The General Agreement on Trade in Services'; website: gats-into.eu.int/gats-info/guide.pl?MENU=bbb

European Services Forum (ESF) (1999) 'Set of Principles', 26 January 1999; website: www.esf.be/f_e_abou.htm

Evans, R. (1999) 'Health reform: what business is it of business?' in D. Drache and T. Sullivan (eds), *Health Reform: Public Success, Private Failure*, London: Routledge.

Gould, E. (1999) 'The Next MAI', Ontario: Council of Canadians, website: www.canadians.org

— (2001) *The WTO General Agreement on Trade in Services: Separating WTO Fact from Fiction*, Ontario: Council of Canadians.

Government of British Columbia (2001) 'GATS and public service systems: the GATS "Governmental Authority" exclusion', discussion paper from international branch of the Ministry of Employment and Investment, Government of British Columbia, Canada (2 April 2001).

Hall, D. (2001a) *Globalisation, Privatisation and Health Care: A Preliminary Report*, London: Public Services International Research Unit (PSIRU).

— (2001b) *The Public Sector Water Undertaking*, London: PSIRU.

Hildyard, N. (1998) *The World Bank and the State: A Recipe for Change?*, London: Bretton Woods Project.

Koivusalo, M. (1999) *World Trade Organisation and Trade-Creep in Health and Social Policies* (GASPP Occasional Paper 4), Helsinki: STAKES/GASPP.

Krajewski, M. (2001) *Public Services and the Scope of GATS*, Geneva: Center for International Environmental Law.

Kuttner, R. (1996) 'Columbia/HCA and the resurgence of the for-profit hospital business', *New England Journal of Medicine*, 335 (5), 362–7.

— (1998) 'The commercialization of prepaid group health care', *New England Journal of Medicine*, 338 (21), 1558–63.

— (1999a) 'The American healthcare system: Wall Street and health care', *New England Journal of Medicine*, 340, 664–8.

— (1999b) 'The American healthcare system: health insurance coverage', *New England Journal of Medicine*, 340 (2), 163–8.

Lang, T. (2001) 'Trade, public health and food', in M. McKee, P. Garner and R. Stott (eds), *International Co-operation and Health*, Oxford: Oxford University Press.

Levins, R. (2000) 'Is capitalism a disease? A report on the crisis in US public health', *Monthly Review*, 52 (4), 8–33.

Macdonald, M. (2000) *From Seattle to Beijing+5: How Can Women's Economic Human Rights be Safeguarded in Times of Globalisation? The Impact of Macro-economy on Women* (WIDE Bulletin), Brussels: WIDE.

Martin, B. (1993) *In the Public Interest? Privatisation and Public Sector Reform*, London: Zed Books.

Pollock, A. M. and Price, D. (2000a) 'Rewriting the regulations: how the World Trade Organisation could accelerate privatisation in health-care systems', *The Lancet*, 356, 1995–2000.

— (2000b) 'Globalisation? Privatisation!', *Health Matters*, 41, 14.

Price, D., Pollock, A. M. and Shaoul, J. (1999) 'How the World Trade Organisation is shaping domestic policies in health care', *The Lancet*, 354, 1889–92.

PSI (Public Services International) (1998) *Transnationals in Public Services*, Ferney-Voltaire Cedex: PSI.

— (1999a) *The WTO and the General Agreement on Trade in Services: What is at Stake for Public Health?*, Ferney-Voltaire Cedex: PSI.

— (1999b) *Health and Social Services*, Ferney-Voltaire Cedex: PSI.

— (2000) *Great Expectations: The Future of Trade in Services*, Ferney-Voltaire Cedex: PSI.

Rayner, G. (2001) personal communication with the author, 11 June.

Sanger, M. (2001) *Reckless Abandon: Canada, the GATS and the Future of Health Care*, Ottawa: Canadian Centre for Policy Alternatives.

Sinclair, S. (2000) *GATS: How the World Trade Organization's New 'Services' Negotiations Threaten Democracy*, Ottawa: Canadian Centre for Policy Alternatives.

UNDP (United Nations Development Program) (1999) *Human Development Report 1999*, New York: UNDP.

UNISON (n.d.) *Public Services Manifesto*, London: UNISON.

USTR (Office of the United States Trade Representative) (1998) *USTR 1998 Trade Policy Agenda and 1997 Annual Report*, Washington, DC: USTR.

Vastine, R. (1999) Statement before the Senate Finance Committee Subcommittee on International Trade, 21 October 1999; website: www.uscsi.org

Waskow, D. and Yu, V. B. (2001) *A Disservice to the Earth: The Environmental Impact of the WTO General Agreement on Trade in Services (GATS)*, Washington, DC: Friends of the Earth US.

Watkins, K. (2000) 'Behind closed doors: why the poor will suffer if globalisation is not controlled', *Guardian* (Society), 13 December, 9.

Wesselius, E. (2001) *Liberalisation of Trade in Services: Corporate Power at Work*, Amsterdam: Corporate Europe Observatory.

Whitfield, D. (2001) *Public Services or Corporate Welfare: Rethinking the Nation State in the Global Economy*, London: Pluto Press.

WTO (1998) Secretariat, 'Health and Social Services: background note by the Secretariat S/C/W50', 18 September.

— (1999) Secretariat, Trade in Services Division, 'An Introduction to the GATS'; website: www.wto.org/english/tratop_e/serv_e/gsintr_e.doc

Zarilli, S. and Kinnon, C. (eds) (1997) *International Trade in Health Services: A Development Perspective*, New York and Geneva: UNCTAD/WHO.

CHAPTER 4

Ethics and Medical Care in a Globalising World: Some Reflections

IMRANA QADEER

Classical thinkers conceptualised an ideal society based on a strong sense of justice that shaped their vision of law, administration, cooperation and individual conduct. As the modern state emerged, however, 'growth' acquired a central space in social thought, with parallels being drawn from the disciplines of economics and biology and the theory of social evolution. According to Durant, Spencer for example believed that organic evolution determined certain ethical conceptions (Durant 1926). Over time, survival of the fittest and competition were easily accepted as legitimate ethical principles of the expanding capitalist societies. Yet, so strong was the notion of justice that neo-classical thought had to anchor individualism, competition and private property around issues of equality of access and opportunity, and the protection of basic human rights. Thus the conflict of interests between classes, individuals and society, freedom and control, continues to unfold within a search for universal ethical principles.

In the field of medicine, basic ethical conflicts are reflected in the struggle for control over knowledge, its use or misuse by professionals/healers, and the role of the state in ensuring equity in health. As the scope of medicine expanded from clinical practice to mass interventions and the realm of public health, ethical guidelines were initially built into a code of conduct for physicians, the rights of patients and informed consent. Later, issues such as the access to healthcare systems, quality of care, and policy choices regarding technology and its organisation became the ethical themes for the international community and the World Health Organisation (Leary 1997).

The post-colonial societies of the Indian subcontinent drew upon the experiences of the social-democratic and socialist countries and set out to build their healthcare systems within the emerging ethical guidelines

(WHO 1989). Although the common goal was to uplift marginalised populations and reduce inequity, the achievements varied, depending on constraints on the political economy of each country. Differentials in wealth and health services continued to exist between the rural and the urban in each context and the rich and poor populations. Preference for clinical specialisation varied, creating different combinations of basic healthcare facilities and hi-tech tertiary care. Sri Lanka and Pakistan presented two extremes of this scenario (Qadeer et al. 2001). It is a fact that these slow growing economies – imprisoned in their feudal and patriarchal structures – could not create the services they had planned for and dreamt of; but it is also true that they attempted to build a responsible and coherent welfare state that encouraged self-sufficiency.

In the subcontinent, some fifty years of planning has created a wealth of knowledge of and expertise in the prerequisites for realising national goals (Banerji 1997a). This has helped to identify the forces that have impeded the pursuit of equity and justice in healthcare (Banerji 1998). The linkages between health and poverty have become increasingly more visible (Qadeer 1985) and the caste–class divides have been identified as a key aspect of existing inequalities in access to healthcare (Banerji 1982). The professed goals of the different states and the insights gained have not, however, been able to combat the combined pressures of middle-class aspirations and the push of international financial institutions on faltering and indebted governments. These governments are then forced to pursue specific strategies that would continue to perpetrate inequality, despite the fact that during this period the health services for the poor improved to some degree.

Such unprogressive policies were seen in the 1980s, when Sri Lanka, for example, opted for restructuring health services for its tea plantation workers and handed over the management of these services to the private tea companies (Hettiarachchi 2001). At the same time, in India, the sixth Five Year Plan proposed that medical care be opened up to the non-government sector (GOI 1980). However, with the rising debt burden, the countries of the subcontinent formally accepted and began implementing structural adjustment programmes during the late 1980s, with little consideration for the consequences. This policy affected the subcontinent at a varied pace over the 1990s. Bangladesh, for instance, with its almost skeletal infrastructure, actually showed an increase in investment in healthcare (Khan 2001). On the other hand, Pakistan was largely dependent upon private sector healthcare and showed a decline in health indicators as the economic crunch affected policies and purchasing capacity across all social groups (Zaidi 2001). Sri Lanka attempted to prevent its reform policies from undermining its primary healthcare infrastructure (Fernando 2001), to a large extent successfully, certainly in comparison to the others.

To understand the implications and related ethical conflicts raised by economic restructuring upon the health sector as a whole, this chapter will focus on four main aspects of medical care: access, disease control, quality and expenditure. The main emphasis will be on the Indian subcontinent, though a regional dimension will also be reflected where possible.

ACCESS TO MEDICAL CARE

Given a progressively emasculated infrastructure for the distribution of health services (Qadeer 2000), food supplies (Swaminathan 2000), and receding job opportunities (Chauhan et al. 1997), it is not surprising that morbidity levels in India have either stagnated or increased over the past decade (Iyer and Sen 2000). This is particularly true for the very poor who constitute 27 to 52 per cent of the population of the subcontinent (Haq 1999: 12). Data on access to medical care from India show that between 1986–87 and 1995–96 the proportion of population opting for private sector healthcare had increased significantly from 50 to 80 per cent of all expenditure on healthcare. In view of the clear decline in investment in medical care over the last decade, this shows that, as the public sector withdraws, more and more people have little alternative to private sector provision (Qadeer 2000).

The relevance of this for the issue of equity is further highlighted when we see that, despite higher utilisation of the private sector on the whole, in case of serious illness a greater proportion of the poor seek public hospitals (Iyer and Sen 2000). It is also known that ill-health is a major cause of indebtedness and economic pressure in rural areas. Inevitably, pushing privatisation of medical care in regions where both the degree and proportion of service deprivation are high transforms privatised healthcare into a tool for marginalisation. The Sri Lankan experience shows that if the infrastructure in the public sector is adequate for secondary and tertiary hospitals, the private sector is used mostly for outpatient care.

Another reason for the displacement of the poor from public sector provision is the introduction of user fees. The argument that such fees generate resources from those who can pay to improve the quality of care for those who cannot has been proven wrong. Not only do they squeeze the non-paying poor out of public hospitals (Krishnan 1999), but the upper middle class stops using these financially constrained hospitals. Thus, articulate voices that could protest against and resist dwindling quality are lost. Even if a hospital somehow manages to improve its services, it fails to improve the system as a whole since there is no mechanism of risk pooling. Together, the general policy of tax reduction and the introduction of user fees shift the burden of hospital costs on to the poor, who suffer a greater burden of sickness owing to poverty, greater exposure to risk and lack of basic services. The rich thus benefit from the current reforms at the expense of the poor.

The strategy of identifying the poor and exempting them from user fees also appears not to have succeeded. In India for example, in Andhra Pradesh green cards were supposed to be provided to the poor, but, more often than not, they went to the non-poor. In our view the strategy of depending upon non-governmental organisations (NGOs) has also failed, because in most parts of India they are mainly involved in providing reproductive and child healthcare. In addition, their limited population coverage does not really improve access to services as a whole. Handing over primary health centres (PHCs) to NGOs has also not worked in India due to political and administrative constraints.

Availability of personnel and drugs often influences access to care. While the nursing and para-medical staff prefer government postings, in India doctors are moving out of the public sector. Drug availability in most public hospitals is poor, hence patients have to buy their own medicines at the time of admission or return without care. In surgical cases the list of purchases invariably includes syringes, needles, valves, lenses etc., depending upon the nature of the surgery. This policy can only promote the interests of the drug industry. The first comprehensive drug policy of 1978 has been scrapped by the government. The number of drugs targeted under price control declined from 343 to 73 in 1994. The profitability allowed in these categories also increased, from 40 to 75 per cent in 1987 to 150 per cent in 1994. Even this scale of profits is to be rendered redundant soon as the drugs under control are to be further reduced (FMRAI 2001).

MEDICAL CARE AS A PREVENTIVE TOOL

Communicable diseases continue to be a major challenge for public health planners in the subcontinent. An important lesson, learnt the hard way, is that these diseases are the product of a milieu largely born out of poverty. Therefore medical/technological interventions have to be part of an overall strategy of development that focuses on improving well-being, reducing inequity, and promoting inter-sectoral linkages (ICSSR and ICMR 1980). Current reforms of the health sector and the restructuring of health financing have not only ignored these lessons, but also strengthened the negative trend of promoting vertical disease control programmes. These programmes are isolated, expensive and use imported hi-tech facilities, and have become the mainstay of the control programmes. Research on the comparative utility of the various possible regimes has been wholly inadequate and has further complicated the problems of access to and availability of services.

In the case of tuberculosis, for example, the relative clinical benefit of a new regime is not sufficient to establish its superiority. Experts suggest that improved availability of drugs, better management, monitoring, and 'case holding' are more crucial factors than a mere change of drugs (Nagpaul 1992). But such indigenous advice has been neglected and, instead, an imported and expensive regime has been adopted. Introducing a more expensive regime has meant reducing total coverage (owing to costs incurred), even though the cure rates among the treated may be higher (Qadeer 1995). Since the new programme, Directly Observed Treatment – Short Course (DOTS), is based on the premise that people are irresponsible, hence the selection of patients has also been extremely biased. It has excluded, for instance, the homeless, migrants and the early defaulters, thus exaggerating the probability of cure among the selected. Patients with resistance or a relapse, and those who need the new drug regime the most, may not get it (Chakraborty 2001). This selective application of hi-tech (which also increases national dependence and debt) is highly questionable from the epidemiological and ethical point of view. Not only has it not achieved the 75 per cent coverage it had aimed for, it also denies the right of individuals to quality treatment (Banerji 1997b). It also treats poor people differently.

Control of malaria and leprosy are other examples of distorted medical care strategies under the reforms package, which provides more support to the drug manufacturing multinational corporations (MNCs) than to the patients. Keeping aside the ecological complexities of malaria, the new 'roll back malaria' strategy provides mosquito nets for people who either have little time to sleep within them, or have no roof from which to hang them. The drugs are a series of third-generation products (WHO 2000) which are expensive and not manufactured in the subcontinent. Similarly, following a decade of Rifampicin use under the leprosy programme, it has only now been acknowledged that we may not be able to eradicate the disease as there is no guarantee that two years is sufficient for cure (Qadeer 1995).

The case of AIDS is yet another example of the reforms process ignoring the socio-economic roots of disease, neglecting the importance of primary healthcare and ensuring that drugs being provided for treatment are inaccessible to those most in need (AIDS Anti-Discrimination Movement 2002). The role of the World Trade Organisation (WTO) in changing the nature of patents and the extent to which MNCs are ready to block other local companies from producing cheaper drugs provide evidence of a trend to strengthen the commercial hold of the MNCs (Balasubramanium 2000). By compelling Third World countries to accept the monopoly of the MNCs and forcing them to buy at high prices through borrowing from the financial institutions, the debt trap is well established in the name of international cooperation and technology transfers.

Another implication of the reforms for the national health programmes is that, due to a weakened public infrastructure coupled with weaknesses in controls and monitoring systems, the interventions of the private sector not only increase but their effectiveness remains unknown. Hence, a major part of the strategy of control and elimination that depends on standardisation, adequate monitoring of treatment, and feedback, is simply not possible. According to one study, for example, 300 combinations of drugs were recorded in the prescriptions of private practitioners in Maharashtra (Phadke 1998). Thus key therapeutic interventions are distorted due to uncontrolled privatisation. This increases the probability of failure to impact upon the strategies supporting epidemiological trends of diseases and an ongoing progression of the commodification of ill-health.

QUALITY OF CARE

There are two uses of medical care: community-level interventions for epidemiological control and clinical care for individuals. The issue of the nature of quality differs in both of these. For the former, especially in a poor country, the issues of cost-effectiveness and coverage of the population are intimately linked to the quality of control programmes based on therapeutic interventions. Even when we examine the quality of clinical care for individuals, a host of problems remain. Quality does not depend upon effectiveness of technology alone. It requires correct and early diagnosis and optimum duration of hospitalisation if and when required. These, in turn, depend upon support from good laboratory, nursing, para-medical and ancillary services. The personnel resource-crunch affects all these services in public hospitals and therefore ultimately also the quality of care. For example, the practice of allowing public sector doctors to indulge in private practice has been further legitimised by the pressures of privatisation. This not only takes away time spent at the hospital, but it diverts hospital resources (human resources and material) into the special care of private patients in general wards. The tenuous links that existed between the public and private sectors prior to the reforms have now been strengthened. What was previously viewed as 'inappropriate' is now known as 'Public Private Partnerships'. Many forms of these partnerships appear to flourish in the neo-liberal climate. These range from the charging of commissions for referrals to private labs, to nursing homes that have been reported as being run in the name of relatives (Baru 1998). Under the reform package these partnerships tend also to breed a kind of indifference among the in-house professionals towards public hospitals. They view them as a means of making personal profits rather than providing a service. By weakening the three-tier health infrastructure that had existed, the reforms have led to overloading of hospitals with not necessarily the most vulnerable patients.

In India, the private sector consists of a small but powerful corporate sector, a rapidly proliferating set of nursing homes, and a vast body of private practitioners ranging from specialists to untrained individuals. The professionals view the latter with contempt and their practice is in the process of being banned, even though they are often the only healers available for the poor. The schemes set in place to upgrade and train these practitioners (often the only resource for the poor) have been severely criticised by professional doctors. Similarly, the nursing homes are a mixed bag of doubtful quality providers, as revealed by the qualifications of their personnel and the quality of their infrastructure (Baru 1998). The claims to international standards in the quality of care are largely derived from the corporate sector.

According to one study, the large private and corporate hospitals are known to spend up to 30 per cent of their total expenditure on salaries. Of this the maximum (50 per cent of the consultation fee paid by users) goes to the consultants (Workers' Solidarity 2000). This explains the shift of public sector doctors to the private sector. Other personnel, however, are fleeced and exploited by private hospitals through long hours, low pay scales, an almost complete denial of benefits and lack of any rational system of work monitoring (Baru et al. 2000). Inevitably, this drastically affects their performance and the overall levels of care.

Similarly, given the range of private institutions, the competence of physicians is also varied. Corporate sector hospitals, run on the basis of share-holdings, often encourage higher rates of invasive procedures, which may raise returns on shares owned by doctors, but not necessarily the quality of care (Baru 1998). Unnecessary and frequent uses of ultrasound and rising rates of Caesarean sections in private clinics are all evidence of indifference towards the quality of care. Often private hospitals prefer to discharge patients once the investigative and invasive phase is over and when their profitability decreases. The slow turnover in public sector hospitals, rather than being labelled inefficient, may in fact reflect a more patient-centred approach. Thus, the usual criteria of lower cost-efficiency and patient turnover, and higher hospital mortality rates, do not necessarily reflect a poor quality of medical care. A more comprehensive definition of quality of healthcare is needed, which goes beyond such narrow/technical indicators and takes into account quality as well as outcome.

The inability of the state to rationalise, control or monitor the private sector is one of the outcomes of the current strategy of decontrol and of building 'partnerships' and 'social contracts' with the private sector. The hold of the private sector on medical care is thus rising and significant, and, in our view, endangering whatever remains of primary healthcare (including secondary and tertiary care). This uncontrolled expansion has led to growing malpractice in the illegal sale of body parts such as kidneys (VHAI 1993), human experiments without informed consent (Rao 1998), and sale of dangerous contraceptives through the private sector (Sathyamala 2000). The private sector, therefore, is highly prone to providing declining quality without adequate checks and safeguards.

MEDICAL CARE EXPENDITURE

In India, the two main resources for health expenditure are the government and the private sector. The state resources come from the central and provincial governments, local bodies and the public sector insurance system. The private sources are mainly the out-of-pocket expenditure and the benefits/insurance for employees. India and Sri

Lanka spend around 6 per cent and 3.4 per cent of their GDP, respectively, on health. Of this, 1.4 per cent and 1.7 per cent come from the state and 4.6 per cent and 1.7 per cent from the private sector respectively. This indicates that both have a high proportion of private investment but India's private expenditure is much higher (75 per cent as against 50 per cent in Sri Lanka). Of the private expenditure in India, 88 per cent is out-of-pocket expenditure. In Sri Lanka insurance accounts only for about 2 per cent of the private expenditure (Gill and Kavadi 1999; Hsiao 2000). Thus, the private sector plays a key role in medical care in Sri Lanka where it mainly provides for outpatient care, while in India it is now focusing on providing secondary and tertiary inpatient care. Private sector investment in India has risen from around 50 per cent to the present level of over 75 per cent. Consequently, government expenditure has declined in medical care (Iyer and Sen 2000). This means hardship for the poor in terms of a rising burden of personal debts due to illness, the economic downturn of families and the increased sale of family assets (Daspattanayak 1996).

To overcome the crunch of resources even if the state proposes 'social contracts', private capital will first ensure its profits. For them the objective is diversification and not the extent of welfare coverage. In this process medical care priorities are invariably distorted. The private health insurance schemes, for example, are targeted only at those groups that can pay high premiums, and the aged and chronically ill will have to pay more as they are considered high-risk cases (Rizvi 1999). In India, the Employees' State Insurance Scheme (ESIS) for workers is trying to lend its hospitals to private agencies to be run as general hospitals. It is likely that this will prevent occupational diseases among workers from obtaining adequate and much needed treatment (*Times of India*, 3 June 2001, p. 10). Since most international aid is tagged to specific programmes such as AIDS, tuberculosis and malaria, it invariably distorts national health budgets. The new financial arrangements under the reforms package, therefore, care neither about epidemiological priorities nor adequate cover for the poor.

The transformation of medical care under the new dispensation – where efficiency and profits prevail – can in no way preserve long fought-for ethical norms. Hence, without actually giving them up, their content is being redefined. Primary healthcare has become 'primary level care', and public health propaganda now exhorts the individual to change lifestyles, fertility behaviour, and adopt technical interventions to control disease. Financial efficiency and profit maximisation have evolved as the measure of quality in medical care, while epidemiology is turned on its head and viewed as a tool for genetic engineering rather than as a science of public health. Without any reference to political economy, prevention has become health education and a search for vaccines. The governments and the private investors from the First World are generously contributing to vaccine research in the Third World – such as in the Indo–US Collaborative Project and the Gates Foundation's donation for global research efforts on vaccines. The answer to the question of who will hold the patents and who will bear the costs appears predictable.

Finally, a new strategy of removing the poor from the metropolis is being encouraged to lessen the moral dilemma of the well-off. In Delhi itself, 360,000 people living in slums have been displaced over the past two years, with little alternative space or basic amenities (Roy 2000). In addition, values such as 'pollution control' and 'healthy environment' are being used to blame the poor and discredit them, irrespective of their actual contribution to these. A growing anti-poor ethos lets the real culprits – the industrial houses and the consumerist classes – get away scot-free. These trends are undoubtedly clashing with the old set of ethical principles. The proponents of reform are trying to re-establish the place of markets in the welfare sector, even though it has not succeeded in the past, especially in relatively poor countries. Those in power have chosen to retain the principles of equity, access and quality, yet in such a way that these principles lose all their substance. The question that needs to be asked is, how ethical are the new ethics and can they save societies from chaos?

REFERENCES

AIDS Anti-Discrimination Movement (2002) 'AIDS therapy in whose interest?', in *Endless and Sickening Therapies for AIDS – A Citizens Report on Anti-AIDS Drugs and the Threat to Public Health*, New Delhi: AIDS Anti-Discrimination Movement, 7.

Balasubramanium, K. (2000) 'Globalisation and Liberalisation of Health Care Services: WTO and the General Agreement on Trade in Services', paper prepared for People's Health Assembly, Dhaka (December), available on www.pha2000.org

Banerji, D. (1982) *Poverty, Class and Health Culture in India*, New Delhi: Prachi.

— (1997a) *Landmarks in the Development of Health Services in the Countries of South Asia* (monograph), New Delhi: Lok Paksh.

— (1997b) *Serious Implications of the World Bank's Revised National Tuberculosis*

Control Programme for India, New Delhi: Nucleus for Health Policies and Programs.

— (1998) 'Trends in Public Health Practice in India: A Place for a New Public Health', B. C. Dasgupta Oration, Thirty Second Annual Conference of the Indian Public Health Association, Hyderabad.

Baru, R. V. (1998) *Private Health Care in India: Social Characteristics and Trends*, New Delhi: Sage.

Baru, R. V., Qadeer, I. and Priya, R. (2000) 'Medical industry: illusion of quality at what cost?', *Economic and Political Weekly*, 35 (28–9), 15–21.

Chakraborty, A. K. (2001) 'Tuberculosis Program in India: Current Operational Issues', in I. Qadeer, K. Sen and K. R. Nayar (eds), *Public Health and the Poverty of Reforms: The South Asian Predicament*, New Delhi: Sage.

Chauhan, D., Antia, N. H. and Sangita, K. (1997) *Health Care in India: A Profile*, Mumbai: Foundation for Research in Community Health (FRCH).

Daspattanayak, R. K. (1996) 'Conditions of work and life of agricultural labourers in Baleshwar district: implications for health', New Delhi: Centre for Social Medicine and Community Health, School of Social Sciences, Jawaharlal Nehru University (unpublished dissertation).

Durant, W. (1926) *The Story of Philosophy*, New York: Salone Press.

Fernando, D. N. (2001) 'Structural adjustment programs and healthcare services in Sri Lanka: an overview', in I. Qadeer, K. Sen and K. R. Nayar (eds), *Public Health and the Poverty of Reforms: The South Asian Predicament*, New Delhi: Sage.

FMRAI (Federation of Medical Representative Association of India) (2001) 'Note on Amendment to the Drug Price Control Order, 1995', presented at the National Drug Convention, New Delhi, 14 June 2001.

Gill, S. and Kavadi, S. N. (1999) *Health Financing and Costs: A Comparative Study of Trends in Eighteen Countries with Special Reference to India*, Pune: Foundation for Research in Community Health (FRCH).

Government of India (GOI) (1980) *Sixth Five Year Plan*, New Delhi: Planning Commission.

Haq, M. (1999) *Human Development in South Asia*, Oxford: Oxford University Press.

Hettiarachchi, I. (2001) 'Structural adjustment policies and health in the plantation sector in Sri Lanka', in I. Qadeer, K. Sen and K.R. Nayar (eds), *Public Health and the Poverty of Reforms: The South Asian Predicament*, New Delhi: Sage.

Hsiao, W. (2000) *A Preliminary Assessment of Sri Lanka's Health Sector and Steps Forward*, Cambridge, MA: Harvard University Press.

Indian Council for Social Science Research (ICSSR) and Indian Council for Medical Research (ICMR) (1980) *Health For All: An Alternative Strategy* (Report of a Study Group set up jointly by ICSSR and ICMR), New Delhi: ICSSR.

Iyer, A. and Sen, G. (2000) 'Health sector changes and health equity in the 1990s in India', in S. Raghuram (ed.), *Health and Equity* (Technical Report Series 1.8), Netherlands: Institute for Effecting Cooperation with Developing Countries (HIVOS).

Khan, A. Q. (2001) 'Health Services in Bangladesh: Development and Structural Reforms', in I. Qadeer, K. Sen and K. R. Nayar (eds), *Public Health and the Poverty of Reforms: The South Asian Predicament*, New Delhi: Sage.

Krishnan, T. N. (1999) 'Access to health and the burden of treatment in India: an inter state comparison', in M. Rao (ed.), *Disinvesting in Health: The World Bank's Prescriptions for Health*, New Delhi: Sage.

Leary, V. A. (1997) 'Human rights and the renewal agenda', in Z. Bankowski, J. H. Bryant and J. Gallagher (eds), *Ethics, Equity and Health for All*, Geneva: Council for International Organisation of Medical Sciences (CIOMS).

Nagpaul, D. R. (1992) 'Surajkund Deliberations' (Editorial), *Indian Journal of Tuberculosis*, 39 (1).

Phadke, A. (1998) *Drug Supply and Pharmaceutical Use*, New Delhi: Sage.

Qadeer, I. (1985) 'Health service systems in India: an expression of socio-conomic inequalities', *Social Action*, July.

— (1995) 'Primary health care: a paradise lost', *IASSI Quarterly*, 14 (1–2), 1–20.

— (2000) 'Health care systems in transition III: India. Part I, the Indian experience', *Journal of Public Health Medicine*, 22 (1), 25–32.

Qadeer, I., Sen, K. and Nayar, K. R. (eds) (2001) 'Introduction', in *Public Health and the Poverty of Reforms: The South Asian Predicament*, New Delhi: Sage.

Rao, M. (1998) 'Quinacrine sterilisation trials: a scientific scandal?', *Economic and Political Weekly*, 33 (13), 692–4.

Rizvi, S. (1999) 'An exploratory study of the place of health insurance in the delivery of healthcare: a focus on India', unpublished dissertation, New Delhi: Centre for Social Medicine and Community Health, School of Social Sciences, Jawaharlal Nehru University.

Roy, D. (2000) 'Organising for safe livelihoods: feasible options', *Economic and Political Weekly*, 35 (52–3), 30 December.

Sathyamala, C. (2000) *An Epidemiological Review of the Injectible Contraceptive, DepoProvera* (monograph), Pune: Medico Friend Circle and Forum for Women's Health.

Swaminathan, M. (2000) *Weakening Welfare: The Public Distribution of Food in India*, New Delhi: Left Word Books.

VHAI (Voluntary Health Association of India) (1993) *Trading of Organs: Need for a Comprehensive Policy*, New Delhi: VHAI.

WHO (World Health Organisation) (1989) *Health Care in South-East Asia*, New Delhi: WHO SEARO.

— (2000) *Implementation of Collaborative Activities on Roll Back Malaria in the South East Asia Region* (Report of an Inter-country Meeting, 4–6 May 1999), New Delhi: WHO SEARO.

Workers' Solidarity (2000) *Critical Conditions: A Report on Workers in Delhi's Private Hospitals*, New Delhi: Workers' Solidarity.

Zaidi, S. A. (2001) 'Structural adjustment and economic slowdown: likely impact on health outcome in Pakistan', in I. Qadeer, K. Sen and K. R. Nayar (eds), *Public Health and Poverty of Reforms: The South Asian Predicament*, New Delhi: Sage.

PART TWO

The Process of Change

CHAPTER 5

Assessing Health Systems' Performance: A Critical Appraisal of the WHO *World Health Report* 2000

CLAUDIA TRAVASSOS

In June 2000 the WHO published the *World Health Report* (WHR 2000), presenting for the first time a ranking of the 191 member countries in relation to the performance of their health systems. The importance of measuring the performance of health systems is that it informs the public and policy-makers about the impact of health policies, so it should be based on clear and meaningful measures. Unfortunately, this was not the case with WHR 2000.

The assessment was based on a new composite index – Overall Health System Attainment – to measure the achievements in the level and the distribution of healthcare, the level and distribution of responsiveness and the fairness in financial contributions. The indicators were weighted – 25 per cent for level and 25 per cent for distribution of health; 12.5 per cent for level and 12.5 per cent for distribution of responsiveness and 25 per cent for fairness of financial contributions. A second measure was developed to compare the attainments with what the system should be able to accomplish – that is, the best that could be achieved with the same resources – the measurement of performance (WHO 2000: 23). Performance was equated with efficiency, which was defined as the extent to which the health system makes the maximum achievable contribution to the defined social goals, given available health system and non-health system resources (PAHO 2001). The methodology was designed to become an annual exercise for monitoring the attainment and performance of the health systems of WHO member states.

Despite the complexity of the analytical work involved in the report, in our view it presented measures that are questionable in terms of their validity and are also quite unclear. For example, regarding data in

general, inferences were drawn from very imperfect baseline data that
also lacked transparency. Only five out of the 191 member states had
provided the information necessary for calculating the indicators, Brazil
being one of them. At the time the WHR 2000 was published, many of
the technical papers with details about the methodology employed were
not available to the member states or to the public. Moreover, the use
of a composite index and the way indicators were aggregated have also
been widely questioned (Navarro 2000; Ugá et al. 2001a; Hurst and
Jee-Hughes 2001; Almeida et al. 2001).

The WHR 2000 presents a new concept of health systems referred
to as 'new universalism'. It means supplying quality essential services,
defined by cost-effectiveness criteria, to the population as a whole. It
implies letting the private market respond to more complex healthcare
needs (Ugá et al. 2001b). In our view this concept questions, on very
superficial grounds, the effectiveness of universal healthcare policies,
primary healthcare and the Alma-Ata Declaration (1978). These are
presented as strategies to be replaced by what is called a third generation
of market-oriented healthcare systems reforms (Almeida et al. 2001).

Despite the fact that countries vary largely in the way they define
and organise their health systems, the monitoring strategy that has been
devised is linked to a very particular view of how health systems should
be defined and structured. This normative approach limits the usefulness
of the evaluation, which should instead be directed at allowing countries
to identify characteristics of health systems in other countries that
perform better, as a means to direct improvement of the performance
of their own health systems.

It also replaces attention to healthcare needs in the population too
simply with the demand for healthcare services. It puts emphasis on the
preferences of individuals – how people prefer to be treated – regardless
of their health needs, access to and the actual utilisation of services.
While it is true that people's preferences play an important role in the
demand for health services, the demand-led explanatory model is much
more complex than the simple straightforward preferences of individuals. It also involves aspects related to the supply side of the market,
social factors and, particularly, healthcare needs in the population as a
whole (Ugá et al. 2001b).

The measure of 'health' used in WHR 2000, Disability-Adjusted
Life Expectancy (DALE), incorporates in the life table the years lost
due to disability. It is a summary measure that includes the burden of
disability from all causes in a population. But DALE is difficult to

measure; presents problems of reliability; there is no consensus on its use for policy decisions; it presents ethical problems and might have adverse consequences for the poor if used to allocate resources (Almeida et al. 2001). DALE was used in the Composite Index of Attainment as the key measure of effectiveness of health systems. As such, it does not acknowledge the impact on the health status of the population of powerful factors other than healthcare delivery. Despite agreeing that the major goal of health systems is to bring health benefits to the population, the use of health as a measure of outcome for health system functioning is questionable and must be supported by a clear understanding of the impact of healthcare on health and of the determinants of health.

In a recent article, Buck et al. (1999) point out that an adequate conceptual framework to measure the benefits of healthcare must deal with the following problems:

- no population health outcome measure can be a perfect indicator of population health status due to contextual factors
- health outcomes are influenced by many factors other than healthcare
- healthcare contributes to welfare other than improvements in health status
- many of the links between healthcare and changes in health status are poorly understood
- many of the influences of healthcare on health status operate over a long period of time

Causal validity (Donabedian 1980), which implies the existence of a causal relationship between an outcome measure and the process that is being evaluated, in this case the functioning of health systems, is an essential attribute of an outcome measure. The absence of causal validity in health outcomes will result in measures that say very little about the functioning of the health systems. What should be good scientific practice in the WHO's document tends to lack causal validity. Apparently, the approaches used do not rely on theory and disregard the existing scientific evidence about the impact of health systems. Actually, in the WHR 2000 there is very little scientific evidence supporting the goals selected and the measures adopted. Furthermore, there are problems with limiting health system monitoring to macro-health outcomes. Reliable measures of health outcomes are difficult to obtain (Hurst and Jee-Hughes 2001), and macro-measures simply cannot supply information about the achievements obtained through specific policies of the Health Ministry.

Another aspect of the approach used in the report, which must be emphasised (although not explicitly stated), is that it did not measure equity in health in relation to the overall system, but simply the variations in health between individuals. Braveman et al. (2001) and Houweling et al. (2001) demonstrate empirically that the indicator of health distribution in WHR 2000 does not correlate with measures of social inequalities in health. Actually, for assessing inequity in health the authors of WHR 2000 prefer to measure health inequalities between individuals instead of the health differences of social groups (Murray et al. 1999). Arguing in favour of the measurement of health differences between individuals, they turn the methodological discussion mainly into an ideological debate. First, by mixing up the monitoring of the distribution of health with the monitoring of equity in health, which has to have a normative approach based on the measurement of social differences in health that are considered by a particular society to be unjust; the monitoring of health differences between individuals without controlling for social conditions might be useful in specific academic studies on the determinants of health, but it is a waste of time if the purpose is to measure equity. Second, despite all existing scientific evidence about the multiple dimensions of health, by suggesting that good (health) science must focus on the individual without any a priori consideration.

There is substantial evidence showing that social factors shape the way biological factors affect health, implying that it is impossible to understand health without considering the social context in which people live (Sen and Bonita 2000). Why then focus the attention on the abstract individual disembodied from social relations?

A single measure of healthcare service – responsiveness – was used in the composite index. 'Responsiveness' is a new concept introduced by the WHO, which might vary from patient satisfaction, and/or acceptability and/or patient experience (Darby et al. 2000). In WHR 2000 'responsiveness' is related to the experience of people with health services in the sense that it is directed to describe objective characteristics and not to measure people's assessment of the healthcare system – satisfaction (deSilva 2001). It refers mainly to the ability of health systems to meet the legitimate expectations of populations for non-health-enhancing aspects of the health system.[1] Responsiveness expressly excludes the expectations of the public for the health-improving dimensions of their interaction, as this is fully reflected in the first goal (DALE) of population health (Gakidou et al. 2000). Responsiveness contains two main aspects: respect for people (dignity, confidentiality and autonomy) and patient orientation (prompt attention choice of care provider and access to social support networks during care).

The report assumes that better responsiveness results in better acceptance of health services on the part of the population and therefore brings about better utilisation of services. Based on the above argument, no direct measure of access was included in the composite index, critical to the overall analysis. The OECD, in its approach to measuring the performance of health systems, will include 'access' as a legitimate component of responsiveness (Hurst and Jee-Hughes 2001). Additionally, since the composite index does not include a measure of technical quality of care, it seems that the authors consider that non-medical aspects of care influence health-seeking behaviour more than its medical aspects. This, again, is a questionable assumption. The limitations with this measure – level and distribution – are such that after the publication of WHR 2000, the WHO recognised that the data used to build this indicator were based on small samples of country-level health system experts (Key Informant Surveys). The latter, in turn, were seen merely as a preliminary and exploratory exercise in data collection (WHO n.d.).

The elements of responsiveness were chosen through literature review, analysis of patient satisfaction surveys and discussion with researchers, and the weights attached to them were chosen through Internet interviews, mainly directed at the WHO staff (deSilva 2001). The responsiveness of the system was also measured using interviews with public health experts, considered more reliable respondents than the general public or the patients (Gakidou et al. 2000). Blendon et al. (2001) question the exclusion of lay experiences and perceptions from official reports that measure the performance of nations in different areas. They show large differences between the WHO responsiveness assessment and data from surveys in seventeen western industrialised countries, based on lay views and expectations of health systems (satisfaction). The USA, which ranked first in responsiveness, was placed thirteenth and tenth in level of satisfaction among the poor and the elderly respectively. Actually, these discrepancies are also explained by the way the indicator of responsiveness was estimated, which is presented below.

A large number of methodological problems are observed in relation to the manner in which this indicator – level and distribution – was estimated, such as: (i) it deals with fairly subjective issues whose basis for comparison in different contexts and diverse culture is highly problematic; (ii) due to lack of data, Key Informants Surveys were conducted in only 35 out of the 153 member countries and used to estimate the indicators in the remaining countries; (iii) none of the countries selected is among the richest countries and data from three countries (Mexico, Chile and Sri Lanka) were not used in the estimation procedures due to problems of quality; although bias related to sample selection is a problem, it is not discussed; and (iv) procedures used to estimate the indicator where no data were available involved various data sources and questionable assumptions.

For example, to estimate responsiveness in 153 member states the authors tested more than twenty-five variables mainly extracted from the United Nations Basic Social Services Statistics, available on the Internet. These are proxies for poverty and social economic development, access to healthcare services, and some odd choices such as happiness scores. Instead of using access, widely agreed to be an important characteristic of health systems, as a legitimate variable for measuring the performance of health systems, it was used as an estimator of responsiveness. It is stated (Valentine et al. 2000) that data for all these variables were available for most countries, a claim which is highly questionable. In Brazil, data for calculating happiness scores and the percentage of the population living within one hour's travel from a health facility (access) are not available on a national basis. Most probably, the majority of these indicators are themselves estimates, or act as hypothesis presented as de facto.

The variables selected through a number of rather confusing procedures to predict the majority of the responsiveness elements were access, wealth and health expenditure (Valentine et al. 2000). The importance of wealth and expenditure in the estimation procedures resulted in a high level of responsiveness in countries that expend a lot on healthcare – the USA is ranked number one and Germany number five. The question that this raises is, should these systems be used as benchmarks for performance improvement in other countries, simply due to their high levels of expenditure?

The approach used to measure the distribution of responsiveness raises even greater concern. Even though the measure of distribution in responsiveness was used in the composite index, the WHO, in a paper published after the release of the WHR 2000, affirms that 'given the paucity of data available from these surveys, this index should be treated more as a qualitative categorisation of countries than as a quantitative exercise' (Valentine et al. 2000). The respondents of the Key Informant Surveys were asked, in an open-ended question, to list the groups of people whom they considered to be discriminated against with regard to responsiveness.

An 'intensity score' was used (number of times a group was cited as being disadvantaged) to select the groups that would be used to estimate the indicator. The groups selected were the poor, women, elderly and disadvantaged ethnic groups. For the countries with the Key Informant Surveys, an 'inequality index' for responsiveness was calculated using the intensity score for each social group selected and its proportion in the population. For the remaining 153 countries, data from multiple sources were used to select the explanatory variables to predict the inequality index. Various imputations were applied to deal with problems of missing data. Statistical modelling was used to identify predictors (Valentine et al. 2000). At the end only two variables were selected to predict the distribution of responsiveness: percentage of people below the poverty line and local access to healthcare services. Once more, access, an important dimension of health systems performance explicitly excluded from the WHO assessment, was used as an estimator only. At the end the indicator of distribution of responsiveness showed very low sensitivity, with a large number of countries arriving at the same index and, therefore, the same rank. In summary, this was an exercise that used Key Informants Surveys to estimate measures of responsiveness, which originated from a whole range of questionable variables derived from unknown sources. Moreover, Key Informant Surveys from a small and specific group of countries were used to estimate responsiveness throughout the world. At the end of this unscientific and very antiquated exercise it is impossible to know what is in fact being measured. On the other hand, the WHR 2000 offered no methodological solution to guarantee comparability for differences existing between countries. It is based on the idea of the abstract universal individual represented as the client/consumer (Oswaldo Cruz Foundation 2000).

For the next round of the monitoring process, WHO is already collecting population data in approximately seventy countries, based on a new questionnaire that will be supplemented with data from Key Informant Surveys in all member states. Nevertheless, the questionnaire and the sampling strategy (www.fiocruz.br/cict/dis/vering.htm) have not been circulated for open discussion with member states and experts outside the organisation. In addition, the entire exercise is being carried out without the necessary transparency and appropriate methodological assessment.

The other indicator – Fairness in Financial Contribution (FFI) – is also very controversial. The FFI index assumes that the financing of a health system is fair when the percentage of household expenditure on health in relation to disposable income (income after subsistence requirements are deducted) is the same regardless of household level of income, health need, access and actual healthcare service utilisation. That is, it assumes the principle that financing for healthcare must be proportional to a household's ability to pay.

A number of papers have been published questioning this indicator on various grounds (Ugá et al. 2001a, 2001b; Almeida et al. 2001; Oswaldo Cruz Foundation 2000; Williams 2001; Wagstaff 2001; Shaw 2001). For example, Wagstaff (2001) identifies three aspects in FFI: (i) the index reflects both vertical equity (households with different ability-to-pay make different payments) and horizontal equity (households with similar ability-to-pay make similar payments); that is, if the indicator is less than 1 it is not possible to know if it is due to vertical inequity, horizontal inequity or both; (ii) it does not distinguish progressivity (the better-off contribute more) from regressivity (the poor contribute proportionally more to income), it only measures if every household contributes with the same proportion of their ability-to-pay (FFI=1) or not (FFI<1); and, (iii) it is sensitive to the mean, so it is not possible to say if countries with different values in FFI are more or less unequal or expend a different average proportion of disposable income in healthcare.

Due to the above limitations, Wagstaff (2001) questions the usefulness of FFI in policy-making, because 'whilst horizontal inequity necessarily increases income inequality, vertical inequity (defined à la WHO) can ... either reduce it or increase it, depending on whether payments are progressive or regressive'. In short, it is useless because it does not measure equity in the financing of health systems, which is a core dimension in the evaluation of health systems throughout the world. Another area of concern is related to the estimation procedures used. Household data were available for only twenty-one countries, and for the remaining countries the indicator was estimated on the basis of three questionable predictors: percentage of public spending on health; the Gini coefficient and the fact of whether or not a country is or has been under a communist regime. The explanatory power of this regression model was also very low – (multiple correlation coefficient) $R^2 = 0.26$ (Oswaldo Cruz Foundation 2000).

In January 2001 the WHO executive board approved a resolution requesting the director-general to initiate a scientific peer review to update the methodology used in the WHR 2000 and to consult member states on the results of the peer review and its recommendations. In May, PAHO organised a Regional Consultation of the Americas on Health Systems Performance Assessment. Some important observations came out from this meeting: (i) health systems performance assessment should be established by consensus; (ii) performance should not be seen as purely efficiency but the quantitative and qualitative appraisal that shows the degree of achievement of the objectives and goals; (iii) efficiency is one among several dimensions of health systems such as equity, effectiveness and quality; and (iv) particular attention should be paid to the functions and intermediate objectives of health systems and not to concentrate on distant final (macro-) objectives (PAHO 2001).

Monitoring health systems is a very complex task because there is no analytical framework thoroughly developed, and methodological issues and lack of good-quality data act as great limitations. However, the above should not represent an impediment to monitor health systems in the short run. Monitoring strategies will have to be designed within these constraints, but directed to produce valid, meaningful and useful information. The experience of countries such as Canada should be considered. Moreover, the state of the art clearly points to the need for research and methodological development to support comprehensive performance monitoring strategies.

NOTE

1. Legitimate expectations were defined 'as conforming to recognised principles or accepted rules and standards' (deSilva 2001).

REFERENCES

Almeida, C. et al. (2001) 'Methodological concerns and recommendations on policy consequences of the World Health Report 2000', *The Lancet*, 26 May, 1692–7.

Blendon, R. J., Kim, M. and Benson, J. M. (2001) 'The public versus the World Health Organization on health system performance', *Health Affairs*, 3, 10–20.

Braveman, P. et al. (2001) 'Scientific concerns regarding the WHR 2000'; www.fiocruz.br/cict/dis/vering.htm

Buck, D., Eastwood, A. and Smith, P. C. (1999) 'Can we measure the social importance of health care?', *International Journal of Technological Assessment of Health Care*, 15 (1), 89–107.

Darby, C., Valentine, N., Murray, C. J. L. and deSilva, A. (2000) *World Health Organization: Strategy on Measuring Responsiveness* (GPE Discussion Paper Series No. 23), Geneva: EIP/GPE/FAR.

deSilva, A. (2001) *A Framework for Measuring Responsiveness* (GPE Discussion Paper Series No. 32), Geneva: EIP/GPE/FAR.

Donabedian, A. (1980) *The Definition of Quality and Approaches to its Assessment*, Ann Arbor, MI: Health Administration Press.

Gakidou, E., Murray, C. J. L. and Frenk, J. (2000) *Measuring Preferences on Health System Performance Assessment* (GPE Discussion Paper Series No. 20), Geneva: EIP/GPE/FAR.

Houweling, T. A., Kunst, A. E. and Mackenbach, J. P. (2001) 'World Health Report 2000: inequality index and socio-economic inequalities in mortality', *The Lancet*, 26 May, 1671–2.

Hurst, J. and Jee-Hughes, M. (2001) *Performance Measurement and Performance Management in OECD Health Systems* (Labour Market and Social Policy Occasional Papers No. 47), Paris: Organization for Economic Co-operation and Development.

Murray, C. J. L., Gakidou, E. E. and Frenk, J. (1999) 'Health inequalities and social groups differences: what should we measure?', *Bulletin of the World Health Organisation*, 7, 537–43.

Navarro, V. (2000) 'Assessment of the World Health Report 2000', *The Lancet*, 9241, 1598–2001.

Oswaldo Cruz Foundation (2000) Health Systems Performance – The World Health Report 2000, Final Report, 14–15 December, Rio de Janeiro; www.fiocruz.br/cict/dis/vering.htm

Pan American Health Organisation (PAHO) (2001) *Final Report. Regional Consultation of the Americas on Health Systems Performance Assessment*, 8–10 May, Washington, DC: PAHO.

Shaw, R. P. (2001) 'Financial fairness indicator: useful compass or crystal ball', commentary presented at the Regional Consultation of the Americas on Health Systems Performance Assessment, 8–10 May, Washington, DC.

Ugá, A. et al. (2001a) 'Consideraciones sobre el informe de la OMS – 2000', *Revista de Salud Pública*, Colombia, 3, 1–10.

— (2001b) 'Considerations on the methodology used in the World Health Organization 2000 Report', Cadernos de Saúde Pública, Rio de Janeiro, 3705–12.

Valentine, N. B., deSilva, A. and Murray, C. J. L. (2000) *Estimating Responsiveness Level and Distribution for 191 Countries: Methods and Results* (GPE Discussion Paper Series No. 22), Geneva: WHO, EIP/GPE/FAR.

Wagstaff, A. (2001) 'Measuring Equity in Health Care Financing: Reflections on and Alternatives to the World Health Organization's Fairness of Financial Index' (mimeo), Washington, DC: World Bank, Development Research Group and Human Development Network.

WHO (2000) *The World Health Report 2000, Health Systems: Improving Performance*, Geneva: WHO.

— (n.d.) 'Responsiveness: Questions and Answers' (mimeo), Geneva: WHO.

Williams, A. (2001) 'Science or marketing at WHO? A commentary on "World Health 2000"', *Health Economics*, 10, 93–100.

CHAPTER 6

Multinational Corporations and the Pattern of Privatisation in Healthcare

DAVID HALL

MULTINATIONALS AND GLOBALISATION

Multinational corporations (MNCs) have come to play an increasingly important role in many spheres over the past two decades. According to the United Nations, by the end of the 1980s, trans-national companies were responsible for some half of all trade in manufacturing and three-quarters of trade in services. In 1994 it was estimated that one-third of the world's output was in the hands of trans-national corporations (Leys 2001). While multinationals continue to play a significant role across all major sectors of the economy, they have in the past few years also been able to penetrate public services.

Since the mid-1980s there has been a transformation in the role of the public sector as a service provider. Often the role is divided into public purchaser and private provider. Hence there is now a dichotomy in public utilities, wherein there is in many cases and in different regions a private provider and public purchaser. This restructuring has been taking place at an accelerated rate and on a global scale over the past two decades. It has strengthened the predominance of multinationals in new sectors and reinforced the process of globalisation. In public services such as water, waste management and energy there are a small number of multinational companies that have spread internationally by acquisition and through the award of concessions, contracts and licences. In water, for example, there are two major French MNCs, Suez and Vivendi, plus a few other much smaller companies – RWE-Thames Water, Anglian, SAUR, International Water – which dominate the world market. The spread of these MNCs is co-terminus with water privatisation, which has been taking place since the mid-1980s in the European region and early 1990s in parts of the developing world. In energy there is a similar picture, although with a greater number of companies involved. The growth pattern is a simple one of horizontal growth, which is consolidated by some vertical integration and mergers between MNCs such as in gas and electricity. For example, the energy industry in the EU is now dominated by a small group of energy companies – RWE and EON of Germany, EDF of France – which have taken advantage of the liberalisation of these sectors to establish themselves in a number of countries, at the same time eliminating potential competitors.

Privatisation invariably involves these MNCs. The privatisation of public services and utilities from the late 1980s was accelerated by the requirements of the IMF, under structural adjustment programmes, and through the conditionalities attached by the World Bank and other development banks to their loans. In addition, services came under the rules of the world trading system in 1995 when the WTO was established. This together with the creation of GATS (General Agreement on Trade in Services) is expected further to consolidate the process whereby most services will be open to tender and competition.

Multinational companies are also increasingly involved in many aspects of healthcare services, in which the impact of globalisation has been considerable The role of pharmaceutical companies is one of the most obvious examples of this. However, there appears to be no simple or general pattern of multinational growth and concentration in healthcare. In the case of healthcare, privatisation involves a diverse set of companies, including local ones as well as some multinationals that operate globally. Privatisation in healthcare is thus an extensive and continuous operation in overall healthcare systems, in both developed and developing countries. It is not restricted simply to multinational activity, nor to the privatisation of a single subsector, such as hospitals, but involves a whole range of activities spanning health services, from cleaning and catering to the purchase and maintenance of equipment, and the organisation of diagnostic and treatment services.

This chapter examines the pattern of involvement of multinationals with the process of privatisation of healthcare, especially in relation to the range of private healthcare ventures promoted by the World Bank and, particularly, the International Finance Corporation (IFC). These organisations have taken an international lead in facilitating the process of privatisation. While a number of features of this pattern of private sector involvement are considered, the major focus of this chapter is its implications for trade unions and workers.

GLOBALISATION, UNIONS AND WORKERS

Among the many effects of privatisation in the service sectors are its damaging consequences for employees. For example, the effect of contracting out of healthcare support services in the UK, under the Thatcher government, was to weaken and reduce the quality of the terms and conditions of employment. This in turn increased stress as well as working hours, segmented the workforce and weakened their ability to form unions. Most significant is the growing evidence in the health sector of the effects of privatisation on the quality of public services; according to reports from many regions of the world, it has been largely negative (Whitfield 2001).

On the other hand, globalisation, through multinational expansion and acquisition, has itself been a major factor in stimulating international trade union solidarity in a number of sectors. As multinational corporations (MNCs) become established in more and more countries, workers and unions in different countries find that they are facing the same employer and a similar set of problems. Therefore, the need for collective international action becomes a natural extension of national trade union organisation. This process has been accelerated by the creation, in the European Union, of European Works Councils (EWCs), which are mandatory for multinationals operating in two or more European countries. The EWCs are consultative bodies, with worker-elected representatives from different countries meeting the management once or twice a year. Although the EWCs themselves have limited powers, they have stimulated strong and regular links between unions, particularly across Europe. The EWCs have also had an impact beyond Europe. They have provided a focus for trade unions in European-owned MNCs to establish global solidarity with workers employed by the same MNC in other countries. For instance, the trade unions on the EWC of the French electricity and gas companies, EDF/GDF, have used the EWC to support the demands of workers in Haiti for better pay and conditions of work, and, on a separate occasion, of workers in Uruguay. Where the MNCs are based in non-European countries, such as in the USA, trade unions have established links with fellow trade unions in the USA. A further extension of EWCs is now being negotiated with some companies through the unions, to establish world councils, covering employees of the group in all countries as with the EWCs. For example, Vivendi has agreed to establish such a world council, with union representation agreed through confederations of international unions.

HEALTHCARE RESTRUCTURING AND UNION ORGANISATION

Often trade unions and organised health workers are a specific target of health restructuring. In Mexico, for example, supporters of privatisation claim that the three biggest problems they face in trying to extend privatisation are the effect on standards of care, the risk-selection policies of insurers, and 'the effect of shifting jobs once under the control of the unions to the private sector'.[1] The unions are not only viewed as obstacles in the way of attempts by private companies to increase the exploitation of health workers, but also as important agents of political resistance to privatisation. The same assessment describes the education union and social security workers union as 'the last bastion of support for preserving the state's role as corporate provider of health care'.

This highlights the two dimensions to trade union and health worker concerns about the privatisation of healthcare. The first is the effect it has on conditions of work, and on the ability of unions to organise and protect and improve these conditions. The second is the delivery of healthcare as a public service, and the ability to organise and promote public healthcare of high standards.

MULTINATIONALS IN HEALTHCARE

The behaviour of multinational companies in healthcare is not as cogent or as expansionist as in other sectors (including other public service sectors such as water, waste management and energy). Despite this lack of coherence, there are areas of health services that have increasingly come within the arena of multinational activity. These fall into four categories and include the insurance sector, hospitals, clinical, laboratory and technical services, and support services. The following paragraphs give a preliminary list, by category, of the main companies which have business in health services in more than one country (Hall 2001a); they do not list private companies which are very important in their own country but do not operate outside it (for example, Clininvest, the healthcare chain of Suez-Lyonnaise des Eaux, which does not operate outside France; or a number of American health insurance and HMO companies which do not operate outside the USA).

Insurance multinationals   Table 6.1 below illustrates the nature and trends in expansion among multinational insurance companies. Insurance is a rapidly expanding area of investment, as privatisation of public sector provision, most notably in healthcare, increases in pace.

The companies identified below and in Table 6.1 frequently change ownership, reflecting a fluid situation, with some having a major interest and others an expanding interest in the health insurance sector. Typically for many developing countries, the rise of health insurance reflects the first stage of the segmentation of healthcare provision into public and private providers. The vast majority of the population in countries such as India and China, for example, do not have health insurance cover and are relegated to utilising a shrinking public sector provision while the insured market serves a better-off elite.

In India, health insurance multinationals have tried to target this elite, but have found difficulty in establishing profitable markets. In November 2001 Cigna closed its Indian health insurance operation after two years,[2] and in 2002 BUPA was also reviewing its HMO joint venture with Piramal[3] (although BUPA has established a call centre in India).[4] Cigna has set up a training centre in Beijing of the Health Insurance Association of America (HIAA)[5] and has stated its plans to enter the health insurance business in China,[6] but its withdrawal from India suggests this is unlikely in the near future. Aetna International was sold by its USA group to ING, the Netherlands insurance and finance company, in December 2000. It no longer has any connection with the US insurance group Aetna. AIG and Allianz are both very large insurance

TABLE 6.1 Insurance multinationals, 2002

Base	Company	Other countries
USA	AIG	Many
Germany	Allianz	
USA	Cigna	Many
Netherlands	ING/Aetna International	Many (excluding USA)
USA	United Health	Philippines, Hong Kong
Spain	Adeslas (Aguas de Barcelona/ Mederic)	Argentina, France
UK	BUPA	Spain, Ireland, Thailand, Hong Kong

Source: PSIRU database 2002

companies for whom health insurance is a small part of their business. Allianz specialises in offering healthcare for employees of multinationals. Cigna has a substantial health insurance business, and has expanded into a number of countries including Mexico. United Health, a large operator of HMOs in the USA, now has health schemes in the Philippines and Hong Kong. Adeslas is the largest healthcare company in Spain. It operates not only as an insurer but also as an owner of private hospitals and clinics in Spain and Argentina (see next section). It is a subsidiary of Aguas de Barcelona, the Spanish water company, which in turn is owned (25 per cent) and controlled by the French Suez group. In January 2002 the French health insurance company Médéric took a 45 per cent stake in Adeslas, and the joint venture is expected to expand into France and other EU countries.[7] BUPA has expanded its insurance services to a number of countries, both in Europe and elsewhere. However, it has private hospitals only in the UK (except in Spain, as a consequence of its ownership of the third largest private insurance company, Sanitas, which owns two hospitals).[8]

Hospital multinationals The big hospital companies of the USA – HCA, Sun and Tenet – have all reduced their international operations in recent years, but HCA and Tenet still have a presence in Europe. HCA's operations in England and Switzerland appear to be making significant losses, according to HCA's reports, and there is no mention of international activity in HCA or Tenet discussions of strategy.[9] Sun Healthcare sold its operations in the UK in 2000, filed for bankruptcy in 2001, and is now operating again without international subsidiaries. Paracelsus operates outside Germany in Switzerland. The former Paracelsus healthcare company in the USA, which had an indirect connection, went into liquidation. Capio has grown rapidly in the last few years from its base in a privatised hospital in Stockholm.

Its other operations, in Sweden and overseas, include both hospitals and specialist clinics. Capio was owned by Swedish venture capitalists Bure but was floated as an independent company in September 2000. Parkway Holdings, owner of the Gleneagles group of hospitals, has a significant number of hospitals in south and South-East Asia. It also owned the London Heart Hospital, but was unable to make it profitable, and in 2001 sold it (to the UK National Health Service). Afrox is a South African company which has operations in Zimbabwe and is hoping to expand outside Africa.

The nature of expansion and acquisitions described to some extent

TABLE 6.2 Hospital multinationals, 2002

Company	Base	Other countries	Activity
HCA	USA	UK, Switzerland	Hospitals
Sun Healthcare	USA	(none)	Hospitals
Tenet	USA	Spain	Hospitals
Paracelsus	Germany	Switzerland	Hospitals
Capio	Sweden	UK, Norway, Denmark, Poland	Hospitals, clinical services
Adeslas (Aguas de Barcelona)	Spain	Argentina	Hospitals, insurance
Parkway Holdings	Singapore	Malaysia, Indonesia, Sri Lanka, India	Hospitals
Afrox	South Africa	Zimbabwe	Hospitals, occupational health

Source: PSIRU database 2002

reflects the type of restructuring taking place in the health sector world-wide, but especially in developing countries. This involves reducing the capacity of public provision, particularly in the secondary sector, and increasing the opportunities for what are often costly and sophisticated diagnostics at outpatients clinics.

TABLE 6.3 Clinical, laboratory and other services, 2002

Company	Home	Other countries	Sector
Fresenius	Germany	USA, others	Dialysis, clinical services
Scanfert Oy	Finland	Portugal, Russia	Clinical services
AstraZeneca	UK/Sweden	(USA)	Drugs, cancer care
Healthsouth	USA	UK, Australia	Clinical services
Quest Diagnostics	USA	UK, Mexico	Laboratories
Worldcare	USA	many	Tele-medicine

Source: PSIRU database 2002

Clinical laboratory and other services   Fresenius is a German company which started by manufacturing kidney dialysis machines and expanded into providing dialysis clinics in many countries. It now offers other clinical services as well as hospital management. Scanfert Oy is a Finnish company which has recently expanded into St Petersburg (Russia) with the backing of the World Bank's IFC division. AstraZeneca is an unusual case of a drugs multinational which also has a subsidiary in health services – a cancer clinic chain in the USA. Healthsouth, a major US company in the business of providing outpatient surgery, has expanded into diagnostic centres and occupational medicine in the USA, Australia, Puerto Rico and the UK. Quest Diagnostics is a major laboratory testing company, which has expanded beyond the USA into the UK and Mexico.

Worldcare is a tele-medicine company which has formed a consortium of leading American hospitals, and seeks to sell tele-medicine services worldwide. Tele-medicine is a new type of venture that has been growing in developed countries in recent years (for example, NHS Direct, UK). Though its efficacy in reducing morbidity remains unclear, it is being promoted in the developing world too.

Support services   ISS is a cleaning and hotel services multinational, with hospital cleaning contracts in a number of countries. It has diversified into residential care in Scandinavia, and is involved in six hospital concessions in the UK under the private finance initiative (PFI), which has encouraged consortia with support services companies.[10] Sodexho is a French-based catering multinational with hospital catering contracts in many countries and a hospital PFI concession in the UK. It has

TABLE 6.4 Support services multinationals, 2002

Company	Base	Other countries	Main service
ISS	Denmark	Many	Cleaning, care homes
Sodexho	France	Many	Catering
Rentokil/Initial	UK	Many	Cleaning
Granada/Compass	UK	Many	Catering
EDS	USA	Many	Computing

Source: PSIRU database 2002

withdrawn from its venture into residential care homes in Scandinavia. Rentokil/Initial and Granada/Compass are the other two major cleaning and catering multinationals, each with many contracts in hospitals in many countries.

EDS is one of the major computing services multinationals, and it is still active in healthcare. A number of other computing multinationals were active in the UK after the computing divisions of the NHS were privatised in the 1980s, but all of them got out of the UK NHS business in the mid-1990s.

From this initial research into activities of multinational companies in healthcare, it emerges that many of the hospital companies and the HMO insurers of the USA have experienced financial and performance problems in recent years. An extreme illustration of the weakness of these groups was the sale of Aetna's entire international health division to the Dutch finance group ING. Healthcare is not unique in this respect: there are similar weaknesses in US companies in water, waste and, to a lesser extent, energy.

The private hospital companies have also not been very successful at expanding internationally. This is especially true for the US groups, which have largely withdrawn from international ventures in the last five years. It is also true for the French companies Vivendi and Suez, although these two groups are extremely aggressive internationally in other public service sectors such as water and waste management. Vivendi withdrew from the UK four years ago and Suez-Lyonnaise has never expanded Clininvest outside France. Within Europe, companies which are very large in their own country, such as Paracelsus, show few signs of expanding into neighbouring countries. The transformation in February 2002 of Adeslas into a joint Spanish/French venture between Aguas de Barcelona and Médéric is a unique development so far. Parkway Holdings (Singapore) has an international network of private hospitals in south and South-East Asia, and expanded into the UK. However, in 2001 Parkway also withdrew from the UK, selling its hospital to the NHS.

On the other hand, cleaning and catering support services exhibit the 'classic' pattern of multinational dominance worldwide, at least in developed countries. These companies may also establish themselves in more general hospital concessions, but so far this has happened only with the PFI scheme in UK. The cleaning and catering companies show no signs of rapid withdrawal from the market in the way the computing multinationals did in the UK in the 1990s. The insurance companies, as insurers or with HMO schemes, are also expanding. Some of this appears to be simply into 'niche' markets, for example, of employees of multinationals, but there is also some investment in HMOs in developing countries. This expansion is obviously dependent on countries adopting policies which create this market.

There is growing evidence of international expansion in clinical diagnostic or therapy services, such as dialysis, blood products, MRI scans. There are examples of this kind of service being privatised in a number of countries, such as in Brazil (see the IFC/MIGA financed schemes below), India (where Delhi council hospitals are to franchise private companies to provide CT scans, cardiac doppler and echo, respiratory lab, incinerator services and other high investment medical technologies),[11] and Canada (where private MRI scans have opened up in a basically public healthcare system).[12] This seems to be the market that companies like Fresenius, Capio and Scanfert are expanding into (and which the World Bank/IFC seem keen to finance) (Lethbridge 2002).

Vertical integration of private healthcare companies, or any consistent pattern of consolidation, remains unusual. De-mergers have been more striking: Aetna sold its international insurance business to ING, Capio was sold off by its parent finance group. The support services groups have been volatile about expansion into residential care.

ISS has twice sought to expand into the sector; Sodexho has sold its care home companies. Globalisation may not necessarily arrive at the first stage of privatisation. In the case of HMOs in Brazil and the Philippines, local companies first established the privatised systems and then the multinationals arrived, through joint ventures or acquisition, during the 1990s.

PROMOTING PRIVATISATION: MULTINATIONALS, WORLD BANK AND IFC

Multinationals and marketing   The marketing activities of multinational corporations are central to the processes of privatisation and globalisation in all sectors. The most conspicuous example of this in healthcare is an annual trade conference on the global potential for private healthcare organised by a body called the Academy for International Health Studies (AIHS) which is not an academic institution but a private healthcare business association in the USA. The proceedings of a conference[13] held in December 2000 reveal how multinationals are working with each other, with governments, and with international bodies in a global marketing effort (Buse and Walt 2000).

The companies involved in the conference were principally concerned with insurance: Aetna International, Allianz Group, Aon Healthcare Alliance (USA); CIGNA International Healthcare and United Healthcare International. Astra/Zeneca Pharmaceuticals (UK) was also involved. The conference treated healthcare worldwide simply as a marketing opportunity. There were workshops and seminars on such topics as 'Private Health Sector Investment – Opportunities and Obstacles, in Countries as Far Apart as Argentina, Australia, Brazil, Chile, Egypt, Germany, Indonesia, Israel, Mexico, Nigeria, Philippines, Poland and South Africa', 'Globalization of American Managed Care: Trends, Opportunities and Challenges', 'Employee Benefits for the Multinational Corporation: Health Plan Challenges' and 'Global Demographic Trends: Implications for Payers, Providers and Pharmaceuticals'. The conference started with a keynote address by Jeffrey Sachs, chair of the WHO Commission on Macroeconomics and Health, on 'Health Care Globalisation in the 21st Century: Issues and Challenges'. It was attended by high-ranking ministers and officials from many countries, and concluded with a 'Ministries of Health' forum on 'Perspectives on Public–Private Partnerships' (the conference had hoped to host a formal inter-ministerial conference). The World Bank and the WHO made a joint presentation to a plenary session of a 'State of the World's Healthcare Report': a remarkable display of unity, for the benefit of a business conference, between the world's leading development bank and the leading international health organisation.

World Bank   The numerous divisions of the World Bank are significant forces driving privatisation in healthcare, through projects, investments and institutional support for the multinationals. The WHO also seems to be associating itself with the policy collapse into 'public–private partnership' that is taking place in other services too. These changes are being effected despite little evidence of workability and amid growing opposition from public health practitioners worldwide (Qadeer et al. 2001).

During the past two decades and especially since the publication of the *World Development Report* (1993), the World Bank has been an active driver of privatisation in a number of ways. This includes the conditionalities and objectives attached to the loans of the WB itself – the IBRD and the IDA. Specific loans from the World Bank often involve, and are conditional upon, privatisation of the provision of the relevant services. This is now quite commonplace in energy (examples include

Uttar Pradesh in India and in the Dominican Republic) and water, where loans to Palestine, Ghana and others have required privatisation of the water service (Hall 2001b; Bayliss 2001; Bayliss and Hall 2000). The imposition of these conditions makes privatisation almost un-avoidable, assuming that the country needs the World Bank loan to develop the service further.

Private sector development strategy The policies of privatisation are now being extended and generalised through the World Bank's private sector development strategy. This strategy, adopted by its executive board in February 2002, sees public services and infrastructure as key areas for development of the private sector. The private sector is ex-pected to finance the development of infrastructure, which is to be paid back through a service delivery contract over many years – like a concession, or a UK-style private finance initiative (PFI) – and then for the WB to offer selective subsidies to support these payments. These concessions and schemes have been highly problematic and contentious in energy, water, health, education and other services both in developing countries (Bayliss and Hall 2001), and in the UK, where one of the main criticisms is that it is merely an expensive means of finance for public services (Pollock et al. 1999).

One arm of this policy has been to extend what it calls 'output-based aid' (OBA). This is based on the assumption that long-term private concessions will be created based solely on private infrastructure de-velopment. It is also assumed that this will be followed by a long period of charging governments or users for such services. The WB, a keen supporter of this strategy, is dividing its financing into two clear streams: financing private sector infrastructure development (through the IFC – see below) and output-based subsidies, such as education vouchers and means-tested water consumption (World Bank 2002) in order to facilitate the process. Given that the social sector will be included, it remains unclear as to how the outputs of the social sector will be quantified and valued. If one is to make a conjecture about this on the basis of recent social sector 'performance measures' undertaken by the WHO in con-junction with the World Bank, then considerable problems could arise in relation to the arbitrary nature of definition and classification (see Travassos, this volume, on the *World Health Report* 2000).

International Finance Corporation (IFC) The IFC is a division of the World Bank that invests solely in the private sector – a global venture capital fund. As such, IFC loans in public services are bound to be restricted to private ventures. Moreover, the IFC has a declared policy of being simply in favour of extending the role of the private sector in public services, including healthcare. The IFC's role has grown sharply in the last twenty years: the share of IFC and MIGA in the total World Bank group financing has increased from 3.3 per cent in 1980 to 25 per cent in 2000 (World Bank 2002). The IFC introduces a further layer of conditionality by persuading governments to modify their policies on any issue, including healthcare, to make the investment climate more favourable for IFC and private sector investments. The WB itself states that: 'The government may be willing to adjust policies, when the IFC is involved as an investor in a particular project. In this case policy reform can be shown to translate immediately into additional investments' (World Bank 2002).

The IFC's investments in healthcare are all financial investments in private facilities, usually private hospitals, or clinics providing various diagnostic and therapeutic services to private patients. These investments bear no relation to public healthcare needs or policies. In some cases the hospitals or ventures are set up for the benefit of tourists. One case is that of the Dominican Republic, where the IFC stated 'the lack of quality healthcare services has been identified as one of the major barriers to the development of tourism in the Dominican Republic'.[14] Or they may be aimed at the corporate market for private health insurance and services, such as the Medicover scheme in central and Eastern Europe. According to recent research (Lethbridge 2002), in Africa, the IFC is investing a total of $6.4 million, all in private hospitals and private medical centres mainly to encourage privatisation. In Asia the budget is larger (nearly $70 million) but the range is similar: a number of private hospitals in China, India, Indonesia, the Philippines, Samoa, Sri Lanka and Vietnam, and a private diagnostic venture in the Philippines.

The IFC investments have been with partly local and partly multinational partners (based in Finland, Portugal, Spain and Singapore). Very few of these investments are to large multinational healthcare companies, apart from two ventures involving subsidiaries of hospital companies Gleneagles (Singapore), and BUPA (UK). In a number of cases powerful local companies feature in share holdings, such as the Lopez Group in the Philippines and Afrox in South Africa. In many cases the investments involve ventures owned by small or medium groups of doctors and financial partners. The relative lack of large multinational partners is not a reflection of IFC policy – in sectors such as water the

IFC has invested heavily with large, dominant multinationals; rather it is a reflection of the fragmentation of private investors in healthcare operations.

Multilateral Investment Guarantee Agency (MIGA)   Another section of the World Bank, the MIGA, provides investment guarantees to protect mainly against political risk. Together with the IFC, MIGA has provided two remarkable forms of support for the private leasing of medical equipment by a USA firm – DVI – in Brazil. DVI Inc. is a company that finances the leasing of medical equipment, mostly MRI scanners, and increasingly treatment equipment such as lasers. In this particular case, first, the IFC formed a joint venture with DVI, called MSF Cayman, in the offshore tax haven favoured by money-launderers, the Cayman Islands. The role of MSF Cayman is to provide 'cross-border loans and lease financing to private hospitals, clinics and physician groups through-out Latin America, for the purchase of state-of-the-art diagnostic imaging and radiation therapy equipment'.[15] Then MIGA's role was to provide insurance worth $75 million to protect the investments against political risks, and, in 2000, $150 million-worth of guarantees against political risks for notes issued by MSF. This insurance raised the credit-rating of the notes higher than the credit-rating of Brazil itself – so international finance could be obtained by MSF at lower interest rates. MIGA claimed: 'This is a project with high development impact, which will help improve the provision of healthcare in Brazil.'[16]

SOME CONCLUSIONS

The processes of privatisation in healthcare are extremely destabilis-ing for health workers. In other sectors such as water there may be relative stability of employment after initial cutbacks. In healthcare the pattern of corporate activity is such that it creates greater instability. Workers may be deployed or redeployed into a new commercial venture, which may then be sold, restructured or closed. Local venture capitalists, frequently including medical partners, are likely to casualise and reduce pay and the work conditions of employees in both developed and developing countries. For trade unions, the attempts to weaken their position are not always offset by the international solidarity engendered by the presence of a dominant multinational. In terms of public policy, the conditionalities and policy changes sought by the IFC are likely to be highly contradictory to public health strategies and needs. The recent pattern of development suggests that as much attention should be paid to the behaviour of the World Bank, especially the IFC, as to the marketing strategies of multinationals or policies of bodies such as the WTO. It also indicates that a much wider range of companies are intervening in healthcare and destabilising public policy than is often recognised, and that the hospital corporations of the USA are not among the leading players.

NOTES

1. 'AIHS country workshop report', *Modern Healthcare International*, 17 July 2000; www.modernhealthcare.com

2. 'Cigna Corp. scraps Indian health insurance expansion plan', *Bloomberg News*, 17 October 2001.

3. Ananth Iyer, 'BUPA–Piramal venture likely to be called off', *Healthcare Management*, 15 February 2002; http://www.expresshealthcaremgmt.com/20020215/cover1.shtml

4. 'Call centre firm claims market ripe for growth', *Scotland on Sunday*, 21 April 2002.

5. *Business Daily Update*, 4 July 2001 (FT Asia Intelligence Wire).

6. *China Business*, 8 June 2001.

7. 'Médéric acquiert 45 per cent de l'espagnol Adeslas', *Les Echos*, 29 January 2002.

8. 'A Spanish revolution; with surging economy, private sector plays vital role in healthcare system', *Financial Times*, 13 November 2000.

9. See the HCA website at http://199.230.26.96/cgi-bin/ir/hca/keystat.html: SEC filings eg 10Q 11/14/2001; Tenet Annual Report for 2001 at http://www.etenet.com/GeneralInfo/annualrpt/AR01.pdf

10. ISS half-yearly results, August 2000.

11. 'MCD move on hospitals to hit poor', *The Hindu*, 18 December 2000.

12. 'Clash in Canada: Privatization legislation and NAFTA open healthcare market to protests', *Modern Healthcare International*, 13 November 2000.

13. See www.aihs.com/summit/summitabout.html for information on speakers and agenda.

14. 'IFC invests in hospital network in the Dominican Republic', IFC Press Release 102, 7 April 2000.

15. 'MIGA insures ground-breaking health care project in Brazil', MIGA Press Release, 6 August 1999.

16. MIGA: 'Latin Report: Public–Private Insurance', September 2000.

REFERENCES

Bayliss, K. (2001) *Privatisation of Electricity Distribution: Some Economic, Social and Political Perspectives*, London: Public Services International Research Unit (PSIRU); www.psiru.org/reports/2001-04-E-distrib.doc

Bayliss, K. and Hall, D. (2000) *Independent Power Producers: A Review of the Issues*, London: PSIRU, www.psiru.org/reports/2000-11-E-IPPs.doc

— (2001) *A PSIRU Response to the World Bank's Private Sector Development Strategy Paper*, London: PSIRU, www.psiru.org/reports/2001-10-U-WB-psd.doc

Buse, K. and Walt, G. (2000) 'Global public–private partnerships: Part I – a new development in health?' *Bulletin of the World Health Organization*, 78 (4), 549–61.

Hall, D. (2001a) *Globalisation, Privatisation and Healthcare – a Preliminary Report*, London: PSIRU, www.psiru.org/reports/2001-02-H-over.doc

— (2001b) *Water in Public Hands*, London: PSIRU, www.psiru.org/reports/2001-06-W-Public.doc

Lethbridge, J. (2002) *Private Investment and International Finance Corporation Investment in Healthcare*, London: PSIRU, www.psiru.org/reports/2002-03-H-capital.doc

Leys, C. (2001) *Market-driven Politics: Introduction*, London: Verso.

Pollock, A., Dunnigan, M. G., Gaffney, D., Price, D. and Shaoul, J. (1999) 'The private finance initiative: Planning the "new" NHS: downsizing for the 21st century', *British Medical Journal*, 319, 179–84.

Qadeer, I., Sen, K. and Nayar, K. R. (2001) *Public Health and the Poverty of Reforms: the South Asian Predicament*, New Delhi: Sage.

Whitfield, D. (2001) *Public Services or Corporate Welfare: Rethinking the Nation State in the Global Economy*, London: Pluto Press.

World Bank (2002) 'Private Sector Development Strategy – Directions for the World Bank Group'; rru.worldbank.org/documents/PSDStrategy-April%209.pdf

CHAPTER 7

Health Systems Solidarity and European Community Policies

MERI KOIVUSALO

Solidarity and universal coverage have been distinctive goals in the organisation and functioning of European health systems. In recent years, though, many European countries have increasingly applied market mechanisms to health with the aim of controlling costs and improving effectiveness. These measures have had repercussions on the abilities of governments not only to maintain solidarity and universal coverage but also, in fact, to control costs. Overall, the quest for effectiveness has compromised the aims of enhancing equity and ensuring cross-subsidisation of resources, both across richer and poorer populations and across areas. Similar changes have been introduced to the health systems in many developing countries as part of sectoral reforms which have been promoted in the context of aid and structural adjustment policies.

More general public sector and policy reforms, such as trends towards limiting the role of public services and regulation, accompanied by the increasing influence of commercial actors and contractual arrangements, have also put pressures on the health sector. In addition, liberalisation priorities in economic and trade policies influence and interfere with the implementation of health policies in all countries.

This chapter examines health systems and the goal of solidarity in the European Union context and in relation to the impact on health policies of European Union policies developed in other sectors. It articulates three main arguments. First, that market-oriented and competitive reforms in health systems have not brought about the promised changes of controlling costs and improving effectiveness (but have introduced problems of their own, particularly related to solidarity). Second, as market-oriented reforms directly within the health sector have lost their popularity, another wave of pressures with similar goals has emerged from other policy sectors such as trade, competition and industry. Their significant influence on the health sector at both national and European level implies that threats to the goal of solidarity are likely to stem from the impact of other policies rather than from direct changes to health policies themselves such as the market-oriented approaches to health systems implemented in recent years. Many structures of the initial market-oriented reforms have remained within health systems, however. They have formed the basis for further changes now being promoted and lobbied for by the pharmaceutical healthcare industry and for technical changes being suggested by trade and finance departments as part of their aims to enhance competition and control public sector costs. And third, while there are cultural and historical contexts and specificities for health systems in all countries, what is happening to health systems within OECD countries affects the developing world through economic, trade and aid policies.

EUROPEAN HEALTH POLICIES

The financing and organisation of health systems within the fifteen countries of the European Union have long varied, but they mainly follow two models: the Bismarckian, social insurance model (Germany, Austria, Belgium, Luxembourg and the Netherlands) or the Beveridge national health system model (United Kingdom, Spain, Denmark, Sweden and Finland). The health systems of the remaining five countries (France, Greece, Ireland, Italy and Portugal) reflect a mixture of both models. Those of Italy, Portugal and Greece also reflect the later de-velopment of an organised country-wide healthcare system, a larger proportion of private services than other EU countries and a lower level of general public spending on health. In terms of total costs, it is generally understood and recognised that the social insurance-based systems (Bismarckian) are better at permitting consumer choice and recognising the concerns of health professionals but are not so good at controlling costs and can provide too much unnecessary care. National health systems (Beveridge), on the other hand, tend to be better at controlling costs but may not provide enough care.

Three aspects of health systems are relevant as far as equity is concerned: (i) the comprehensiveness of the care package provided by the health system; (ii) coverage of the population; and (iii) financing of care. Equity issues are relevant to variations in all these aspects as far as poorer and richer individuals are concerned and poorer and richer populations. This chapter emphasises the effects on equity of changes to the financing of healthcare in Europe.

Wagstaff and Doorslaer (1992) compared the financing of health systems of various European countries and the United States in their effects on equity and concluded that tax-financed systems tend to be mildly progressive, social insurance systems regressive, and private systems very regressive. In most countries, out-of-pocket payments by patients are an especially regressive means of raising healthcare revenues. This would probably be little different in developing countries except where the access to and functioning of health systems has been geared towards serving predominantly the wealthy, i.e. where health services are affordable only by the rich. To ensure equity, the financing of health systems needs to focus on the overall short- and long-term costs and their impact on the distribution of services in such a way that allows for cross-subsidisation between people and regions (see Taroni in this volume).

In most European countries, cross-subsidisation is fundamental to the overall practice of health systems. Yet some mechanisms of health-care financing which are now being promoted as development aid (medical savings accounts, some types of private health insurance and some forms of community-based insurance, for instance) do not allow for redistribution and will not attain any level of cross-subsidisation unless supported by and combined with specific regulatory measures.

At the core of the practice of solidarity is the pooling of people's health risks and financial contributions in a way that ensures that treatment is provided according to need and is financed according to ability to pay. Solidarity has been promoted through support for universal coverage of services; services and mechanisms which are targeted for the poor, in contrast, tend to end up simply as poor services. If public services are left for the poor only, it is hard to maintain their quality. This recognition has led to an emphasis on 'keeping the rich' within the same healthcare system as the poor. This approach contrasts with the views and emphases now prevalent within the donor and broader aid community to target all public resources towards basic (in effect, reproductive) services for the poor. These policies implicitly promote a two-tier service, whereby the rich and healthy are encouraged to use services provided through the private sector and outside the public system.

EUROPEAN EXPERIENCES WITH MARKET-ORIENTED REFORMS

A recent Eurobarometer survey of consumer points of view on health systems suggests that both social insurance and national health systems had broad support in the 1990s. The strongest support for their health systems came from Denmark and Finland, which have Beveridge models of national health systems (Mossiailos 1997; European Commission 1998). The Eurobarometer survey confirms that the general public in all European countries supports the principle of a universal health service and that most people are not ready to abandon the commitment to provide care for all citizens (European Commission 1998). The European analyses on consumer points-of-view also contrast with the recent WHO *World Health Report* analysis, which tried to assess the responsiveness and effectiveness of health systems in different countries (WHO 2001).

In general, an interest in applying market and competition principles to healthcare systems has now become less fashionable in European health policies than it was in the 1980s. The shift away from competition-led models can be partially attributed to changes at the political level (from right to left) in many countries and partially explained by problems in implementing the principles, by failures of the reforms to render the promised benefits and by their adverse effects. In particular, using market forces did not introduce fully functioning markets but rather monopolies while generating problems in implementing regulations and ensuring quality control.

In terms of health systems development, moreover, stressing competition, economic incentives, outcomes and cost-effectiveness have produced their own biases and adverse effects. These often include changes in the values held by public service workers (Seagall 2000). A Swedish study showed that the adoption of economic incentives in the form of performance-based reimbursements led to health workers internalising an awareness of costs which in turn led to problems in the quality of care provided. The study found that a high awareness of costs was a negative predictor of the quality of care (Forsberg et al. 2001). In the context of public service reform in developing countries, Mackintosh (1995) has drawn attention to the fact that public service ethics are much easier to destroy than to build up. She also contests the aim of splitting policy from management upon which the edifice of much public sector management reform is now built. In the United States, one of the most serious problems of market-driven, investor-owned healthcare that has been identified is the embodiment of a new value system which breaks the communal roots and Samaritan traditions of hospitals, makes doctors and nurses the instruments of investors, and views patients as commodities (Woolhandler and Himmelstein 1999).

Two recent overviews have analysed the background and current state of market-oriented reforms in health policies in various OECD countries and report, at best, very mixed results (*Social Science and Medicine* 2001; *Health Policy, Politics and Law* 2000). Another European analysis of the impact of market forces on health systems concluded that there was no evidence of increased productivity but some evidence of increased administrative costs. Thus the enthusiasm for healthcare markets has now generally faded in health sector reform efforts, possibly implying a return to more traditional notions of public service. But while reforms of Beveridge-type national health systems have often introduced purchaser/provider splits in previously integrated systems, consumer choice reforms in Bismarck-type social insurance systems seem to have led to closer relationships between purchasers and providers and tighter contacts between sickness funds and health service providers. According to the study, planning for populations and for appropriate services both argue against markets. Reconciling consumerism with effective planning and effective provision may, therefore, best be achieved through regulatory means rather than through market mechanisms (European Health Care Management Association 2000).

Even if health administrations have swapped their enthusiasm for market forces for a more cautious, even negative, approach to health services, arguments in favour of competition, markets and consumer choice have nevertheless found their way into more general policy debates within the European Community. Health policies are thus increasingly influenced by and under pressure from policies drawn up outside the health sector, such as those promoted by commercial service providers or trade and competition authorities at both national and EC levels.

EUROPEAN COMMUNITY POLICIES AND HEALTH SYSTEMS

European Community policies are governed by the treaties of the European Community. The treaties of Maastricht (1992) and Amsterdam (1997), as well as changes agreed at the intergovernmental conference in Nice (2001), are all relevant for the development of health systems.

The main framework of European Community policies, which is set by the treaties, relates to internal market regulations and commitments to the four freedoms of movement of goods, consumers, services and capital within the area of the European Union. The European Union is thus primarily based on legal governance. The European Court of Justice (ECJ) deals with legal matters in the European Community to which both individuals and corporations may appeal.

The European Community has a mandate to establish public health policies. The most recent version of its approach to health, however, covers issues related to health systems as well as those related to public health. The 1997 Treaty of Amsterdam explicitly obliges the European Community to take into account in all policies the high level of health protection, its Article 152 stipulating that:

> A high level of human health protection shall be ensured in the defini-
> tion and implementation of all Community policies and activities ...
> Community action, which shall complement national policies, shall be
> directed towards improving public health, preventing human illness,
> and obviating sources of danger to human health. Such action shall
> cover the fight against the major health scourges, by promoting research
> into their causes, their transmission and their prevention, as well as
> information and education. (European Community 1997, Article 152)

Member states value highly the principle of subsidiarity, reflected in European policy debates on health services. The essence of the principle limits in theory the scope of community policies. It stipulates that whatever can be done better at national level should not be done at community level. The principle is also explicitly reflected in Article 152: 'Community action in the field of public health shall fully respect the responsibilities of the Member States for the organisation and delivery of health services and medical care' (European Community 1997, Article 152). But concerns have also been raised that the European Commission aims to incorporate health services into its mandate by expanding the scope of 'public health' to encompass health services. The stipulations of the Treaty of Amsterdam may provide avenues to argue that health concerns should be taken into account in other EU policies, but this may be difficult to ensure, especially as resources and interests within the European Commission to take Article 152 more seriously are limited. The stipulations in the Treaty of Amsterdam on integrating health in other policies tend to be interpreted as a commit-ment applying only within the countries of the European Union. They are thus not considered to relate to the substantial tobacco subsidies as cultivated tobacco is exported. In comparison to the rather meagre public health budget of the EU, tobacco subsidies are substantial. According to Eisma (1999), the total health budget of the EU is less than 5 per cent of the EU support paid for tobacco (more than €999 million).

There are six policy areas within the mandate of the European Commission which have an impact on health policies: internal market regulations; competition; European Monetary Union and general economy; trade; aid; and industry.

Internal market regulation policies Internal market regulations and commitments to the four freedoms of movement (of goods, services, consumers and capital) form the legal 'hard core' of European Community policies. It is from these regulations and commitments that new challenges to the organisation and financing of health systems have emerged. The cross-border trade in health services is increasingly raised in the context of internal healthcare markets. This debate is apparent in a background study of the European Single Market and health which analysed European Court of Justice decisions between 1958 and 1998 (Busse 2001). It found 233 Single European Market regulations, directives, recommendations and rulings directly referring to healthcare.

Underpinning and fuelling this debate are recent European Court of Justice cases dealing with the cross-border movement of services and goods, which may have important implications for health services. In the Kohll and Decker cases, which dealt with the reimbursement of the costs of medical treatment or products (such as spectacles) obtained in another member state, the European Court of Justice decided that national rules which make the reimbursement of the costs of medical treatment or medical products obtained in other member states subject to the prior authorisation of sickness funds are, in principle, incompatible with the provisions of the EC Treaty on the free movement of goods (Article 30) and services (Article 59) (Van der Mei 1999). The Kohll and Decker cases were considered to have implications primarily for social insurance health systems (Bismarck) only, but two more cases, Smits and Peerbooms, have demonstrated that the rulings could apply to other types of health systems as well (European Court of Justice 2000a, 2000b; Wismar 2001; Nickless 2001a, 2001b; Grinten and Lint 2001). These rulings in effect mean that member states' claim that health systems are a national, and not community, matter has not been upheld. Furthermore, as internal market rules and priorities are rooted in policies and policy priorities other than health, there is a danger that health policies may be compromised in this process.

The recognition of the problem was clearly stated by Andrea Fischer, German Federal Health Minister, in a policy statement during the German EU presidency in 1999:

> It is feared – primarily in Germany – that the application of European Community law, especially along the lines of the decisions by the European Court of Justice, might eventually erode the national responsibility of the Member States for their own healthcare systems …This indisputably problematic situation must be defused by means of political decisions. It would be fatal and a political testimonium pauperitatis if the development of health policy in the EU were left mainly to the jurisdiction of the European Court of Justice. (Fischer 1999: 4)

A recent report of the High Level Committee on Health on the internal market and health services clearly states that internal markets do have implications for health services: 'Generally speaking, the principle of the free movement of services applies also to health services. This means that health service providers can offer their services in another Member State without any discrimination vis-à-vis national providers' (European Commission 2001a: 20).

While the matters on which decisions were sought at the European Court may not necessarily represent concerns of large numbers of European consumers, their legal implications may well be broader. On the legal side, an emphasis on the rights of consumers to choose health service providers in another country effectively promotes the case for a common healthcare market. The extent to which people wish to be treated in another European country is open to question, however, accompanied as it is by problems of language and follow-up care. A broad patient-centred movement to lobby for this freedom is thus unlikely. The emphasis on the free movement of services, however, might well be more important for private and for-profit actors who are seeking new entries throughout the European market area as contractors for services. It is thus the freedom to provide services that may end up as being most significantly affected by the ECJ decisions.

Competition policies   Countries such as the Netherlands regard health services as sufficiently mature to be included in the sphere of competition policies. The Dutch competition authority, for instance, which is responsible for anti-competitive behaviour under Dutch competition law, has ruled that social health funds in the Netherlands should be regarded as enterprises, irrespective of their public status (European Health Care Management Association 2000). In practice, this means that regulations relating to competition policy will apply also to social and health funds.

In countries where the health system includes a lot of private health insurance and/or for-profit providers, competition policy arguments may well become more important in the future. But competition arguments may also be used in national-health-type systems if reforms resulting in purchaser–provider splits have been implemented. In Finland, for example, the National Competition Authority (Kilpailuvirasto 2001) has drawn attention to the lack of competition in healthcare in Finland and now promotes competition and competitive mechanisms in basic services, including healthcare (Kauppa ja Teollisuusministeriö 2001). The 'government and the markets' project of the National Competition Authority states the following in relation to health services: 'The Finnish Competition Authority finds that the healthcare markets are one of the major sheltered sector markets where public regulation and public procedure cause competition restraints' (Hagman 2001).

In all health systems where public authorities contract out to service providers, the role of government procurement practices becomes more important. In the European Union, public procurement theoretically comes under internal market regulations, but its practice is often tackled in the context of competition policies. European Court of Justice rulings have again been used to define the scope and practice of government procurement (European Court of Justice 1998a, 1998b). In a proposal for a new European directive on government procurement, health and social services are classified as those services to be governed mostly by national laws (category B services) as opposed to those services to be governed mostly by EU regulations (category A services) (European Commission 2000). But if health services are interpreted as comparable to other services, this might gradually change in many countries. Technical changes in listing services as either category A or B, in national laws governing competition and/or government procurement, or changes brought about as a result of international agreements governing trade in services could shift the mandate for national governance quite quickly.

When national laws and their interpretation do not exclude social and health sector services from government procurement rules, as in, for example, Finland and the Netherlands, both these rules and those governing competition may quickly create problems when services are bought or sold within a health system based on contractual arrangements if competition requirements are not taken into account in the contracting process (see, for example, Grinten and Lint 2001). In Finland, the legal arm of the National Competition Authority has ruled that social and health services should abide by the general practice of government procurement and thus be subject to competitive bidding. Should health services become subject to competitive bidding, European service providers would probably need to have the same access to potential contracts as local or national providers.

To understand competition and health policies, it is important to look not only at EU level policies which may seem to exclude health and social services, but also at national competition policies and at links with other regional and international legal agreements and policies. In practice, competition policies might be effective in opening markets to private providers. According to Palm and Nickless (2001), if the policy implications of the Kohll and Decker judgments are considered in the context of discrimination between providers rather than of the free movement of patients, these could force national mechanisms governing contracting to be opened up to all healthcare providers in the European Union. If government and public services are conceptualised in the same way as private corporations are, policies will be decided on the basis of pro-competitiveness and may result in a strong mechanism favouring privatisation and commercialisation of service provision. This could also mean that, if services are provided by public sector actors too cheaply, they could be challenged. In Finland, for instance, the Competition Authority required the public sector laboratories to bill for their services according to a more market-based pricing policy rather than its current practice of charging the actual costs of the service (Kilpailuvirasto 2001).

European Monetary Union and general economic policies The financial and economic policies that set the requirements for joining the EMU (European Monetary Union) favour limited public budgets and prudent economic policies. This approach extends to social and welfare services and how they are financed. It becomes an incentive to shift financing of health systems away from the sphere of public budgets towards individual/personal or employer contributions to private providers, even though the overall result is a more expensive health system.

According to Pitruzello (1997), implementing the fiscal convergence criteria as laid out in the Treaty of Maastricht has driven attempts in

Italy and France to reform welfare and pensions. The Maastricht fiscal convergence criteria require prospective member countries of the EMU to cut their deficit and debt ratios to 3 per cent and 60 per cent, respectively, of public expenditure by 1997. Restructuring welfare systems thus emerged as a central strategy to achieve these fiscal balances. In the context of healthcare reforms, the fiscal convergence criteria have been cited as factors contributing to changes in the Greek health system, in particular the shifting of financing from taxation to social insurance (Liaropoulos and Tragakes 1998)

'Globalisation' is often given as the main reason why the scope of public budgets should be limited. This in turn propels changes towards more privatised and individualised health systems. But a recent overview of social policies and globalisation would suggest that this should not necessarily be the case (Scharpf 2000). According to Scharpf, both Scandinavian and US social policies seem to respond to incentives from the globalisation process better than social insurance-based schemes. But as Scandinavian and US policies differ substantially from each other in terms of solidarity and social responsibility, it must not be blindly assumed that globalisation necessitates shifts towards US-type social policies. At the European level, a major concern is that the EU's internal market and European Community policies may generate a kind of 'globalisation process' leading towards more market-oriented policies. A key issue is therefore the extent to which the European fiscal convergence process creates pressures which may lead to further privatisation and marketisation of health policies rather than promoting universal services and cost-containment. Some aspects of this can already be seen in social insurance markets where international agencies and corporations have endeavoured to influence the framework of European policies in social insurance (Holzmann and Rutkowski 2002).

Trade policies   In international trade negotiations, the European Commission represents the fifteen European member states on issues related to the cross-border trade of goods. The competence has traditionally been shared between the Commission and the member states which means effectively that European Commission positions have had to respect the will of individual member states. The intergovernmental conference in Nice (2001) saw the first attempt to give more competence to the Commission on investments, services and intellectual property rights, a change intended to give the EU more opportunities for effective negotiation and the capacity to act more quickly. But the negotiations in Nice led to a rather unclear mandate: competence was defined in terms of internal and shared competence (implying the subsidiarity principle) and in terms of commercial policies in relation to trade-related intellectual property rights (European Community 2001). The Treaty of Nice deals explicitly with health and social services, according to paragraph 6 of its Article 133:

> An agreement may not be concluded by the Council if it includes provisions which would go beyond the Community's internal powers, in particular by leading to harmonisation of the laws or regulations of the Member States in an area for which this Treaty rules out such harmonisation ... In this regard, by way of derogation from the first subparagraph of paragraph 5, agreements relating to trade in cultural and audiovisual services, educational services and social and human health services, shall fall within the shared competence of the Community and its Member States ... (European Community 2001, Article 133, para 6)

This means that the European Community is the main actor in negotiations concerning international trade in goods, but that many aspects of trade in services and in intellectual property rights still fall within the category of shared competence.

In the context of the renegotiations of the World Trade Organisation's General Agreement on Trade in Services (GATS), however, it is clear that the EU is reviewing all service sectors. The Commission represents the EU on most of the WTO working groups, including one looking at GATS Article VI which covers domestic regulation. This working group is leading negotiations on, for example, possible requirement concerning proportionality in relation to the desired outcome of regulatory activity, necessity of the regulatory measure and pro-competitiveness of domestic regulation. This has raised concerns about the possible implications of GATS stipulations on domestic regulation for health systems (Price et al. 1999; Pollock and Price 2000).

Another WTO agreement with implications for health systems is the Agreement on Trade Related Intellectual Property Rights (TRIPS). In the context of access to pharmaceuticals in developing countries, intellectual property rights have become the subject of a hotly contested debate in which the European Commission has traditionally represented the view of the rights holders — in practice, the research-based pharmaceutical industry (T'Hoen 2000). Yet in many cases, the interests of European health systems are not the same as those of the rights holders.

In fact, in many ways the interests of health systems in European countries are closer to those of developing countries when considering past European Commission positions on compulsory licensing and interpretations of the TRIPS Agreement. The pharmaceutical industry has been active in gaining support and ensuring that regulatory measures which protect the interests of the industry, especially from the alleged threat of parallel imports of lower priced pharmaceuticals from poorer countries, and which favour them, such as incentives encouraging research and development, are implemented.

Within the European Community, trade policy issues are dealt with by Committee 133 which is run by the trade and foreign policy departments of member states. Thus health administrations have little clout in these negotiations. They often find it difficult to understand and analyse the health policy implications of very specific technical decisions made by the committee. The services and pharmaceutical industries are much more prominent in the committee's base of Brussels than national Ministries of Health and Social Affairs. The rapid pace of consultations within Committee 133 limits the scope and opportunities for national administrations to influence its agenda and decisions unless they have firm views and a capacity to respond quickly. European civil society consultations with non-governmental organisations (NGOs) and industry provide an important forum for debate and may well end up influencing the trade agenda far more than national health administrations. Many vocal development NGOs, for example, have no interest in containing the costs of European pharmaceutical policies. In practice, therefore, there is a growing gap between the European and national levels as far as health policy is concerned. This gap acts against health policy interests especially in relation to policies concerning areas where commercial interests are high, such as pharmaceuticals, research and intellectual property rights.

This means that trade policies may have important systematic implications for health systems and development and aid policies. It is not surprising that health systems are neglected in European trade policies – as well as in those of most other countries – given that such policies are guided primarily by the interests of exporters – in other words, private sector interests. One consequence is a systematic bias against public regulatory measures and public interest concerns affecting all countries over the long term. Finally, the neglect of health concerns is not a problem solely for European countries. It is frequently argued that European public health regulations and precautionary measures act as trade barriers, an argument sometimes regarded as legitimate within the development and trade community. In the sphere of public health, however, this argument could lead to the dismantling of public health regulations because they often limit commercial prospects.

Aid policies Worldwide, the European Union is the single largest aid donor. It is in a strong position, therefore, to make a major contribution to development policy options. But recent trends in the European aid regime clearly illustrate that aid policies are influenced primarily by European economic interests (selling European products and services) or emerge in an ad hoc manner. This is illustrated by the G8-driven approach to the 'three diseases' (HIV/AIDS, malaria and tuberculosis), which was influenced more by the US stance than European ones. In the sphere of health policies, moreover, links with the UN agencies such as the WHO and ILO are relatively weak, while policy guidance is often sought from the OECD or international financial institutions.

EU documents provide evidence to support each of these trends. For example, an EU communication in 2001 on poverty and the 'three diseases' is clearly based more on trade-related and other interests than sound consideration of policy choices to support poverty reduction (European Commission 2001b). It emphasises support for the research and development efforts of European industry and European researchers in national developing country strategies but omits to mention health systems in its actual programme for action. Thus, while the EU emphasises the lack of capacity and ability of health systems in developing countries to provide adequate services to deal with HIV/AIDS, its own emphasis on disease programmes could weaken further the capacities of these health systems (European Commission 2001b).

The Programme for Action of the European Community's 2001 development policy highlights poverty reduction in its analysis, but its suggested measures to tackle it are based on initiatives from the OECD, IMF and World Bank. As part of the policy framework, there seems to be a commitment to support those IMF and World Bank sectoral programmes in health and education which are consistent with the macro-economic framework of the international financial institutions (European Commission 2001c). The main question left unanswered is how poverty is to be reduced and to what extent this programme will result in European aid for health being tied more closely to the macro-economic policies of the Bretton Woods institutions.

According to Wade (2001), the European states and Japan have been inactive in steering the World Bank, which has thus been left to the vagaries of US policies. The Nordic States have been investing millions of dollars in trust funds for Bank work on the 'social' aspects of development, an area where the US Treasury has been happy to let them take the lead and pay the costs. In practice, however, the situation is perhaps even more problematic for the Nordic and European countries which have supported World Bank social policies than Wade has described. As the content of World Bank social sector support has been more informed by market-oriented and US models, it is highly likely that at least some part of European support to the World Bank has resulted in the promotion of US-style social policies and the commercial interests of the healthcare industry. The World Bank and its private sector wing, the International Finance Corporation (IFC), are actively promoting market-oriented reforms in the developing world and expanding the markets for the international healthcare industry, especially in Latin America (Iriart et al. 2001; Armada et al. 2001).

As European aid policies emphasise coherence between European positions on aid and on other policy issues, it is important to ensure that such coherence is not guided primarily by European economic and private, for-profit interests or that it becomes too tightly driven by requirements for aid to be effective. A fundamental problem stems from the lack of EU attempts to use the political and policy opportunities in development policies to promote health and social policy issues. As the European Community seems increasingly to seek to talk in 'one voice' within international fora, it is important to know whose voice is speaking on behalf of the European Community and its members in health and social services.

Industry policies In industrial policies, health-related matters are important in the context, for example, of health technology assessments, regulatory policies concerning occupational health and safety and, last but not least, pharmaceutical policies. In the EU, pharmaceutical policies have by and large been considered in the context of industrial policies which has led to a bias towards industry-led policies and market orientation in an area where public regulation is necessary. The bias is also problematic in the context of steadily rising pharmaceutical costs. As the public health sector buys most pharmaceuticals, pricing policies clearly matter to national Ministries of Health. Generous commitments by European policies to industry on data exclusivity in the licensing regulations governing pharmaceuticals mean higher prices of drugs in

European countries in spite of stated efforts to support and increase the use of generic drugs in European health systems.

The pharmaceutical industry is one of the most effective lobbying groups within the European Community and is clearly able to influence policies. According to Greenwood (1997), it has become normal practice for the industry to second its staff to work in the Commission. The European Federation of Pharmaceutical Industry Associations is just one example of an intermediary which has an ingrained interest; the association's involvement in the governance of selling standards in medicines at the European level bears all the hallmarks of neo-corporatism. The federation provided the blueprint for extending the patent period for medicines in Europe, something the Commission had initially been reluctant to accept; encouraged the idea of a European Medicines Agency; and prevented a 'social acceptability' criterion from being inserted in the registration of medicinal products (Greenwood 1997). In the development context, the most problematic aspects of European pharmaceutical policies relate to trade-related intellectual property rights and to development aid and trade policies. The strong influence of the pharmaceutical industry on European policies ensures that attention is paid to the interests of the rights holders (in most cases, the research-based pharmaceutical industry) in the field of trade, patenting and intellectual property rights.

TOWARDS MORE 'HEALTHY' PUBLIC POLICIES

All the examples explored above highlight how European policies that fall outside the health sector have an impact on health systems' priorities and practices at both national and local level. The Treaty of Amsterdam requires the European Community to promote health protection to a high level in all policies, but this principle is generally not implemented.

Economic policies and commercial and trade interests clearly do not mesh well with many aspects of health policy, a conflict that needs to be recognised at the European level. Currently, national reactions to this conflict have primarily consisted in taking out issues relating to health services on the grounds of subsidiarity – member states can deal with national health systems more effectively than the European Commission. But it is more urgent to ensure that health and social policies are not further marginalised as the result of Community policies in other fields which influence health policies indirectly. Even if health administrations are consulted in terms of these policy issues, they may lack the willingness and expertise to envisage the implications for health systems of legislative changes at Community level. This gap needs to be recognised but is not an argument for shifting more policy competence from member states to the European level.

The gap between member states and the European Commission in health policy, and the lack of knowledge at the national level about other matters relating to health, extends to external aid and trade policies, which are weak in substance and tend to be dominated by narrow economic and trade interests and policies promoted by the private sector. At the same time as European health systems have problems due to the higher costs of pharmaceuticals, competition policies, internal market regulations and some aspects of government procurement, the European trade agenda is keenly promoting many of these problems in its international trade negotiations and debates. In aid policies, the promotion of European interests seems to have been easily moulded with the promotion of the interests of European private health service providers. This elision may contrast with the solidarity principles of the health systems of recipient countries and represent corporate greed more than human needs.

Three issues deserve specific emphasis in the context of European policies:

1. *The common nature of the problems*. In many countries, the pressures upon and problems of health systems are perceived as particular national problems. This perception further marginalises the potential political power that could be mobilised through citizens articulating their views and priorities in the context of European policies. At issue is not the extent to which specific national ('good') policies are compromised by European ('bad') policies, but rather a more systematic problem of conflicting interests and practice of policy-making at the European level with relevance to each of the member states.

2. *Democratic accountability*. In principle, democratic accountability in the European Union should lie in national parliaments and the European parliament. The European Union needs to consider the basis and nature of the European Community from citizens' viewpoints. Also, in these perspectives lies the possibility of articulating health concerns more strongly. European policies are already facing both anti-globalist and nationalist social movements and cannot provide more ground for the critics to blame the European Union for neglecting European citizens or for undermining health, equity and social security.

3. *Invisibility of incremental changes and complexity of different levels*

of governance. In many ways, the policy issues addressed in this chapter relate to incremental processes of policy change. The nature of the changes are difficult to follow and are made explicit primarily through rulings of the European Court of Justice, national rulings on competition law or in relation to trade-related interpretations and negotiations of new treaties or amendments to old ones.

The EU is primarily a legal and financial actor and is therefore mainly influenced through these areas. It is unlikely that its enlargement towards Eastern Europe will strengthen considerations of the social aspects of the European Community. The critical task for those concerned with health is to bring politics back into health policy-making and to work towards strengthening citizens' rights to public services in general and towards maintaining the capacity for adequate public health policy at both national and European levels.

At the moment, the magnitude of the various changes to health services in many European countries is limited, but there is a grave danger that incremental change will produce broader changes backed by legislation at national and/or regional (European) level. Such changes will predominantly relate to other sectors such as trade, industry and competition and are likely to be guided by economic and market-oriented principles. The same danger applies to the European Union's external policies and development aid. The lack of a social agenda is further aggravated by the influential role of international financial institutions, and trade and European business interests in health-related issues.

REFERENCES

Armada, F., Muntaner, C. and Navarro, V. (2001) 'Health and social security reforms in Latin America: the convergence of the World Health Organisation, the World Bank and the transnational corporations', *International Journal of Health Services*, 31 (4), 729–68.

Busse, R. (2001) 'A single European market in healthcare?', *Issues in European Health Policy*, 4, 3–5.

Eisma, D. (1999) 'How to build a better EU public health budget', *Eurohealth*, 5 (1), 12–13.

European Commission (1998) *Citizens and Health Systems: Main Results from a Eurobarometer Survey*, Luxembourg: European Commission DG V/F.1. European Communities.

— (2000) *Proposal for a Directive of the European Parliament and of the Council on the Coordination of Procedures for the Award of Public Supply Contracts, Public Service Contracts and Public Works Contracts* (VOM [2000] 275 Final/2. 2000/0115 [COD]), Brussels: Commission of the European Communities.

— (2001a) *The Internal Market and Health Services* (Report of the High Level Committee on Health, Directorate-General Public Health), Brussels: Commission of the European Communities.

— (2001b) *Communication from the Commission to the Action on HIV/AIDS, Malaria and Tuberculosis in the Context of Poverty Reduction* (EN/D/347.2001), Brussels: Commission of the European Comunities.

— (2001c) *Commission Staff Working Document. The European Community's Development Policy. Programme of Action* (SEC [2001] 150), Brussels: Commission of the European Communities.

European Community (1997) *Consolidated Version of the Treaty Establishing the European Community*, Luxembourg: Office for Official Publications of the European Communities.

— (2001) 'Treaty of Nice. Amending the Treaty on European Union, the treaties establishing the European Communities and certain related acts', *Official Journal of the European Communities*, 10 March, 2001/c80/01.

European Court of Justice (1998a) Judgment of the Court, 24 September 1998. Case C-76/97. Walter Tögel vs. Niederösterreichische Gebietskrankenkasse.

— (1998b) Opinion of Advocate General Fennelly, 2 April 1998. Case C-76/97. Walter Tögel vs. Niederösterreichische Gebietskrankenkasse.

— (2000a) Julkisasiamiehen ratkaisuehdotus 18 päivänä toukokuuta 2000, Asia C-157/99 B.S.M. Geraets-Smits vs. Stichting Ziekenfonds VGZ ja H. T. M. Peerbooms vs. Stichting CZ Groep Zorgverzekeringen.

— (2000b) Judgment of the Court, 12 July 2001. B.S.M. Geraets-Smits vs. Stichting Ziekenfonds VGZ and H. T. M. Peerbooms vs. Stichting CZ Groep Zorgverzekeringen.

European Health Care Management Association (2000) Council of the European Parliament, *EC Programme for Action: The Impact of Market Forces on Health Systems. A Review of Evidence in the 15 European Union Member States*, Dublin: EHMA.

Fischer, A. (1999) 'A new health policy in the EU', *Eurohealth*, 5 (1), 4–5.

Forsberg, E., Axelsson, R. and Arnetz, B. (2001) 'Financial incentives in healthcare: the impact of performance-based reimbursement', *Health Policy*, 58, 243–62.

Greenwood, J. (1997) *Representing Interests in the European Union*, London: Macmillan.

Grinten, T. and Lint, M. (2001) 'The impact of Europe on healthcare: The Dutch case', *Eurohealth*, 7 (1), 19–22.

Hagman, R. (2001) 'More competition into healthcare'; www.kilpailuvirasto.fi/cgi-bin/view_text.pl?id=governmentandthemarkets

Health Policy, Politics and Law (2000) Special Issue, 25 (5).

Holzmann, R. and Rutkowski, M. (2002) *Conference on European Pensions: A Public–Private Partnership*, Munich, 11–13 February 2000; www.malekigroup.com/newhome/termine/peafu/2002/einfuehrung.html

Iriart, C., Merhy, E. E. and Waitzkin, H. (2001) 'Managed care in Latin America', *Social Sciences and Medicine* (Special Issue on Comparative Studies of Competition Policy, 52 (8), 1243–53.

Kauppa ja Teollisuusministeriö (2001) *Laatua ja tehokkuutta palvelujen kilpailulla. Kilpailupolitiikan ohjelmatyöryhmän raportti julkisten palvelujen markkinaehtoistamisen mahdollisuuksista ja merkityksestä* (Kauppa ja teollisuusministeriön yuöryhmä ja toimikuntaraportteja 17/2001), Helsinki: Edita. [Ministry of Trade and Industry (2001) *Quality and Efficiency through Competition in Services. Report on the Potential and Significance of the Market-basedness of Public Services* (Competition Policy Programme Committee, ad hoc Committee Reports 17/2001), Helsinki: Edita.]

Kilpailuvirasto (2001) Asia kasmaksusäännösten laboratoriopalvelujen kilpailua vääristävä vaikutus. Kilpailuvirasto. DNRO 391/71/2001. 23.04.2001.

Mackintosh, M. (1995) 'Competition and contracting in selective social provisioning', *European Journal of Development Research*, 7, 26–52.

Liaropoulos, L. and Tragakes, E. (1998) 'Public/private financing in the Greek healthcare system: implications for equity', *Health Policy*, 43, 153–69.

Mossiailos, E. (1997) 'Citizens' views on healthcare systems in the 15 member states of the European Union', *Health Economics*, 6, 109–16.

Nickless, J. (2001a) 'Kohll and Decker: a new hope for third-country nationals', *Eurohealth*, 5 (1), 20–2.

— (2001b) 'Smits/Peerbooms: Clarification of Kohll and Decker?', *Eurohealth*, 7 (4), 7–10.

Palm, W. and Nickless, J. (2001) 'Access to healthcare in the European Union: the consequences of the Kohll and Decker judgments', *Eurohealth*, 7 (1), 13–15.

Pitruzello, S. (1997) 'Social policy and the implementation of the Maastricht fiscal convergence criteria: the Italian and French attempts at welfare and pension reforms', *Social Research*, 64 (1), 589–642.

Pollock, A. and Price, D. (2000) 'Rewriting the regulations: how the World Trade Organisation could accelerate privatisation in healthcare systems', *The Lancet*, 356, 1995–2000.

Price, D., Pollock, A. and Shaoul, J. (1999) 'How the World Trade Organisation is shaping domestic policies in healthcare', *The Lancet*, 354 (27), 1889–92.

Scharpf, F. W. (2000) 'Globalisation and the Welfare State. Constraints, Challenges and Vulnerabilities', paper presented at the International Social Security Conference, Helsinki, 25–27 September; www.issa.int/engl/homef.htm

Seagall, M. (2000) 'From co-operation to competition in national health systems – and back? Impact on professional ethics and quality of care', *International Journal of Health Planning and Management*, 15, 61–79.

Social Science and Medicine (2001) Special Issue on Comparative Studies of Competition Policy, 52 (8).

T'Hoen, E. (2000) 'Europe is beginning to address the crisis of global access to medicines', *Eurohealth*, 6, 23–4.

Van der Mei, A. P. (1999) 'The Kohll and Decker rulings: revolution or evolution', *Eurohealth*, 5 (1), 14–16.

Wade, R. (2001) 'Showdown at the World Bank', *New Left Review*, 7, 125–37.

Wagstaff, A. and Doorslaer, E. (1992) 'Equity in international finance of healthcare: some international comparisons', *Journal of Health Economics*, 11, 361–87.

WHO (2001) *World Health Report 2001*, Geneva: WHO.

Wismar, M. (2001) 'ECJ in the driving seat of health policy. But what's the destination?', *Eurohealth*, 7 (4), 5–6.

Woolhandler, S. and Himmelstein, D. (1999) 'When money is the mission – the high costs of investor-owned healthcare', *New England Journal of Medicine*, 341 (6), 444–6.

PART THREE

Case Studies of Restructuring: Comparative Perspectives

CHAPTER 8

The Impact of Social Health Insurance Reform on Social Solidarity in Four European Countries

HANS MAARSE AND AGGIE PAULUS

Health insurance is the most important tool of healthcare finance in Western Europe. Schneider and his colleagues (1998) estimated its share in healthcare expenditures at 53 per cent in 1994, compared to 31 per cent for tax funding and 16 per cent for private payments. Within health insurance, the share of social (statutory) health insurance far exceeds that of private health insurance. Whereas social health insurance accounted for 47 per cent of healthcare expenditure in 1994, private health insurance covered only 6 per cent of revenues of healthcare expenditures (Schneider et al. 1998).

HEALTH INSURANCE AND HEALTHCARE REFORM

The terms social and private health insurance suggest that both regimes have a homogeneous structure. This suggestion, however, is wrong. In reality, we find a great variety in the way both regimes – as well as their interrelationship – are shaped (Glaser 1991; Mossialos et al. 2002). Generally speaking, we may say that social health insurance is based upon the principle of solidarity whereas private health insurance rests upon the principle of ability to pay. 'Under a social health insurance scheme,' Stone explains, 'individuals are entitled to receive whatever care they need, and the amounts they pay to finance the scheme are totally unrelated to the amount or cost of care they actually use' (Stone 1993: 291). The principle of private insurance, on the other hand, means that the insurer has the 'responsibility to treat all its policyholders in accordance with ability to pay and by establishing premiums at a level consistent with the risk represented by each policyholder' (p. 293).

Over the last two decades, healthcare policy-making in the industrial-ised world has been dominated by the search for reform (Saltman and Figueras 1997). Healthcare reform comprised a range of programmes most of which were directed at cost control and efficiency. These goals also evolved as prime targets in health insurance reform as illustrated by the emergence of new policy issues such as the appropriateness of the benefit package, priority setting, the role of market competition among health insurers and the need for change in the insurer–provider relationship, as well as the use of private payments.

There has been growing concern that reform programmes will have adverse effects upon solidarity in social health insurance (Ter Meulen et al. 2001; Morone 2000; Chinitz et al. 1997). The assumption is that the need for cost control, efficiency and consumer orientation conflicts with the principle of solidarity. The introduction of market competition in social health insurance will inevitably put limits on solidarity. These concerns and assumptions will be investigated in this chapter. What is the influence of reform programmes upon solidarity in social health insurance? Does a deeply rooted 'culture of solidarity' (Hinrichs 1995) still exist in European healthcare? Does solidarity operate as a political constraint to reform? Or is it gradually losing ground as a constitutive principle of health insurance?

In order to find an answer to these questions, we will briefly present the results of an international comparative analysis of the impact of recent health insurance reform upon solidarity in four Western Euro-

TABLE 8.1 Key figures of social health insurance

	% Share in healthcare finance (1994)	Coverage of the population (%)
Belgium*	40.6	99
West Germany	66.0	88
Switzerland*	35.9	99
Netherlands	73.8	65 (acute care)
		100 (long-term care)

Note: * In both countries, social health insurance is heavily subsidised by the state. The figures on the share in healthcare finance underestimate the prominent role of social health insurance.

Source: Schneider et al. 1998

pean countries: Belgium, Germany, Switzerland and the Netherlands. In each of these countries, social health insurance plays a prominent role in healthcare finance and ensuring access to healthcare (see Table 8.1). Everywhere the reform of social health insurance has emerged as a key issue in healthcare reform. Our comparative investigation will be restricted to reforms undertaken in the 1990s.

CONCEPTS OF SOLIDARITY

In Western European countries there is a widespread belief that solidarity and risk-sharing should form a key element in the finance of healthcare. It has always been part of the 'moral infrastructure' (Hinrichs 1995) of the modern welfare state. National social health insurance laws had great influence upon the concrete meaning of solidarity. Solidarity turned from a voluntary into a state-supported arrangement. Membership became mandatory for those who were entitled to it. Furthermore, state laws markedly extended the scope of solidarity, not only by enlarging the portion of the population entitled to social health insurance, but also by broadening the package of healthcare benefits. Ever more people were given access to ever more health services throughout Western Europe, underpinning the legacy of social welfare.

The concept of solidarity points to collective and redistributive activity. There are two types of solidarity. The first is risk solidarity. This concept means that everybody should have access to health insurance, independent of their risk profile. Thus, whether a person is sick or healthy, old or young, male or female, has an unfavourable medical track record and so on, is completely irrelevant for acceptance. There is universal coverage and any kind of risk selection (medical underwriting) on the part of health insurers is, by law, forbidden. 'Risk' solidarity also implies that the contribution the insured must pay is unrelated to health risk.

Risk solidarity sharply contrasts with the principle usually underlying private health insurance, premised upon ability to pay and related to risk profile. This principle holds that the premium the insured must pay should be related to risk. Higher risks should be normalised by higher premiums. Exclusion waivers for pre-existing medical disorders and a non-acceptance policy are also considered fair under the principle of ability to pay and are therefore widely used, especially by commercial insurers (Stone 1993; Light 1992).

The second type of solidarity is income solidarity. The contribution that policy-holders must pay for health insurance should be related to their ability to pay. In other words, the contribution rate (premium, payroll tax) varies with income. A special kind of income solidarity, for example, is family solidarity. In private health insurance, an individual's income is irrelevant. Cross-subsidies from the rich to the poor are often even considered unfair.

Risk solidarity and income solidarity are constitutive principles of social health insurance that must be made operational. Their implementation varies across countries. There exists no one-to-one relationship between principle and concrete regulations since these depend upon historical, legal and socio-economic circumstances. This observation also applies to another dimension of solidarity – scope. Here, a distinction must be made between content and membership. Content refers to the package of health services (benefits) that the insured has access to when sick; membership to the group of people entitled to join the collective arrangement. It is fair to say that social health insurance programmes are characterised by a rather broad package of health services. They also cover a large portion of the population (see Table 8.1).

Solidarity can be conceptualised as an essential component or dimension of the wider concept of equity or fair access. In the European tradition, equity means that all citizens are given a social right to have fair access to progressive achievements in society such as the advance of healthcare, education, and so on. Fair access in the European tradition requires solidarity in healthcare finance. But it also relates to medical consumption. The principle of fair access is not only violated to the extent that solidarity is absent or has only a limited scope, but also to the extent that the sick are discriminated against in medical care. However, what kind of discrimination is considered fair or unfair will again vary across countries (Payer 1988).

REFORM AND RISK SOLIDARITY – SOME FINDINGS

It is often assumed that health insurance reform directed at effective cost control, better efficiency, more consumer sovereignty or a stronger emphasis upon financial accountability could adversely affect risk solidarity. Market competition, for instance, may tempt insurance companies to practise risk selection as the most promising strategy to save costs and to gain competitive advantage. From an individual insurer's point of view, it is not efficient (rational) to have a large number of bad or high-risk cases among its insured.

Contrary to what is commonly expected, our examination of the impact of the introduction of market competition into social health insurance does not confirm an adverse effect upon risk solidarity. The picture is more complicated. In the Netherlands, for instance, there are no clear signs of risk selection. If it exists, it is only a small-scale phenomenon. This is hardly a surprising conclusion. Health insurance reform brought only some market competition under the sickness fund insurance scheme, mainly covering acute and short-term care, but not under the exceptional medical expenses scheme for long-term care (Schut 1995). Risk selection also remained explicitly ruled out in health insurance legislation. The insurers must accept all applicants, medical underwriting is forbidden, and flat-rate premiums[1] (charged in addition to income-dependent contributions to allow for some market competition between the insurers) should remain unrelated to risk. In order to counteract risk selection, a system of prospective risk pooling was also introduced, replacing the old system of full retrospective risk pooling between the insurers (Schut and Van Doorslaer 1999).

Belgium is another country where risk solidarity has remained a cornerstone of social health insurance (Observatory 2000c; Hermesse et al. 1999). This cannot be seen separately from the structure of the health insurance market. The mutual funds are organised in five national alliances. Two of these, the National Alliance of Christian Mutual Funds (45 per cent) and the National Union of Socialist Mutual Funds (29 per cent) together cover almost 75 per cent of the population. Traditionally, they have strong alignments to different political and ideological positions. As a result, relations between the mutual funds have always been characterised by political and ideological overtones (Nonneman and Van Doorslaer 1994). Political and ideological alignments also reinforced the sense of sharing risk and solidarity among its group members. This situation has not been fundamentally changed in the 1990s by the reform programme of the Belgian government to introduce limited financial self-responsibility of the mutual funds (Schut and Van Doorslaer 1999).[2] The culture of risk solidarity is also present in complementary health insurance. Contrary to practice in the other countries where the purchase of a complementary health plan is voluntary, Belgian mutual funds usually resort to enforced solidarity. An applicant subscribing to a fund must also purchase its complementary health plan. Enforced solidarity is considered an effective tool to avoid adverse risk selection by the insured and to facilitate risk solidarity (Van der Oever and Volckaert 1999).

Switzerland is a country where one of the prime goals of health insurance reform in 1994 was precisely to increase risk solidarity (Observatory 2000b; Hermesse et al. 1999). Prior to reform, risk solidarity was gradually weakened by intense market competition between the funds (*Entsolidarisierung*). Furthermore, women had to pay a higher premium than men premised on the argument that average healthcare costs for women are higher. The reform put an end to this 'discriminatory' practice. More generally, healthcare reform abolished any form of pre-existing risk selection on the part of insurance companies. Under a specific new regime of market competition, insurance companies have to accept all applicants; premiums should not be related to risk but based upon community rating. A risk equalisation scheme was introduced for a ten-year period (expiring in 2006) to level off differences in risk profile.

Germany has always been a country with a segmented structure in social health insurance. Segmentation means that risk solidarity holds only for group members (group-based solidarity) but not between groups. Three types of insurers have traditionally dominated the market: the local sickness funds (AOKs) being open to every applicant; the company-based funds (BKKs) accepting only company workers and their family members; and substitute funds (EKKs), with one exception only accepting white-collar workers (Observatory 2000a). This type of segmentation is clearly a source of indirect risk selection, as demonstrated by Wysong and Abel (1990). They found, for instance, clear evidence that higher income groups were underrepresented in the AOKs and that the unemployed were overrepresented. Because health risks correlate with income and social status, they inferred from this that the risk profiles of the three types of funds were different. These differences are a major cause of the variation in contribution rates.[3] In 1993, for instance, they ranged from 10.6 per cent to 16.8 per cent with an average of 13.4 per cent in West Germany (Greiner and Von der Schulenburg 1996).

Social health insurance reform in the 1990s brought an important alteration in this situation. In order to facilitate market competition and to give the insured a greater freedom of choice, new legislation opened the substitute funds (EKKs) to all applicants. The BKKs, or company funds, were also given the option of 'opening their door' to non-company members. If they opted for that strategy, however, they had to accept every applicant. Furthermore, a risk equalisation scheme with transfer payments between the funds was implemented to remove unfair practice. This was an innovation because risk pooling did not really exist in Germany, except for pensioners.

The perhaps paradoxical conclusion to be drawn from social health insurance reform in Germany is that the reforms in the 1990s to stimulate market competition among the funds and to enhance the consumers' freedom of choice led to greater risk solidarity in social health insurance. This is because company funds, guild funds as well as substitute funds, now have to accept all applicants and, by implication, are sharing their risks. By risk pooling, risk solidarity has been extended from a purely within-group arrangement to a between-group arrangement.

From the above observations it follows that, contrary to what is often assumed, reforms aimed at market competition in social health insurance and more freedom of choice for the insured have increased the extent of risk solidarity in social health insurance. However, simple and premature conclusions should be avoided. One should not forget that the arrangements for prospective risk pooling are deficient, particularly in Germany and Switzerland. Short-term effects may also be different from long-term effects. Furthermore, it is important to note that reforms directed at market competition were not the only reforms that occurred in the 1990s. Another reform was to increase private payments by means of cost sharing and co-payments. This reform, which particularly occurred in Belgium and Germany, reduces risk solidarity to the extent that it connects private payments with medical consumption. The negative impact of private payments upon risk solidarity has been somewhat limited by means of compensatory programmes linked to risk (for example, no cost sharing for prescription drugs for life-threatening disease). In the Netherlands, however, the share of private payments decreased from 10 per cent in the early 1990s to 6 per cent in 1999.

REFORM AND INCOME SOLIDARITY

Income solidarity means that a person's contribution is dependent upon his ability to pay. Thus, the rich pay more than the poor; often the state pays (part of) the contribution for the very poor. The relationship between contributions and income varies (Glaser 1991). For example, in the Netherlands, Germany and Belgium, the contribution rate is a fixed percentage of a person's salary. In Belgium, there is a ceiling to the contribution an insured person must pay. In Germany and Switzerland, rate setting is delegated to the insurers. Consequently, contribution rates are different for each fund. In the Netherlands and Belgium, rate setting is centralised and contribution rates are uniform across all insurers (with the exception of the flat-rate premiums in the Netherlands where rate setting is delegated to sickness funds).

Switzerland differs significantly from the other countries in the way income solidarity is shaped – income-dependent premiums have always been politically unfeasible. Under the new health insurance Act, premium setting by the insurers must be based upon community rating per canton: one rate for each insurer per canton.[4] State and canton subsidies are used as a tool to implement income solidarity. Each canton may follow its own compensation policy, resulting in differing compensation arrangements for each. No income solidarity exists between cantons. Another innovation of insurance reform is that, under the new health insurance Act, subsidies are paid directly to the insured instead of the insurance companies as happened before reform. Targeting subsidies at the insured put an end to the old situation when all insured benefited from state and canton subsidies (Observatory 2000b).

How has health insurance reform affected income solidarity over the last decade? We will direct our analysis here at private payments and mandatory contributions that the insured must pay, which are unrelated to income. These instruments reduce income solidarity, since a person's expenditure on healthcare no longer solely depends on income but also on medical consumption. In particular the chronically sick may be worse off. The adverse impact of co-payments and a mandatory deductible is dampened to the extent that compensatory arrangements are used to protect the poor.

The instrument of private payments has always been unpopular in the Netherlands. Various proposals for such payments were voted down or were cancelled only a few years after introduction (Starmans 1998). Most co-payments are for the 'hotel costs' of long-term residential care. These payments are related to income and there is a maximum payment. In 1994 they accounted for 7.3 per cent of costs in healthcare in Europe – the lowest percentage in Europe (Schneider et al. 1998). However, the introduction of market competition in social health insurance had some negative effects upon income solidarity. Since the early 1990s, the insured must not only pay an income-related contribution but also on top of that a flat-rate premium to create some room for competition. The underlying assumption was that efficiently operating insurers would charge lower premiums than insurers operating inefficiently (Schut 1995). A flat-rate premium is a fixed sum and, therefore, reduces income solidarity, the more so because not only the principal insured (head of family) must pay it but all dependants as well.

In Belgium, where private payments already accounted for some 17.8 per cent of healthcare expenditures in 1994 (Schneider et al. 1998), the reform of social health insurance led to a further increase of cost sharing and co-payments (*remgelden*) with the purpose of making patients pay for healthcare costs. A recent study of the National Alliance of the Socialist Mutual Funds found that the chronically sick pay on average 23 per cent of their income to medical care and social services (Peers et al. 1999). A study by the National Alliance of the Christian Mutual Funds demonstrated that 5 per cent of the population covers 50 per cent of the total sum of co-payments – obviously a byproduct of the very uneven distribution of healthcare expenditures over the population in Belgium (quoted in Peers et al. 1999). There is increasing concern about the negative effect of private payments on solidarity. Therefore, proposals are under way to put an overall annual limit on private payments in social health insurance.

Private payments play an important role in Swiss healthcare finance. In 1997 they accounted for 27.6 per cent of healthcare expenditures. Most health plans require the insured to pay a fixed part of the costs by means of a mandatory deductible. Furthermore, the Swiss must pay a 10 per cent co-payment rate for all medical care under the social health insurance programme (Observatory 2000b). The share of private payments has remained more or less the same following the new legislation on health insurance in 1994.

Germany also has a long tradition of private payments, particularly for pharmaceutical drugs. Health insurance reform in the 1990s led to a substantial increase in these payments, not only for pharmaceutical drugs, but also for dental care, physiotherapy, hospital stay and stationary rehabilitative treatment following a hospital stay, ambulance transportation, and so on. The tool of payments increasingly evolved as a contested issue in German healthcare politics (Busse and Howarth 1999). When the new left-wing government came to power, a Law to Strengthen Solidarity in Statutory Health Insurance was adopted (1998). Under this law, some arrangements for cost sharing and co-payments, for instance, for pharmaceuticals and dental care, were lowered. The law also put an end to the option for the insurers to introduce a 'no claim' bonus, deductibles, and higher co-payments.

From the above analysis, we may conclude that social health insurance reform has influenced the degree of income solidarity under social health insurance. The increase in the use of cost sharing and co-payments in some countries as a tool for cost control has reduced income solidarity. Compensatory arrangements have somewhat reduced this effect.

REFORM AND SCOPE

How did reform in each of the four countries influence the scope of solidarity or, more precisely, the benefit package and membership of social health insurance? As a general observation, we may say that the benefit package evolved as a new issue in healthcare policy-making, although in some countries more than in others. Everywhere extensions of the package were more critically considered than before. This trend – sometimes framed as priority setting – was propelled by the search for efficiency and equity. In the Netherlands, for instance, the Dunning Committee proposed a framework for 'package decisions' based upon necessity and evidence-based medicine. The framework was not only intended for decisions on extensions, but also for a critical screening of the current package. The screening operation, however, did not prove to be a success mainly because the criteria of necessity, effectiveness and efficiency were difficult to apply in concrete cases and the abundance of conflicting interests difficult to sort (Van der Grinten and Kasdorp 1999). To date, priority setting has hardly developed as a critical issue in healthcare policy-making in Belgium, Germany and Switzerland.

To the extent such 'package decisions' would lead to an elimination of unnecessary, ineffective and inefficient healthcare, we can reasonably argue that those decisions do not reduce risk and income solidarity. The problem is, of course, that most decisions were not made on a rational basis but on a political one, and that they were always considered unfair by patient groups, providers and industrial stakeholders, and so on. The political character of package reform is nicely illustrated by the fact that some package reductions were cancelled in a later reform. An example of remedial reform is the relisting of large parts of dental care in 1996 in the Netherlands, after they had been delisted in 1994. The aforementioned Law on Strengthening Solidarity in Social Health Insurance in Germany was also intended as a political step to rectify a number of earlier package reforms.

Again, it is too simple to conclude that health insurance reforms led only to a back-door erosion of solidarity (the terminology is derived from Poullier and Sandier 2000). In some cases it also increased it. Germany, for instance, enacted new legislation on nursing care (*Pflege-*

gesetz) in the 1990s – not really a new advance in medicine but rather a traditional part of it. The new law was intended to strengthen fairness in German social health insurance by ensuring every German better access to nursing care. Healthcare reform in Switzerland also contained steps to greater solidarity by extending the benefit package as part of the health insurance reform in 1994.

Health insurance reform also relates to membership. In the Netherlands, some reform programmes enlarged membership. For instance, health insurance was opened to the elderly whose income was below a state-set level. Recently, self-employed workers whose income was below a state-set level were transferred from private to social health insurance. But membership decisions always proved very political, not only because of people resisting being shifted from a private to a public arrangement (membership is mandatory), but also because of the delicate balance between social health insurance and private health insurance in Dutch healthcare policy. Understandably, the private health insurance market did not want to lose its market share to social health insurance. More generally, we can say that the coexistence of social and private health insurance has always proven a formidable obstacle to health insurance reform, in particular to proposals for the introduction of a universal social health insurance programme for acute care. Nowadays, a universal programme exists only for long-term care. There is a political trade-off between the membership and package issue: for some policy-makers, a universal scheme is acceptable only if the package is considerably reduced, leaving substantial room for the private market of complementary health insurance.

The balance between social and private health insurance has also proved to be a delicate issue in Germany. It has remained more or less stable over the last ten years. There is an important structural difference between Germany and the Netherlands here. Under Dutch social health insurance, people who do not meet the entitlement criteria cannot enrol in the Statutory Health Insurance Programme (enforced exit). They must purchase a private plan. German social health insurance gives its members an opt-out option. Those who are not a mandatory member of social health insurance are given the option to contract with a private health insurance company.[5] This is particularly the case for people whose earnings exceed the state-set income level. In this segment of the market, social health insurance competes with private health insurance. An important reform in the 1990s put an end to switching freely between social and private health insurance.

In Switzerland, health insurance reform has increased its membership. The former option for the well-to-do to opt out has been abolished. Following reform, membership has become mandatory. In Belgium, membership has not been an important issue over the past decade, because 99 per cent of the population is already covered by it.

In summary, we can conclude that health insurance reforms have varied in form and in content. Overall, it has not significantly affected the scope of solidarity, despite the rhetoric about priority setting. Where health services were shifted from the public to the private sphere, remedial programmes were started to redress some of its effects. The remarkable exception to this conclusion is Germany because of the adoption of the *Pflegegesetz* in 1994. The package was also extended in Switzerland. In respect to membership, we did not find much sign of either a positive or negative effect.

CONCLUSIONS

In each of the four countries studied we found no clear evidence that social health insurance reform programmes had had an adverse impact upon solidarity and its scope. Even contrary to that, we saw various examples of reform programmes strengthening risk solidarity and scope. On the other hand, there were also examples of a negative effect, in particular the increase of private payments by new cost sharing and co-payment arrangements. It would be naïve, however, to assume that the future of solidarity in social health insurance lies only in the past. New developments may have a strong impact upon the future shape of solidarity. In this final section, we will briefly digress on how these developments may influence solidarity in social health insurance in future. In fact, our theme is the future of social health insurance itself.

The principle of solidarity may be depicted as a key principle of the welfare state in Europe. It is a constitutive element of the 'moral infrastructure' of the welfare state, as Hinrichs (1995) put it. But will it survive? If we may believe the results of the study of a Dutch research group, the answer tends to be in the affirmative. The study left 'no doubt about the overwhelming support for public health services in Europe. In all countries (of the European Union HM/AP), positive attitudes towards public healthcare prevail, demonstrating "a general preference for a universal healthcare system with a broad range of health services"' (Gevers et al. 2000: 319). Indeed, the success of the collective arrangements in the welfare state is critically contingent upon the presence of a culture of solidarity.

Yet, there are also factors at work that may reduce solidarity in social health insurance and even question the viability of it as it exists today. The first factor is concerned with the rise of healthcare expenditures. The growing share of the elderly and the advance of medicine will lead, beyond any doubt, to further cost increases. Not only will more treatments become available, but the scope of medicine will also extend as ever more knowledge becomes available on the origins of diseases and how they may be prevented. We may speculate that in future an increasing number of potential patients will enter the medical world. The political issue, then, is to what extent the costs of these developments will be borne by welfare arrangements like social health insurance.

One scenario is that governments under great pressure to reduce public expenditure will cope with the financial challenge by playing the 'card of privatisation', for instance by 'package decisions', enhancing the private payment component in healthcare finance or by giving more people the option of going private. Consumers and employers may also turn to private arrangements because of dissatisfaction with the public sector or a growing emphasis upon the capacity of individuals to pursue their own interests and to develop their potentialities. Advocates of privatisation not only use the rhetoric of efficiency, consumer orientation, innovation and so on to argue for the need for a shift from public to private, but also postulate what may be called a collapse theory of the welfare state. In future, collective arrangements will no longer be financially affordable. There are limits to intergenerational solidarity. The only way to cope with this problem is to extend the private basis in healthcare finance. Opponents to such ideas put forward that solidarity could be saved by extending its financial basis. There is also a debate on the issue of whether family solidarity has not gone too far.

Our four-country case study points to the conclusion that social health insurance has survived the fiscal crisis of the state in the past twenty-five years of the last century. The political debate on the future of the welfare state appears to have hardly affected the definition of solidarity contained within it. At the same time, we conclude that the debate on the attainability and desirability of public welfare arrangements has been far from silent. However, so far there is no definite answer to the political question about the extent to which we are indeed 'beyond the welfare state' (Pierson 1998).

Finally, we point to the impact of technological change upon solidarity. Stone (1989) has correctly observed that the concept of risk is gaining ever more importance with the advance of medicine and the rapid invention of new technologies to identify people who are likely to develop disease or disability. Her observation is particularly important in the light of the ongoing revolution in genomics. This revolution will open the way to risk individuation – the identification of health risks at the individual level given a person's genetic predisposition. The paradox of risk individuation is that it makes risk solidarity more needed than ever and at the same time more difficult than ever to implement since health insurers do not like 'to insure a burning house'. Risk individuation may also strike off a process of blaming individuals for abstaining from appropriate preventive action by means of diet programmes, prescription drugs or other activity. Blaming will put risk solidarity at risk.

It is impossible to predict how these factors will influence the definition of solidarity in the future. It is too simple, however, to believe that they will leave its definition unaffected. We may conclude, therefore, that the definition of solidarity and, indeed, the concept of social health insurance in European healthcare are now at a crossroads.

NOTES

1. Flat-rate premiums are charged by the insurers. Sickness funds compete on flat-rate premiums that must be calculated according to the principle of community rating.

2. Health insurance reform has always been less dominated in Belgium by the rhetoric of market competition. Policy-makers prefer to speak of a *responsabilisering van de mutualiteiten*.

3. In Germany and Switzerland rate setting is delegated to the sickness funds; in the Netherlands rate setting is a state affair, with the exception of the flat-rate premiums that are set by the sickness funds themselves. In Belgium rate setting is also centralised.

4. In fact, there are more rates because an applicant may opt for an affiliation to an HMO, a family physician model or a higher deductible. Rates also vary with age: one rate for children up to sixteen years, one rate for seventeen- to twenty-five-year-olds, and one rate for those over twenty-five.

5. However, some categories are excluded from social health insurance.

REFERENCES

Busse, R. and Howarth, C. (1999) 'Cost containment in Germany: twenty years experience', in E. Mossialos, J. Le Grand (eds), *Health Care and Health Care Cost Containment in the European Union*, Aldershot: Ashgate.

Chinitz, D., Preker, A. and Wasem, J. (1997) 'Balancing competition and solidarity in healthcare financing', in R. Saltman, J. Figueras and C. Sakellarides (eds), *Critical Challenges for Health Care Reform in Europe*, Copenhagen: WHO.

Gevers, J., Gelissen, W., Arts, W. and Muffels, R. (2000) 'Public healthcare in the balance: exploring popular support for healthcare systems in the European Union', *International Journal of Social Welfare*, 9 (4), 301–32.

Glaser, W. (1991) *Health Insurance in Practice*, San Francisco, CA: Jossey Bass.

Greiner, W. and Von der Schulenburg, J. M. (1996) 'The health system of Germany', in M. Raffel (ed.), *Health Care and Reform in Industrialised Countries*, University Park, Pennsylvania: State University Press.

Hermesse, J. et al. (1999) *Health Protection Systems Today: Structures and Trends in 15 Countries*, Brussels: Association Internationale de la Mutualité.

Hinrichs, K. (1995) 'The impact of German health insurance reforms on re-distribution and the culture of solidarity', *Journal of Health Policy, Politics and Law*, 20 (3), 653–83.

Light, D. (1992) 'The practice and ethics of risk-rated health insurance', *Journal of the American Medical Association*, 267, 2503–8.

Morone, J. (2000) 'Citizens or shoppers? Solidarity under siege', *Journal of Health Policy, Politics and Law*, 25 (5), 959–68.

Mossialos, E., Dixin, J., Figueras, J. and Kutzin, J. (eds) (2002) *Funding Health Care: Options for Europe*, Buckingham: Open University Press.

Nonneman, W. and Van Doorslaer, E. (1994) 'The role of the sickness funds in the Belgian healthcare market', *Social Science and Medicine*, 39 (10), 1483–95.

Observatory (2000a) *Health Care Systems in Transition: Germany*, Copenhagen: WHO.

— (2000b) *Health Care Systems in Transition: Switzerland*, Copenhagen: WHO.

— (2000c) *Health Care Systems in Transition: Belgium*, Copenhagen: WHO.

Payer, L. (1988) *Medicine and Culture*, New York: Penguin Books.

Peers, J., Gillet, P., Hermesse, J. and Polus, C. (1999) *Gezondheidszorg in België: uitdagingen en opportuniteiten* (Health Care in Belgium: Challenges and Opportunities), Brussels: Landsbond Christelijke Mutualiteit.

Pierson, C. (1998) *Beyond the Welfare State: The New Political Economy of Welfare*, Cambridge: Polity Press.

Poullier, J. P. and Sandier, S. (2000) 'France', *Journal of Health Policy, Politics and Law*, 25 (5), 899–905.

Saltman, R. and Figueras, J. (1997) *European Health Care Reform*, Copenhagen: WHO.

Schneider, M. et al. (1998) *Gesundheitssysteme im internationalen Vergleich* (An International Comparison of Health Care Systems), Augsburg: Basys.

Schut, F. (1995) *Competition in the Dutch Health Care Sector*, Ridderkerk: Ridderprint.

Schut, F. and Van Doorslaer, E. (1999) 'Towards a reinforced role of health insurers in Belgium and the Netherlands', *Health Policy*, 48, 47–57.

Starmans, B. (1998) *The Effects of Patient Charges on Medical Utilisation, Expenditures and Health: Dutch Investigations and International Evidence*, Maastricht: Datawyse.

Stone, D. (1989) 'At risk in the welfare state', *Social Research*, 56 (3), 591–633.

— (1993) 'The struggle for the soul of health insurance', *Journal of Health Policy, Politics and Law*, 18 (2), 287–317.

Ter Meulen, R., Arts, W. and Muffels, R. (eds) (2001) *Solidarity in Health and Social Care in Europe*, Dordrecht: Kluwer.

Van der Grinten, T. and Kasdorp, J. (1999) 'Choices in Dutch healthcare: mixing strategies and responsibilities', *Health Policy*, 50, 105–22.

Van der Oever, R. and Volckaert, C. (1999) 'Evolutie in de rol van de ziekenfondsen in Vlaanderen als zorginkopers met betrekking tot de aanvullende verzekeringen' (Evolution in the role of sickness funds as purchasers in complementary health insurance), *Acta Hospitalia*, 27–39.

Wysong, J. and Abel, T. (1990) 'Universal health insurance and high-risk groups in West Germany: Implications for U.S. health policy', *Milbank Quarterly*, 68 (4), 527–60.

CHAPTER 9

Restructuring Health Services in Italy: The Paradox of Devolution

FRANCESCO TARONI

The idea that the nation-state as we know it appears simultaneously both too small and too large to serve the preferences of the global consumer and the desires of the local citizen has spread rapidly and widely (Courchene 1995). The pressure for global markets has taken the form of international agreements on trade and investments, while the desire to make governments more responsive to the expectations and preferences of the individual citizen lies behind moves to fragment the nation-state into smaller, self-governing political units. A resurgent federal idea promises to provide a way of putting together the needs of the global economy with the preferences of the local community, and devolution is the worldwide buzzword of the day. The financing and organisation of healthcare delivery, which is one of the most politically sensitive activities of governments and among the most demanding of public expenditure, is no exception to this trend of 'glocalisation'.

Decentralisation of health services is the goal and focus of the current wave of healthcare reforms in a number of countries which have successfully implemented the market-oriented reforms of the early 1990s. Canada regionalised the administration of healthcare in its long-established federal system, with provincial governments delegating administrative powers to regional units (Lomas 1997). The United Kingdom, whose NHS has long been the prototype of centralised command service, has devolved legislative powers to Scotland and Wales, and granted fiscal autonomy, albeit limited, to Scotland (Klein 1998; Pollock 1999). In England plans have been issued to decentralise administrative powers to local health services and to reorganise the regional health authorities (Department of Health 2001).

After a twenty-years-long process, Spain has also recently finished constructing its particular form of asymmetrical federalism in healthcare (Reverte-Le Judo and Sanchez-Bayle 1999). In Italy, two separate processes of reform are running in parallel: the implementation of political and fiscal devolution to regional governments, which already enjoy considerable administrative autonomy in the healthcare sector, and the reform of the healthcare system, its fourth reorganisation since the establishment of the Italian National Health Service (Servizio Sanitario Nazionale – SSN) in 1978 (France and Taroni 2000).

The design of devolving political and fiscal responsibility for healthcare to subnational units has not provoked the fierce ideological debate which was associated with pro-market healthcare reforms. This may be because of the ambiguity of the concept of federalism, which is sufficiently vague to accommodate neo-liberal, communitarian and social democratic visions of the welfare state. In fact, the term 'decentralisation' disguises a complex set of phenomena, ranging from intergovernmental reforms which define the forms and the boundaries of governance (between levels of governments), to devolving governmental activities to non-governmental organisations operating in private markets (Bennet 1990). Moreover, federalism is on occasions presented as a viable alternative to the classic opposition between the public sector and the market, putting together individual freedom, social solidarity and cost control.

Political and fiscal decentralisation may have advantages, such as promoting efficiency, diversity, responsiveness, accountability and public participation. There are also relevant theoretical reasons for concern that egalitarian principles and universal interests, as well as the equality and autonomy of the subnational units, might be adversely affected (Prud'Homme 1994). Furthermore, accumulating empirical evidence suggests that fiscal federalism helps the retrenchment of the welfare state (Pierson 1994). However, while abundant literature exists examining its impact on environmental issues, the downsides of federalism for egalitarian healthcare systems have been largely overlooked. This chapter will focus in the main on the risks of political and fiscal federalism on healthcare systems organised under the principles of universality of access, solidarity of contribution and comprehensiveness of coverage. The chapter begins by describing briefly the Italian plans for devolving political and fiscal powers to its twenty regions. The possible consequences of this reform for the SSN are then identified. The chapter concludes with some comments on the pertinence of the Italian case to strategies for devolution in other countries with egalitarian and solidaristic healthcare systems.

FEDERAL REFORM AND HEALTHCARE IN ITALY

Italy has had a regional system of government since 1971 and a national health service since 1978. The Italian SSN has been modelled along the principles of universality of access, comprehensiveness of coverage and solidarity of financing through general taxation. It is egalitarian in that it seeks to ensure for all citizens equal access to the same set of 'essential' services (livelli essenziali di assistenza – LEA). LEA are defined by the central government with reference to four criteria: human dignity, clinical effectiveness, appropriateness and technical efficiency.

'Local' governments in Italy include twenty regions, around 100 provinces and over 8,000 communes. There is no hierarchical relationship between these levels of government (which have instead their own finance and direct links with the central government), but five regions have a special statute of fiscal and political autonomy. The fifteen 'ordinary' statute regions have enjoyed considerable legislative, administrative and regulatory autonomy in the healthcare sector since the early 1990s but, until recently, they lacked virtually any own-source revenue. In 1992, regional resources covered only 3 per cent of their expenditure. Responsibility for funding rested with the central government, which defined both the size of the National Healthcare Fund (NHF) and its distribution across the regions. The criteria used for the NHF appropriation formula (modelled along the English Resource Allocation Working Party formula) were inspired by principles of geographic equity, granting each region an amount of resources that were commensurate with its healthcare needs.

The twenty Italian regions show extreme disparities in population and territorial size, and are characterised by inequalities in health, healthcare services, wealth and socio-economic development (see Table 9.1). Regional economic contrasts are considerably more pronounced in Italy than in other European Union countries. The coefficient of variation in average regional per capita income in Italy was 26.6 per cent, compared to 14.3 per cent in Germany, 7.7 per cent in the United Kingdom and 4.5 per cent in France (Watts 1999). This is because of the existence of an Italian dual economy, which follows a clear-cut north–south divide. Income levels and healthcare needs are inversely related, as they usually are: infant mortality, for example, is twice as high in Campania as in Emilia-Romagna. Availability of healthcare facilities and actual provision of healthcare also show extreme differences in terms of both capacity and utilisation. Healthcare spending per capita is higher in the more affluent and older regions of the north than in southern regions.

Constitutional reform, approved by a national referendum in October 2001, provided regional governments with concurrent or exclusive legislative powers in several areas, including healthcare, education, scientific research, land use, energy production and distribution, transport and so on. The constitutional foundation of the healthcare system is based on a joint jurisdiction, with the regions holding the legislative powers on healthcare within the general principles set out by the central government. Essentially, the central government has the role of the 'guarantor' of citizenship rights through its exclusive powers over the definition of 'essential and uniform levels of services concerning civil and social rights', including the essential levels of healthcare. The constitutional reform, however, does not consider new institutions for governing the transition to a federal state and for fostering intergovernmental collaboration.

From its very inception, the Italian SSN has endured massive onslaughts from four major reforms and yearly adjustments, as well as from continuous intergovernmental contention about the adequate level of funding and its fair distribution across the regions. Bailing out of regional deficits in health expenditures has been a structural characteristic of the Italian system of intergovernmental relationships. A new electoral majority law has made more clear and visible the political boundaries between central and regional governments, as well as between regional

TABLE 9.1 Selected indicators of inter-regional diversity

Indicators	Italy	Regions	
		Low	High
Population (× 1,000)	57,680	330	8,988
% > 65 yrs	18.0	13.5	24.7
Infant mortality rate %	5.6	3.2	7.9
Public healthcare expenditure, per capita *	2.3	2.0	3.1
Hospital beds (× 1,000 inhab.)	4.9	3.9	6.1
Hospitalisation rate (× 1,000 inhab.)	163.9	151.1	203.4

Note: * million Italian lire

Source: ISTAT 2000

governments. This has quickly propelled almost any particular issue in dispute into an ideological one, which has led to national health policy becoming a pawn in a much larger political game. Intergovernmental relations have developed under a sort of 'executive' or 'cabinet' federalism, with little or no external public inputs, resulting in a process in which each regional government acts solely in its own areas of jurisdiction.

Opinion polls have repeatedly shown that a slight majority of the general public is generally in favour of devolving powers to the regions, but is not clear about which order of government is accountable for the performance of the health system or its financing. For example, only 24 per cent of citizens correctly put healthcare under the responsibility of the regional government (Vassallo 2001). However, in this climate of ill-informed 'trust', no rational government would even consider increasing the tax burden of its constituency for improving health services, which another level of government could have undertaken.

FISCAL FEDERALISM, ITALIAN-STYLE

Healthcare is, by far, the most important regional function, since it is a politically sensitive issue which affects voting behaviour, and because public health expenditure absorbs, on average, about three-quarters of regional revenues. Transport, the second most important budget item, accounts for less than one per cent. Between 1998 and 2000, the centre-left national government published detailed plans to grant greater political, administrative and fiscal powers to the regions. Healthcare was, of course, principally affected. The intention of the 2000 fiscal plan was to introduce virtually complete fiscal decentralisation over a period of thirteen years. The fiscal plan assigns both own taxes and pre-specified shares of central government tax revenues to the regions, with corresponding reductions in central transfers (see Table 9.2). A business tax (IRAP) is the major source of regional revenues, accounting for some 72 per cent of their total finance. This tax on public and private productive activities has an extremely large base, approximating 50 per cent of the GNP, which is also the most volatile and unequally distributed across the regions. For example, the per capita revenue of the private part of the tax base (over which the regions exert their autonomy) in 1998 was 1,208,700 It. lire in Lombardia and 180,400 It. lire in Calabria. The second most important tax is a regional surcharge on the individual income tax (IRPEF), providing an estimated 6.4 per cent of regional revenues. In addition, the regions do not have borrowing powers but are allowed to vary the rates for the business tax and the personal income tax surcharge within a band set by the central government.

An equalisation fund has been established in order to adjust for the large interregional differences in fiscal capacity and expenditure requirements, during a thirteen-year transition period. The fund carries about 10 per cent of total regional revenues and is modelled along the lines of a 'vertical equalisation' principle. However, it is entirely financed from consumption tax revenues, which are more uniformly distributed across the regions than IRAP and IRPEF, with no additional transfer from the central government. The fund involves an unconditional transfer intended to adjust for interregional differences in standardised per capita fiscal capacity (but only up to 90 per cent, one-year over the other), healthcare expenditure 'needs' and the economies of scale enjoyed by the larger regions. The design of this equalisation fund provides explicit incentives for interregional competition, and implies the optimistic assumption that regional governments will be able to close the gap, both between interregional fiscal capacity and each regional historical and optimal expenditure, in a little more than a decade.

In addition, the 1999 healthcare reform introduced a new source of healthcare funding, the complementary mutual funds (Fondi Integrativi del SSN), covering private expenditure for healthcare services, including user fees for specialist services. Mutual funds enjoy higher fiscal incentives than pure private insurance, and are expected to open up new opportunities for private markets, including the promotion of private practice within the SSN. Additional revenue opportunities come from the regional power to impose user fees.

TABLE 9.2 Sources of regional revenues

Revenue source	(%)
Business tax (IRAP)	72.8
Personal income tax (IRPEF)	6.4
Tax on motor vehicles	11.0
Petrol excise	8.0
Surcharge on natural gas	1.5
Other sources	0.4

The Finance Act for the year 2000 imposed severe budget constraints on regional expenditures, based on the Internal Stability Pact (ISP) between the central government, the regions and the local governments, transferring to regional and local governments the obligations assumed by the Italian government on entering the European Monetary Union. For example, the Finance Act for 2001 went so far as to allow the central government to oblige regional governments to raise their tax rates, in case healthcare expenditure exceeded agreed-upon limits. Hard budget constraints tend to clash against the strong ties that regional governments have developed with the spending commitments they inherited when administrative responsibilities were passed down.

Two questions are crucial in evaluating the design of the regional tax system: does devolved fiscal capacity adequately match regional expenditure responsibilities? How responsive is the regional tax system in matching the expected rate of increase of healthcare expenditure? There is a huge mismatch between regional own-source revenue and expenditure commitments; a few regions barely make sufficient revenues to match their inherited healthcare expenditure, since this is where the equalisation fund comes into operation during the transition period. In 2001, for example, six regions were 'net donors' to the equalisation fund, with Lombardia alone providing 55.2 per cent of the total (see Table 9.3). The constitutional amendment currently under discussion, which proposes assigning exclusive regional powers for healthcare, education and local police, will make this condition more extreme. Current estimates predict that about half of the total state revenues must accrue to the regions, posing the serious question of transferring to them also a significant part of the national debt, including its servicing. The net fiscal benefit will amount to one-third of total regional

TABLE 9.3 Regional contribution to the transfer fund, 2001

Region	(%)
Lombardia	55.2
Lazio	13.5
Veneto	12.1
Emilia Romagna	11.4
Piemonte	7.8
Total (billion It. lire)	12,074

revenues and it will be negative for ten of the fifteen regions. This requires an extensive redistribution programme, where ten regions are net receivers for as much as 5 million Italian lire per capita, more than twice as much as the current per capita expenditure in healthcare.

The principles of regional equality and regional autonomy seem difficult to hold in the face of such an economic imbalance. Heavy economic dependence by most of the southern regions on a few northern regions (even if hidden under the thin veil of a vertically modelled equalisation fund) risk eroding their autonomy and negating their equality. During the transition period reliance on central transfers constrains the freedom of action of southern regional governments and magnifies the political power of the wealthier regions in the north. This will most likely cause political instability within the new federation, and could encourage regions which are net donors to the equalisation fund to fiscally 'secede', for example by lowering their fiscal effort, which is not easily observable, both by the central government and by the other regions. In order to preserve their full autonomy during the transition period and after the end of it, the less developed regions are caught in a sort of 'poverty trap'. On the one hand, they would prefer high tax rates, in order to increase revenues and match expenditure responsibilities; but on the other hand, and in order to attract business and promote economic growth, the least developed regions need to reduce their tax rate, accepting a fall of their revenues in the short term in the hope of enlarging their tax base.

Ideally, the regional tax system should be responsive to the expected evolution in healthcare expenditures. Instead, the regional tax system seems designed to impose a structural deficit in regional budgets. While healthcare expenditure tends to grow faster than personal income or the regional Gross Product, for all regions revenues will rise more slowly than healthcare expenditure, even if regional taxes were to capture economic growth to the maximum. The regional tax system featured by the Italian fiscal federalist reform seems to have fully embraced both the Tibout vision of the local public sector as a competitive marketplace and the Weingast concept of market-preserving federalism (Tibout 1956; Qian and Weingast 1997). Hard budget constraints from the central government and competition among regional governments are assumed to ensure cost control and foster efficiency in the supply of local public goods, just as competition among firms and individuals ensures efficiency in the supply of private goods. Furthermore, interregional tax competition is hypothesised to constrain local governments' appetite for tax revenue, to reduce the size of the government, and to promote a 'race-to-the bottom' for public services (Kenyon 1997).

A FUTURE FOR THE SERVIZIO SANITARIO NAZIONALE?

This mismatch between hard budget constraints, low revenues and inherited spending commitments can possibly be rolled back but only at great political cost. Meanwhile, it provides regional governments with plenty of incentives for the 'passive' privatisation of publicly provided health services, regardless of whether they are in favour of this, or simply because they are unable to halt it. Regional governments could find their options restricted to either explicitly rationing healthcare services or introducing substantial charges for their users. Ultimately, both options shift the burden of responsibility for funding healthcare services from the public purse to the individual.

'Delisting' of medical services previously covered by the SSN is tantamount to creeping privatisation of public healthcare. Private insurance and/or the mutual funds legislated for in the 1999 healthcare reform provide financial coverage for the services excluded by the SSN provision, which will be available in private markets from public and private providers. Therefore, the first scenario for the future of the SSN is a process more aptly described as the 'commodification' rather than the 'privatisation' of healthcare, whereby the formerly universal and comprehensive SSN develops a second tier of 'commodified medicine' alongside a slimmed-down publicly financed one. Similar results might result from a different strategy. The national government (possibly under the pressure of the cash-strapped southern regions, or, for opposite reasons, from the wealthier northern regions) might explicitly define the content of the 'essential benefit package' as the minimum amount of SSN coverage afforded by the lowest fiscal capacity of the regions. This would transform the SSN into a safety-net for the poor, on top of which a second tier of commodified healthcare can flourish.

In December 2001, the central government set forward the 'livelli essenziali di assistenza' (LEA), that is, the levels of healthcare, which the regions are under an obligation to provide in their territory. Delisting reduced public coverage for a minimal number of services can potentially save only modest amounts. The negative list includes three categories of ambulatory and hospital services (see Table 9.4). Category 1 includes a few, miscellaneous services which are excluded outright from the SSN coverage because of their proven clinical ineffectiveness or because they are not pertinent to the goals and aims of the SSN. Category 2 is an open list of ambulatory services to be excluded from public coverage on a case-by-case basis, based on their appropriateness for individual clinical indications. Category 3 includes a DRG-based indicative list of potentially inappropriate hospital admissions, which the regions are required to move to alternative levels of care. Examples include carpal tunnel release (DRG 16), hypertension (DRG 119) and diabetes (DRG 294). Both the soundness of the conceptual approach and the effectiveness of this policy are open to debate (Charles et al. 1997). Certainly, the negative list confounded the expectations of those hoping that delisting would make a significant dent on public expenditure, providing ample space for complementary mutual funds.

A third and novel path is therefore emerging, assuming that the constitution obliges regional governments only to ensure the provision of LEA, not that they must be publicly funded. This strategy aims at 'diversifying the revenue stream' for funding healthcare through a blend of public, private and not-for-profit organisations, opening the way to the overt marketisation of healthcare. Following this path, devolution might well progress as far as the complete retreat of public services from the SSN field. In Italy, increasing attention, particularly from the most conservative part of the political spectrum, has been given to one interpretation of the principle of 'subsidiarity'. That is, the notion that

TABLE 9.4 The negative list of healthcare services excluded from public coverage

Category 1. Outright exclusion
Circumcision
Cosmetic surgery, except for malformations and injuries
Medical certification, for individual use
Non-conventional medicine
Vaccinations, other than compulsory

Category 2. Open list
Bone density
Excimer laser surgery
Orthodontic interventions

Category 3. Indicative list
44 DRG-based categories of potentially inappropriate hospital admissions

a higher political body should take up only those tasks that cannot be carried out by organisations generated spontaneously by civil society, such as cooperatives and mutual funds. The declared goal is to transform the 'welfare state' into a 'welfare community', shifting the boundaries between the civil society and a slimmed-down state. After being part of the electoral promises of the coalition of parties which won the general elections in May 2001, this is now the official policy of the Italian government, part and parcel of the devolution process:

> the devolution of powers, from the State to the regions, involves not only the transfer of political power but also opens up vast sectors of activity (health, education) to providers different from those organised along bureaucratic lines. Devolution offers great and new opportunities to become part of the service production chain to families, voluntary organizations, mutual funds, foundations, etc. (*Documento di Programmazione Economica e Finanziaria*, Instituto Poligrafico dello Stato, Roma, 2001, 5)

CONCLUSIONS

Italy is in the middle of a complex and difficult process of devolving political and fiscal powers to regional governments, a process riddled with confusion regarding both the process and its ultimate goals. The change of the political majority just after the first constitutional reform and the ongoing discussion of a second, supposedly 'extreme', constitutional reform is certainly not helping in smoothing out this process. Political platforms apart, however, there are reasons to argue for a substantial continuity between the implicit effects of the fiscal policy of the centre-left government and the explicit political goals of the new centre-right majority.

Current healthcare organisation places strong fiscal and political stress on interregional differences in revenue-raising capabilities, making the poorest regions heavily dependent on the wealthier regions. Abstracting from the thin veil provided by the equalisation fund, the plan for fiscal federalism designed by the centre-left government is tantamount to a collective version of funding healthcare according to regional fiscal capacity, that is, ability to pay, instead of according to regional need. Furthermore, it provides the incoming federation with a built-in political asymmetry, in terms of distribution of power, influence and relations, both within regional governments and between them and the central government. These built-in political tensions are not accompanied by the institutional tools to provide the common interest of the federation to hold together.

Hard budget constraints and the incentives for interregional tax competition impose significant fiscal stress on regional governments which will eventually force most regions into choosing between raising taxes or reducing public expenditures and services. Ultimately, this will adversely impact upon the egalitarian and solidaristic core principles of SSN, promoting a two-tier system both between the regions, according to their fiscal capability, and within each region, based on the extent of the 'passive' privatisation of its healthcare system.

The provisional lessons from the ongoing Italian healthcare reforms process raise some general issues. First, that the thorny issue of devolution in healthcare is trading off local autonomy and individual preferences with policy orientation and a collective commitment to, an egalitarian distribution of, and access to healthcare benefits, and fairness in its public financing. Second, that decentralisation implies a break with uniformity in the provision of healthcare services, while devolution of fiscal powers provides strong incentives for welfare retrenchment. Both avenues offer ample opportunity for increasing inequalities in health and the creeping privatisation of healthcare. The 'remoteness' of the central state from expectations and preferences of individuals and groups has been persuasively described as the Achilles' heel of solidaristic healthcare systems (Mays 2000).

However, the distinction between the process of devolving powers to local communities and the goal of creating political and economic markets is blurred. Some advocates of federal reform seem more concerned with redesigning the boundaries between markets and a slimmed-down state, than with defining the responsibilities and interdependences of different levels of government. Some unexpected similarities can be found between federal reforms and pro-market reforms, which took place in the early 1990s in several European countries. Both focus on the alleged insensitivity and inefficiency of public services delivered by centralised, command-and-control healthcare systems. Then pro-market incentives were to provide the dynamic of the 'internal' markets. Now, being 'closer to the people' is expected to promote greater efficiency and responsiveness to citizens' preferences. However, from the perspective of the potential impact of fiscal devolution on solidaristic national healthcare services, the current trend towards the devolution of powers to local governments looks more like an exercise in downloading, cost cutting and diffusing and deflecting blame than a bold new experiment in deliberative democracy and community empowerment.

REFERENCES

Bennet, R. J. (1990) 'Decentralisation, intergovernmental relations and markets: towards a post-welfare agenda', in R. J. Bennet (ed.), *Decentralisation, Local Government, and Markets*, Oxford: Clarendon Press.

Charles, C., Lomas, J., Giacomini, M. et al. (1997) 'Medical necessity in Canadian health policy: four meanings and ... a funeral?', *Milbank Quarterly*, 75, 365–94.

Courchene, T. J. (1995) 'Glocalization: the regional/international interface', *Canadian Journal of Regional Science*, 18 (1), 1–20.

Department of Health (2001) *Shifting the Balance of Power within the NHS*, London: Department of Health.

France, G. and Taroni, F. (2000) 'Starting down the road to targets in health. The case of Italy', *European Journal of Public Health*, 10 (4s), 25–9.

ISTAT (2000) *Indicatori Socio Sanitari nelle Regioni Italiare*, Roma: Instituto Poligrafico dello Stato.

Kenyon, D. A. (1997) 'Theories of interjurisdictional competition', *New England Economic Review* (March/April), 13–35.

Klein, R. (1998) 'Why Britain is reorganizing its National Health Service – yet again', *Health Affairs*, 17 (4), 111–25.

Lomas, J. (1997) 'Devolving authority for healthcare in Canada's provinces: 4. Emerging issues and prospects', *Canadian Medical Journal*, 156 (6), 817–23.

Mays, N. (2000) 'Legitimate decision making: the Achilles' heel of solidaristic healthcare systems', *Journal of Health Services Research and Policy*, 55 (2), 122–6.

Pierson, P. (1994) *Dismantling the Welfare State ? Reagan, Thatcher and the Politics of Retrenchment*, Cambridge: Cambridge University Press.

Pollock, A. M. (1999) 'Devolution and health: challenges for Scotland and Wales', *British Medical Journal*, 318, 1195–8.

Prud'Homme, R. (1995) 'The dangers of decentralisation', *World Bank Research Observer*, 10 (2), 201–20.

Qian, Y. and Weingast, B. R. (1997) 'Federalism as a committment to preserving market incentives', *Journal of Economic Perspectives*, 11 (4), 83–92.

Reverte-Le Judo, D. and Sanchez-Bayle, M. (1999) 'Devolving health services to Spain's autonomous regions', *British Medical Journal*, 318, 1204–5.

Tibout, A. (1956) 'A pure theory of local expenditure', *Journal of Political Economy*, 64 (5), 416–24.

Vassallo, S. (2001) '"Governatori" e federalismo, Le istituzioni del Federalismo', 3–4, 643–74.

Watts, R. L. (1999) *Comparing Federal Systems*, Montreal: McGill-Queens' University Press.

CHAPTER 10

Global Capital and Healthcare Reform: the Experience of the UK

JEAN SHAOUL

This chapter outlines and explains the rise of neo-liberal policies that have been applied to healthcare provision in the UK in the context of globalisation. Healthcare 'reforms' – the introduction of financial targets, quasi-markets, creeping privatisation, public–private partnerships, outsourcing of 'non-core' services, hospital and ward closures, user charges, 'targeting', cuts in funding and social division – are being introduced by governments of every political persuasion in every country at the behest of the financial markets and giant corporations. Where services cannot be entirely removed for political reasons, then they must be turned over to the private sector to provide a new source of profit. Such policies have led to a drastic decline in access to healthcare and the quality of service, a decline in the standard of public health, and a reduction in the jobs, wages and conditions of those employed in the sector. These changes are not simply the product of a policy shift that can be reversed or of the poor judgement of individual politicians; the changes and policy shift have an objective basis. They reflect the response of business leaders to the profound structural changes that have taken place within the world economy.

The purpose of this chapter is threefold. First, it outlines the range of measures that have been implemented in Britain over the past twenty-five years. Although the examples cited refer to the UK, they are of international relevance since similar measures have been implemented in most of the advanced capitalist countries and developing countries that had a public healthcare system, whether funded by taxation or insurance contributions. Furthermore, since the National Health Service (NHS) was held up as a model to be emulated, its decline has an additional resonance. Second, this chapter explains the international and systemic character of the economic and political processes that led to the adoption of such measures. Third, the final section explains the source of the reforms won in the post-war period and their decline. While the neo-liberal policies that have driven the changes in healthcare policy are attributed to globalisation, a distinction is drawn between the globalisation of production and its control by global capital. The chapter concludes by drawing out the implications of this distinction for opposing the reform of public services and the decline of public healthcare.

HEALTHCARE 'REFORMS': THE EXPERIENCE OF BRITAIN

Public healthcare policy in Britain has been profoundly affected by a series of interrelated and overlapping measures over the last thirty years (Table 10.1). First, a series of institutional measures to control healthcare expenditure as a whole and generate income; second, measures to cap the activities and scale of the public sector; and third, a whole raft of financial, organisational and managerial measures to increase outputs and reduce costs through greater efficiency at the point of service delivery. These are broadly encapsulated under the rubric of the New Managerialism in line with neo-liberal economic policies. Fourth is the introduction of quasi-markets and the reconstitution of healthcare providers as business units charging purchasers the full costs of service provision on a competitive basis. Finally, there is the use of the private sector to finance, build and operate non-clinical services. Each of these will be summarised very briefly in order to indicate how they have affected the work-force and service delivery.

Macro-economic measures aimed at curbing public expenditure on health were introduced in the mid-1970s as a result of conditions imposed by the International Monetary Fund (IMF). The then Labour government sought to cut public expenditure as a percentage of GDP. It moved from a system of volume planning and funding to a system of cash limits for departments and units within departments in order to provide greater financial autonomy. Budgets were devolved to the lowest possible unit to force departments to eliminate loss-making units and minimise cross-subsidisation. Ceilings were placed on annual public expenditure based on assumptions that real growth would not exceed a certain percentage, for example, 2 per cent. In the 1990s, a unified budget was introduced so that central government spending proposals would be considered alongside taxation. User charges and co-payments were

TABLE 10.1 Restructuring of UK health services, 1975–2001

Measures	Outcomes
Curbs on public expenditure	
Cut public expenditure as % GDP	
Volume planning abandoned	
Cash limits	
Devolved budgets	
Ceiling on public expenditure growth	
Unified budget for tax and expenditure	
User charges and co-payments	Lowest % of public expenditure on health in EU/ACCs
'New Managerialism'	
Managerial responsibility for budgets	
Devolved budgets, cost centres, internal payments between departments	
New procedures for capital budgeting and project appraisal based upon discounted cash flow techniques	
Value for money studies	
Three Es	
Performance measurement, league tables, etc.	
Increased use of audit techniques and establishment of National Audit Office and Audit Commission	Managing by financial numbers, not need, and decision-making and control by managers, not health professionals

Reduced scope of public sector activity	
Relatively little privatisation as such	Carried out in private sector for a fee (certain categories of people exempt, means testing, some public funding)
Treatments excluded from NHS, e.g. some dental treatments, ophthalmics, long-term care	
Some treatments excluded locally on the basis of cost	
Outsourcing of 'non-core' services	
Concordat with private sector for treatment of patients at public expense	Growth of new corporations servicing the NHS and delivering healthcare treatments
Quasi-market for health	
Purchaser–provider split	
Providers reconstituted as commercial units in the public sector with financial targets	
Providers required to charge full cost of treatments with no cross-subsidisation	
Publication of costs per hospital of all DRGs (reference costs)	Average cost = basis to fund hospitals, reduce funding and/or increase outputs
	Health services produced for profit in both public and private sectors
Use of private finance	
Private sector to design, build, own and operate hospitals in return for annual payment	
Private sector to build and finance doctors' surgeries	
Doctors able to set up commercial ventures with private sector	
Doctors now able to charge for some personal care	International market for healthcare

introduced, as in other parts of Europe, and increased so that for a number of services, patients were paying almost the full cost, albeit with exemption for certain categories of people; for example, for dental treatments, eye tests, prescription medicines. The net result is that the amount spent on public healthcare provision is now among the lowest in Europe. Services were allowed to 'wither on the vine', fuelling public discontent and encouraging a belief that the problem was public sector 'inefficiency' that could be cured only by a dose of private sector management.

Second, these institutional changes were accompanied by a series of measures to reduce costs and increase outputs, and a culture that became known as the New Managerialism or the New Public Sector Management. This took a variety of forms. Management was reorganised along private sector lines with emphasis on management's responsibility to achieve a balanced budget, limited in cash not volume terms. At a time of high inflation this led inevitably to a reduction in real wages. Devolved budgets and cost centres leading to decentralised decision-making and internal payments between units and departments were introduced. More explicit procedures for capital budgeting and project appraisal, based on the financial methods of private sector corporations seeking finance from the capital markets rather than social objectives, were prescribed. There was an ever-increasing emphasis on audit techniques through the establishment of the National Audit Office and the Audit Commission to audit and monitor the NHS. These changes marked a move away from planning on the basis of need, to managing by financial numbers, and decision-making and control by managers instead of healthcare professionals.

Third, there have by and large been no direct privatisations in healthcare – in the sense that assets and enterprises were sold to the private sector – for both financial and political reasons. Healthcare is simply not cash generative enough to be privatised in the way in which public utilities have been privatised (Shaoul 1998). At the same time, because it is also such an extremely sensitive political issue, no political party can call for the outright privatisation of healthcare. Nevertheless, the scope of health service activities has been curtailed. First, a whole range of healthcare services, for example, long-term care, and certain ophthalmic and dental treatments, were excluded from the NHS. Henceforth they were to be provided by the private sector. In some cases, there were full cost user fees, while in others, certain categories of people and individuals were paid for by the state on a means-tested basis. Second, some treatments were excluded locally on an ad hoc basis on the grounds of cost. Third, many of the 'non-core' low-paid manual services, such as cleaning and catering, and, more recently, the higher-paid professional services such as laboratory and IT functions, have been contracted out. Finally, the government has initiated the Concordat: an agreement whereby healthcare purchasers commission the private sector to treat patients at public expense. As a result of this creeping privatisation of healthcare, there has been a growth in the number of new and the size of existing corporations that service the NHS and deliver healthcare treatments.

Fourth, the Conservative government (1979 to 1997) introduced a quasi-market into healthcare. Health Authorities would commission and pay healthcare providers such as hospitals and general practitioners for healthcare treatments on behalf of the population in their area. Integral to the introduction of the market was the policy of corporatisation – the reconstitution of the hospitals as businesses. They were required by statute to take responsibility for their capital infrastructure and operate as private sector corporations by making a financial surplus or profit, equal to 6 per cent of the value of their capital base, to be paid to the government. Hospitals were required to charge for individual treatments on a full cost basis, that is, including the cost of capital. Cross-subsidies would not be permitted. The hospitals' charges for each diagnostic-related group (DRG) were compared and the average cost was used as the basis for funding them. In other words, cost comparisons were used to force down costs and/or increase outputs for the same level of inputs. The combined effect has been to render healthcare a commodity pro-duced for profit, irrespective of whether it is publicly or privately provided, to enable direct comparisons with costs in the private sector and to make it possible for the private sector to deliver healthcare treatments and services.

More recently, there has been a turn to the private finance initiative (PFI): the financing of new investment in hospitals, clinics and doctors' surgeries by the private sector which would design, build, finance and operate (DBFO) the facilities for the public sector in return for annual payments over thirty years. In the earlier part of 2000, the government rushed through new legislation that allowed family doctors and the health authorities to form commercial ventures with private healthcare organisations and set up new one-stop primary care centres that would include pharmacy, dental and some social services all on one site. For the first time, family doctors would be able to charge for some services. A recent survey of nurses, reported in the press, revealed that one-third of nurses believed that within a decade the NHS would no longer be free at the point of use. Under the Concordat, healthcare purchasers will be able to make contracts with private hospitals, including hospitals overseas, on behalf of their patients. Indeed, the internationalisation of healthcare flows inexorably from recent European Court of Justice decisions and EU Directives. The net effect of this and other healthcare reforms is to develop an international market for healthcare (Koivusalo and Ollila 1997).

While this list is not exhaustive or very detailed, it does give some idea of the wide range of measures introduced by successive governments. The chief characteristic of all these economic, financial and organisational measures is that they are the techniques used by the private sector to generate profit out of the production of commodities for distribution to the providers of finance. Henceforth, state services were to be organised on a similar basis. Furthermore, there was an emphasis on financial management as a proactive tool to manage public healthcare in order to achieve objectives, not simply as a passive tool to record income and expenditure – its role in the past.

This approach was accompanied by an emphasis on the three Es – economy, efficiency and effectiveness – and the growth of performance measures which attempted to capture and compare the performance of public sector providers and thereby ratchet up output or throughput. Underpinning almost all these measures was the assumption that the toolkit of private sector management could improve output and thereby resolve or at least contain the 'problem' of the rising cost of healthcare provision. It represented a very real change in the way that public health was managed in two significant respects: from planning on the basis of perceived need to managing by financial numbers; and from decision-making and control by the service professionals to decision-making and control by managers.

A financial regime has been set in place that is analogous to running public services as private sector operations in the public sector. Like privatisation, this adds a new set of stakeholders and another dimension to conflict, as these stakeholders have claims on the surplus for the physical replacement and improvement of the capital infrastructure and the repayment of finance capital that must be met. But in the context of declining resources for the public services, this means that management can balance the books only by some combination of drastically reducing the number of staff, wages, conditions of employment, the range and quality of services offered, and the physical infrastructure used to deliver the services, and introducing user charges. It means more direct control by management over the work of service professionals, a further intensification of work effort, and a reduction in access to and the quality of healthcare services. It presages increasing conflict between the government and public service workers over jobs, pay and conditions, and between the government and the broad mass of the population over the basic right to good-quality healthcare.

These changes mark a very definite transformation of social relations in a number of important respects. First, the relations of production in health are being realigned so that they match those of the private sector. Henceforth, healthcare must make a surplus over and above the operational costs of the services provided by its work-force in order to pay for capital. In other words, some of the main differences between the forms and practices of the public and private sectors have in practice been eliminated. Second, services funded by the public through taxation are being organised by the state to serve more directly the financial interests of private corporations, not the public, via outsourcing and partnership arrangements. Third, the public is being reconstituted as the customer for the goods and services so produced.

While these measures may appear and indeed were often presented as a form of decentralisation that permits local decision-making, their real function was to create the structures and mechanisms for the private sector to more easily control, own and direct public services and public policy. Furthermore, these changes are part of an ongoing process whereby the social and public services pass into the private sector through buy-outs, subcontracting and sale and lease back operations such as the PFI. Finally such services, following the path of the former nationalised industries before them, are then integrated into the wider international economy as they are taken over by the trans-national corporations. In other words, the social welfare functions of the nation-state are being integrated into the world economy, but for the benefit of capital, not labour or the population at large. The significance of these neo-liberal policies is that they provide the ideology and mechanisms to accomplish an international market for health.

THE DECLINE OF SOCIAL REFORM AND THE CRISIS OF THE PROFIT SYSTEM

While there have been many reviews of neo-liberal policies, there have been few attempts to explain its source and development within the workings of the economic system itself. These policies and attacks on public services are widely viewed as the outcome of the 'free market' ideology rather than as an expression of the crisis of the profit system as a whole.

The ideological sea-change, known as the New Right Agenda, that took place in the mid-1970s was and is presented as simply a policy shift that occurred during the 1970s (and could therefore be reversed by another policy change). In fact, it reflected the response of business leaders and their governments to the objective changes that had taken place in the world economy (ICFI 1998; Beams 1998). The downturn in the rate of return on capital employed in the 1960s and 1970s was the driving force for several interrelated processes: the globalisation of production in order to lower costs, and the development and application of new technologies of production such as computers and telecommunications. Changes in technology enabled ever fewer productive units to supply a world market. Together these processes have been responsible for a transformation of the structure of the capitalist economy. The resulting global mobility of capital spelt the end of the programme of Keynesian national regulation that formed the basis of the post-war welfare state, and the state-owned enterprises and services.

At the same time the enormous technological innovations in the production process, based on the computer chip, enormously intensified the crisis of the profit system. The mission of a capitalist enterprise is to make not simply an absolute level of profit, but a level of profit proportional not to sales but to the amount of capital employed. This is typically 10–15 per cent, and must always be higher than the prevailing interest rate, since this represents the basic return that is available to the providers of finance. As the amount of capital employed – its productive capacity – in an enterprise increases, so must the profit.

The cash surplus or surplus value (the basis of profit) represents in the final analysis the surplus labour extracted from the work-force. But the essence of new technology and cost-cutting is the replacement of value-creating labour by capital equipment in the production process. Consequently, rather than alleviating the tendency of the rate of profit to fall, new technology has worked to exacerbate it (Armstrong et al. 1984). While the falling rate of profit was and is largely invisible in the public debates, it was this that lay at the heart of the policy shift and the New Right Agenda. It is this falling rate of profit relative to the amount of capital employed (even though the absolute amount of profit may be rising in particular industries or companies) that lies behind the successive waves of mergers, cross-border mergers and plant closures in the 1980s and 1990s. Corporations sought to cut costs and sell off surplus assets, thereby reducing the amount of capital employed.

Under conditions where the overall mass of surplus value was expanding, as in the first twenty-five years after the Second World War, capital was able to tolerate the welfare state and even welcome the nationalisation of basic industries. Such policies provided a means of containing and regulating the class conflict since the government as owner was able to pay higher wages and improve working conditions in the mines and railways in Britain. The existence of the welfare state also meant that employers did not have to make extensive provision for health insurance and retirement for its work-force, as employers in the USA did in the period of the long boom. They shifted the cost of investment in capital-intensive industries on to the taxpayers while allowing their former owners to reinvest the proceeds from compensation in more profitable ventures. At the same time the nationalised industries and services could be run in ways that constituted a subsidy to industry. Indeed, the nationalisations in the 1940s were justified with claims of the increased efficiency that would flow from the restructuring and increased investment that only government could provide (Armstrong et al. 1984).

Under conditions where the tendency is for the mass of available surplus value to decline, deductions in the form of corporate taxation to finance social welfare became increasingly intolerable. One of the responses of ruling elites everywhere was to attempt to claw back a portion of the surplus value previously appropriated by the state in the form of social welfare provision to the working class. Furthermore, the 40 per cent or so of GDP that did not directly yield a profit must now be opened up, via privatisation, PFI 'partnerships', outsourcing and all the rest, to private profit. The past thirty years have been characterised by an ongoing assault on the social position of the working class as capital seeks to overcome the pressures on the rate of profit. But all these measures have failed to establish a new equilibrium based on the expansion of the mass of surplus value. Hence the continuous rounds of privatisations and cost-cuttings. No sooner is one round of cuts completed than another begins.

The use of public–private partnerships is an international phenomenon promoted by global institutions such as the World Bank, International Monetary Fund (IMF), World Trade Organisation (WTO), the European Union (EU) and governments around the world. Private finance for public services is integral to the structural adjustment programmes imposed by the IMF and World Bank and a prerequisite for loans for developing countries (Millward 1999). Both promote the use of 'markets in infrastructure provision' (World Bank 1994). Over the past seven years the European Commission has advocated the use of public–private partnerships and has used government grants to set them up. This market was worth more than €720 billion in 1994 (11.5 per cent of the gross national product of the fifteen member states of the European Union). The number of notices in the *Official Journal of the European Community* announcing large procurement projects rose from 12,000 in 1987 to about 200,000 in mid-1999 (European Commission 1997). The World Trade Organisation seeks to open up health, education and social services as new sources of profit for the medico-pharmaceutical and facilities management corporations through its General Agreement on Trade and Services (GATS) and Government Procurement Agreement (Shaoul 2001).

The attempt to extend the GATS to public services reflects the sweeping changes in the global economy over the last two decades. To cite but one example, the development of trans-national corporations (TNCs) has meant that of the 100 largest economic entities, more than half are corporations and the rest are national economies. The driving force behind the GATS is the requirement for new sources of profit and a reduction in restrictions imposed upon their activities by national governments as they undertake the production of and investment in goods and services on an international scale. The TNCs seek to extend and deepen their global reach at the expense of the universal right to water, sanitation, transport, energy, healthcare and education and basic democratic rights. But the GATS also expresses more fundamental and more progressive processes – the inherent drive of the productive forces to break free of the constraints of the outmoded nation-state system.

OPPOSITION TO GLOBAL CAPITAL

This analysis has attributed the neo-liberal policies that are so detrimental to healthcare to the economic system itself, not simply to an ideological sea-change that has occurred in isolation from the changes in the structure of the international economy. It therefore raises important questions about the character of any oppositional movement against such control by the giant corporations. While there has been widespread opposition to the policies of the international financial institutions of global capitalism, the opposition has largely taken the form of opposition to globalisation as opposed to global capitalism. Furthermore, it was unclear on what basis individuals and groups were opposing global capital or globalisation, whether they agreed with each other and, crucially, which social layers were they addressing: international institutions, governments, trade and labour leaders, or the broad mass of the world's population?

In other words, there has been a basic confusion that has identified 'globalisation' with 'global capitalism'. Globalisation refers to the increasingly global character of the production and exchange of goods and services, and in this view is in itself a progressive development. The destructive consequences flow not from globalisation as such, but from the subordination of all economic life to the anarchic pursuit of private profit, based upon national forms of political organisation. Thus, the real question is not how to return to some mythical golden age of national economic life, but who will control the global economy and in whose interests it will be run.

It is impossible to succeed against the restructuring of health services in the era of neo-liberalism, in isolation from any wider social and political struggle in the working class. An examination of the past century shows that whatever gains were made were byproducts of the major political and social struggles of the working class, struggles that were led by socialists against the existing opportunist leaderships. As was pointed out by Rosa Luxemburg 100 years ago: 'Work for reform does not contain its own force, independent from revolution. During every historic period, work for reforms is carried on only in the direction given to it by the impetus of the last revolution, and continues as long as the impulsion of the last revolution continues to make itself felt' (Luxemburg 1988: 49). Consider the origins of the NHS itself. The NHS was the product of a big movement in the working class. The British ruling class had become acutely conscious of the Russian Revolution in 1917 and the revolutionary upheavals in Europe that followed the Russian Revolution and the First World War. It grudgingly granted the NHS and other welfare reforms in the period following the Second World War in response to the threat of revolution posed by the sustained upsurge of the working class and the oppressed masses internationally in the mid-to-late 1940s.

Conversely, the erosion of the welfare state not just in Britain but all over the world in the last twenty-five years has been directly bound up with the absence of any politically conscious movement in the working class. The socialist conceptions that animated large sections of workers in the aftermath of the Russian Revolution came under sustained attack from Stalinism, labour reformism and trade unionism, which together attacked genuine socialism and above all, internationalism. In short, the defence of public services such as health entails the conscious recognition that capitalism, not the increasingly global character of modern society, is the real enemy.

Global capitalism – that is, the subordination of humanity to the financial interests of a few hundred giant trans-national corporations – cannot be fought by seeking to return to a historically outmoded system of relatively isolated and unintegrated national economies. The point is not to reject the advances of science and technology or to return to local, small-scale production, but to wrest control of the enormous productive forces created by human labour from the TNCs and nation-states, and place them under the common ownership of all humanity, with their development subordinated, in a rational and planned way, to human needs (Editorial Board 1999).

In other words, the defence and extension of the gains made by the working class in an earlier period require the development of a conscious political movement of the working class, capable of challenging the very basis of the profit system itself. It implies a very definite social orientation and programme – that of revolutionary scientific socialism as opposed to the dominant, politically liberal, programme of national reformism – which is why the traditional organisations of the working class and intellectuals have been unable to mount any effective opposition or critique of the neo-liberal agenda.

REFERENCES

Armstrong, P., Glyn, A. and Harrison, J. (1984) *Capitalism since World War II: The Making and Breakup of the Great Boom*, London: Fontana.

Beams, N. (1998) *The Significance and Implications of Globalisation: A Marxist Assessment*, Detroit, MI: Mehring Books.

Chossudovsky, M. (1998) *The Globalisation of Poverty: Impacts of IMF and World Bank Reforms*, London: Zed Books.

Editorial Board (1999) 'The social meaning of the anti-WTO protests in Seattle'; www.wsws.org/articles/1999/dec1999/wto-d06_prn.shtml

European Commission (1997) *Public Procurement in the European Union: Exploring the Way Forward*, Brussels: European Commission, Directorate General.

ICFI (International Committee of the Fourth International) (1998) *Globalization and the International Working Class – A Marxist Assessment*, Detroit, MI: Mehring Books.

Koivusalo, M. and Ollila, E. (1997) *Making a Healthy World – Actors, Agencies and Policies in International Health*, London: Zed Books.

Luxemburg, R. (1988) *Reform or Revolution*, New York: Pathfinder Press.

Millward, R. (1999) 'State enterprise in Britain in the twentieth century', in F. Amatori (ed.), *The Rise and Fall of State Owned Enterprises in the Western World*, Cambridge: Cambridge University Press.

Price, D., Pollock, A. and Shaoul, J. (1999) 'How the World Trade Organisation is shaping domestic policies in health care', *The Lancet*, 354, 1889–92.

Shaoul, J. (1998) 'Critical financial analysis and accounting for stakeholders', *Critical Perspectives on Accounting*, 9, 235–49.

— (2001) 'World Trade Organisation agreement aims at privatising public services', www.wsws.org/articles/2001/apr2001/wto-a26.shtml

World Bank (1994) *World Bank Development Report 1994: Infrastructure for Development*, Oxford: Oxford University Press.

CHAPTER 11

The Trouble with Conservative Healthcare Counter-reforms in Spain

M. SANCHEZ BAYLE AND HIXINIO BEIRAS

Spain returned to democracy in 1978 when the constitution became law after forty years of a dictatorship with long periods of suffering and exile for its people, as well as almost complete international isolation. With the constitution of 1978, a state with autonomous regions was created, granting the historic national groups in Catalonia, the Basque country, Galicia and the other regions one of the greatest degrees of decentralisation and independent authority in the international context. Spain's integration in 1986 into the European Union ended the cycle of international isolation (Cortes Españolas 1978).

Since then Spain has been governed first by the political centre, and then (from 1982 to 1996) by the socialists, followed by the conservative Partido Popular (PP – the People's Party). With a population of some 39.5 million and a gross domestic product (GDP) which places it seventh in the world, Spain is the ninth greatest consumer of energy and third in the list of most favourable countries to live in Europe, according to *The Economist* (September 1994). Spain has more doctors per thousand head of population than any other country in the world, and in 1992 Spain's healthcare expenditure per inhabitant placed the country in eighteenth position globally (Gavira 1996; OECD 1996).

HEALTHCARE IN SPAIN

The Spanish National Health Service (NHS), as defined by the General Health Law, was created in 1986 by the then socialist government (Spanish Government 1986). It developed out of a configuration of the national health system, which is the sum of the regional health systems. The system may be summarised as follows:

- it has universal coverage (greater than 99.9 per cent) for all residents in Spain (recently, illegal immigrant children have also acquired the right to universal healthcare)
- development of primary healthcare as the first step in care and the starting point for prevention and promotion; a powerful impulse under this has been the creation of the speciality of family and community medicine and investment in new and better facilities
- free primary healthcare at the point of use, excluding dentistry and community care (pharmaceuticals are free for pensioners and the chronically ill; for the rest, contribution of the patient is 40 per cent)
- a pyramidal organisation of salaried public servants which, in primary healthcare, is complemented and supported by a capitation
- the objective of developing health policies based on integrated health plans
- low cost for healthcare (less than US $2 per citizen per day), making it one of the lowest percentages of GDP dedicated to healthcare in the European Union, which has an average expenditure of 8.3 per cent of GDP
- considerable public approval: public surveys suggest that 73.5 per cent of people are satisfied with the Spanish NHS, 80 per cent would prefer to be admitted to a public hospital in case of severe illness and more than 83 per cent reject NHS privatisation; in addition, 48 per cent would accept higher taxes earmarked for the NHS (Sanchez Bayle 1999c)

The Spanish National Health Service also has high international standing. For example, its method of organ transplantation has developed into an international model; in addition, the WHO recently placed Spain's health service seventh in the international ranking.

THE CONSERVATIVE COUNTER-REFORMS OF THE 1980S

Despite the breadth of the approach to a national health service, the effects of conservative policies and the neo-liberal approach have been dominant in the overall economy since the mid-1980s, and have also been felt in the healthcare systems. The strategies of globalisation, which places the market at the centre of all activity in society and 'trusts' the ability of the market to provide all kinds of goods and services efficiently and effectively, have been extended into the field of healthcare, despite all the evidence that indicates their limitations.

In spite of the positive results and the relationship of costs to benefits in the Spanish NHS, the conservative government of the People's Party has devoted itself to strategies for dismantling the public health system. This has meant a preference for opening up avenues for the privatisation of healthcare, along the lines of the European conservative approach to health services management and organisation. This approach has been focused upon four areas: the privatisation of national health services, increasing of patient co-payments, rationing publicly financed benefits and increasing the role of private insurance companies in health cover and healthcare. Following these trends, the conservative government is now applying important modifications to the Spanish NHS. These involve:

- introduction of the market through the separation of financing and provision with the intention of transforming the public network into a large number of smaller enterprises known as 'fundaciónes' in the case of hospitals, similar to the UK's Hospital Trusts; these are independent businesses, legal bodies, acting independently and in competition with other public health centres
- an increase in outsourcing, to private enterprises, some or all public health services, such as hospital patient archives, laboratories, high technology services and even awarding public companies the special-ised and hospital care of some local communities, as in the case of the Alzira hospital, a policy inspired also by the UK's Private Finance Initiative (PFI)
- placing restrictions on a number of areas of healthcare services, such as some drugs and medicine, since this remains problematic for costs and has previously not been acted upon due to public opposition, most notably from pensioners
- reinforcing of private health insurance, mainly through economic support to MUFACE (private mutualities for some public servants), with a 36 per cent tax reduction as an incentive for companies who privately insure their workers

The privatisation of health centres The privatisation of public health systems is a key strategy followed through systematic dismantling of public health provision in countries where a national health service exists. This paradigm of a policy for example was perfected by the Conservatives in Great Britain and created many problems of function and provision for the British health service (Fisher 1999). The present model of the Spanish conservative government is based upon the separation of purchasing and provision, thus promoting the setting up of an internal market, commercialisation of public health centres and competition between these centres, despite international evidence which shows this to be an economic failure.

The experience from Spain also shows that the 'fundaciónes' in those areas that are under the national government (that is, not yet devolved to the regional governments), as in the case of the hospitals of Manacor and Alcorcón, or in Galicia (the hospital 'fundación' of Verin), have been unable to achieve better results in the quality of their services than in the previous set-up. This is so despite the special budgetary treatment they have received. There are also other experiences such as the presence of publicly funded companies working in some public hospitals and the simple concession of health centres to private enterprises (the Alzira Hospital) (Sanchez Bayle 1996; Martín 1999, 2000; Ponte 2000).

It is evident, therefore, that behind the proposals for reorganisation and the separation of purchasing and of provision, there is a clear intention to encourage the privatisation of the health system. This is also being done through subcontracting undertaken either through renting facilities and the technology of state-owned facilities to private companies, or more simply through the disposal of the overall assets of the centres.

Finally, it has become increasingly evident that this model disrupts the crucial aspects of coordination and integration of the services which form the basis of the national health service (Sanchez Bayle 1999a; de la Mata 1999).

Cuts in healthcare services The reduction of health services is another conservative strategy. This reduction assumes that those citizens who need to use them should pay according to their means. This method has been widely used in Europe by a number of conservative governments, as in Portugal and Italy. However, in Spain the impact of this method has been limited, until now, to the exclusion from public financing of a group of medicaments (although it is a feature which remains available via the euphemistically named 'Agreement on the Modernisation and Consolidation of the National Health System' – Acuerdo sobre Modernización y Consolidación de la Sistema Nacional de Salud). But since March 2000, it has been easier to apply due to the absolute PP majority in Parliament.

However, the main obstacle to this process of privatisation is the potential political cost that its inception would involve, especially among patients with chronic conditions and pensioners (Ministerio de Sanidad y Consumo 1998). The most obvious problem is that such policies penalise the sector of the population who have the least economic resources and for whom it may mean actual exclusion from access to the health system. This would include groups of the population with more severe illnesses and therefore those with the greatest need for treatment within the national health service.

The promotion of private health insurance   A final aspect of privatisation concerns the fostering of private insurance, linked to the segregation of public cover for large groups of the population, so that they are covered by the private sector, maintaining total or partial public financing. The promotion of private health insurance (which is relatively new and small-scale in Spain due to the strength of the public system) is another conservative policy. The authorities try to facilitate its growth and most civil servants may choose between the normal public insurance or private insurance paid by the government through taxes. The most popular modality is through MUFACE, an insurance company allowing members to choose either private insurance or staying within the public health service (NHS) and readdressing their choice annually.

Research suggests that those with private cover would receive greater choice in healthcare, which is in effect maintained by a high level of double cover (around 20 per cent are covered by MUFACE and by the NHS at the same time), and the shifting of the more severely ill and the aged from the private to the public sector. Inevitably this results in a loss to the public sector and a gain for private insurers since they would eliminate from their systems the higher-risk persons, as defined by age and social vulnerability. This form of targeting within the overall system has received special economic support for expansion (Martín 1998).

Therefore, the general public are not only paying for their own public healthcare, but also for others with 'for profit' insurance company policies through a public subsidy. This also applies to some recently privatised public companies such as Telefónica, who have insured their workers with private companies while still receiving funds from the government for public cover. The growth of private insurance, however, brings with it one fundamental problem: limitation of cover. It also promotes what is known as the 'cherry picking' of the best risks. In essence this means that insurance companies seek out the healthiest section of the population and exclude the poorest, which include those with most health risks.

It is known that illness is concentrated among a small number of people, and that these generate the largest part of the costs of healthcare (for example, in the USA in 1987, the 5 per cent of the population who generated the greatest health expenditure 'consumed' 58 per cent of all expenses, while the 50 per cent who caused the least expense 'consumed' 3 per cent of the total). Therefore, the greatest incentive for any insurance company, and also for those who provide healthcare (hospitals, etc.) is not to improve their efficiency, but rather to target that 50 per cent who create the least expense, and to avoid the 5 per cent who are very expensive. If, furthermore, we take into account that the latter group is precisely the one section of the population which has the greatest need for the health system, we can appreciate the gravity of the problem with regard to equitable treatment and health levels in the population. These problems have been outstandingly demonstrated in recent years, in the attempts to promote health insurance systems in Holland and New Zealand (Kutner 1999; Rey 1999).

THE STRATEGY FOR PRIVATISATION

The central problem is that public health personnel within the health system are faced with a very clear strategy: that of a merger of conservative economic interests, which are trying to do business in the Spanish NHS, since the latter has access to more than 3,000 billion pesetas annually. Considering the fact that it is not possible immediately to privatise the NHS, the strategy for privatisation is based upon a series of complementary measures that are well backed up by 'marketing', and use of grandiloquent expressions to conceal and camouflage, all in the hope that we will eventually find ourselves in a situation where it is difficult or impossible to backtrack.

In short, we are looking at the dismantling of the NHS into multiple micro-enterprises (thus making easier the selection of those economically viable segments of healthcare) and offering an infrastructure sufficient in quantity and quality to put an end to state insurance. If we reach this point, the establishment of patient contributions and the limitation of state welfare for the poor to a new system akin to charity would be almost inevitable. The phenomenon of inequality would spread, since the marketplace has no interest in looking after the health problems of citizens, but rather only in assuring the profitability of its investments. We are essentially faced with the intention of converting a basic right, the right to healthcare, into merchandise, with the problems that this will bring for the sector of the population with the least economic resources (Sanchez Bayle 2000).

PUBLIC OPPOSITION TO HEALTHCARE PRIVATIZATION POLICIES: THE EXPERIENCE OF GALICIA

The aforementioned reforms were initiated in the north-western region of Galicia during the late 1980s and are being extended to the rest of the country. Galicia is one of the three nations or nationalities which include the Basque country and Catalonia, and which, along with other regions, form the kingdom of Spain. Owing to its landscape, wet climate and an ageing population of some 2.7 million (with a low per capita income of US $7,300, lower than the average Spanish income), which is widely scattered in numerous country villages, and with a long tradition of emigration, Galicia very much resembles Brittany, Wales or Ireland. In Galicia there is also a declining rural world with an industrialised and densely populated Atlantic coastland, with a good communications system. It is indeed a community with a newly formed middle class, in transition from a rural society to a not yet consolidated urban one, based on industry and services, and is vulnerable to European agricultural policies and the growing difficulties of fishing. It is one of the world's leading fishing regions and is dependent upon public and European funds (22.7 per cent of the population lives on state retirement pensions) (Xunta de Galicia 1997).

In accordance with the Spanish constitution, Galicia has an autonomous parliament and government, with full powers regarding the health administration (devolved by the central government in 1991). The present government is conservative (forty-three seats), and the opposition (thirty-two seats) is composed of Galician nationalists, socialists and a minority of communists.

The Galician public healthcare system The Spanish General Health Law of 1986 decentralised the NHS into regional health services (Reverte Cejudo and Sanchez Bayle 1999), and based it upon universal coverage, equity of access, solidarity, coordination and integration of care and decentralisation. It is mainly public and manages 78 per cent of overall expenditure (5.6 per cent of GDP). The Galician Health Service (SERGAS) was devolved in 1991 but has not yet developed a regulatory legal framework. It has an acceptable network of public hospitals for acute illnesses (with three beds per 1,000 of the population, lower than the Spanish average of 4.3), but performance indicators are adequate, though somewhat worse than the Spanish national figures. Otherwise, the 'reformed' primary healthcare network is underdeveloped in relation to the Spanish average; in 2000 only 50 per cent of the population was covered, as compared with 88 per cent throughout Spain. Long-term and psychiatric hospitals remain insufficient. Hospitals and primary healthcare centres are organised as in the rest of the nation, and professionals and health workers are salaried under conditions similar to those of civil servants (Sanchez Bayle 1996).

Healthcare privatising policies in Galicia   The absence of a regional legal framework in the Spanish health system has helped to set up privatisation experiments in the health services in Galicia as a first step towards their extension to the rest of the nation. These are similar to the policies adopted by the Conservative Party in the UK during the 1980s and 1990s (such as the introduction of internal markets and competition).

The new county hospitals, regional blood bank, some areas of ophthalmologic care, high-technology services, maintenance, advice and medical emergency services were given over to private management under two new legal frameworks, the aforementioned 'fundaciónes' and publicly funded companies, both in open contrast to traditional public management (Martín 1997). The most ambitious enterprise was the Galician Institute for Technical Medicine (MEDTEC), designed to take over all new technologies such as haemodynamics, cardiac surgery, nuclear medicine, oncology and nuclear magnetic resonance. This was set up in the two public hospitals of the city of Vigo, but met with hostility from professionals and trade unions from within. As a result, the deregulation of medical and administrative procedures was concurrent with the absence of any team work, and reduced communication between the public hospital and MEDTEC staff. The use of the new technology among public sector employees in particular, such as physicians, postgraduates and technicians, was forbidden (Martín 1999).

Public opposition to privatisation of healthcare   Inevitably, protests grew and the rejection of such measures has spread among public health workers. In addition, different sections of the public health sector organised the 'Platform for the Defence and Improvement of the NHS' (PNHSD – Plataformas para la Defensa y Mejora de la Sanidad Pública). Those involved have brought together the political parties (with the exception of the party in power), trade unions, professionals, the Federation of Associations for the Defence of Public Health Care (FADSP – Federación de Asociaciones para la Defensa de la Sanidad Pública). The PNHSD has published documents and manifestos, organised meetings, debates and activities in different hospitals. Over a period of three years, four substantial civic demonstrations have taken place, which have unexpectedly drawn more than 25,000 demonstrators each time, reflecting the strength of public feeling about the proposed changes.

The success of this experience of opposition to privatising reforms has led to the creation of a regional committee designed to extend the movement. Over the past two years it has become possible also to draw the attention of the media and public opinion to the implications of the attempts at privatisation of the Spanish health service, and towards public health policy in general. As a result, parliamentary groups, political parties and trade unions are much more alert to the functions and value of the public healthcare system, and have developed joint activities despite their political differences. This is manifested in the express rejection of such policies in their electoral programmes. After all these steps were completed, the need was felt for an instrument that could strengthen the new local platforms with a sustained and 'low intensity' campaign, suited for long-term resistance and awareness, and based upon a strong civic component and a low non-radical political profile. This activity also sought the broadest support and unity, enhanced by one simple and specific aim, that of sustaining a national health service, as well as drawing the attention of the media to the pertinent issues.

The People's Legislative Initiative campaign The Spanish Constitution allows citizens to present a Bill to the regional or national parliaments under a legal disposition, called the People's Legislative Initiative (PLI – Iniciativa Legislativa Popular), provided they manage to present a certain number of signatures in proportion to the electoral roll. For example, the required number of signatures in Galicia for such a bill is 15,000 (Parlamento de Galicia 1987). The PLI aimed at forcing the health authorities to present a Galician Health Ordination (GHO) Bill, in order to put an end to uncontrolled private health investments and budget cuts, to promote integration between primary care and specialised care, to develop greater participation of community health workers and, above all, to stop privatisation and restore to the public sector those services that had been already privatised. The health authorities immediately produced their own draft GHO Bill (Beiras and Alvarez 1998), because the pressure of public opinion had placed them in an embarrassing situation.

Other important aims of this initiative were to make citizens aware of the complex governmental strategies adopted in the privatisation programme, which transformed institutions into independent enterprises that would compete against one another, thus breaking up the unity of the NHS. It also aimed at making clear the advantages of the current public system and the destructiveness to be expected from privatisation policies. The intention of the campaign was to look for a didactical method, both for the speaker and the audience, with an agreed simple and attractive message for the general population. The logo was a hand with a pen signing over the logo of the Galician Health Service. The method chosen was a standard forty-slide presentation, accompanied by an instruction manual and a set of notes for the speaker, and the general themes were a reminder of what the NHS means for the population. It also described the variety and the camouflage of privatising policies, the interest of private insurance companies in the funds currently operated by the Spanish NHS, and the risks for equity, efficiency and quality due to the break-up of public insurance.

The results The campaign ended with a parliamentary debate on 27 April 1999 and the PLI was defeated by the expected Conservative majority of thirty-seven votes against thirty-one. In spite of these anticipated results, the overall aims were achieved and it was felt that it was possible to build a movement in favour of the Spanish NHS and against privatisation even in an adverse global, national and regional climate. In our view it is essential to come to an understanding with trade unions, progressive, political, professional and social organisations, not just in support of the health service. There is also need to raise awareness about neo-liberal policies and the weak, unsubstantiated and often unconvincing arguments put forward in support of privatisation. Therefore, progressive doctors, nurses and other health workers should not become resigned to loss and wait for trends to develop, but rather take the initiative and look to social organisations with the critical appraisal and alternatives they currently offer. The process will move slowly at the beginning, but when it gains enough 'critical mass' in public opinion and in the media, the rate of advance will increase and make the movement less vulnerable.

CONCLUDING REMARKS

Privatising policies, which began in Galicia under the Conservative government, have been extended to the rest of the nation. However 'Platforms' are being organised all over the country (Sanchez Bayle 1999a), and during 1999 and 2000 the mobilisation of public opinion extended across the whole of Spain with great enthusiasm. The campaign achieved great importance with regard to social participation in localities, linking them to problems in each of the cities and autonomous regions. Furthermore, in the autumn of 2000, the Galician regional government decided to transfer its privately managed 'fundaciónes' to the public sector, only a week before the central authorities announced they were to abandon their previous principal policy of transforming public hospitals into 'fundaciónes'. This represents a major success for Spanish National Health Service supporters and for the anti-privatisation movement. It also adds strength to social and professional distrust of neo-liberal healthcare policies in Spain.

REFERENCES

Beiras, H. and Alvarez, L. (1998) 'Anteproyecto de Ley de Sanidad para Galicia' (Health Law for Galicia), *Salud 2000*, 68, 8–12.

Cortes Españolas (1978) *Constitución Española*, Madrid: Cortes Españolas.

de la Mata, I. (1999) 'El mito de la gestión privada: el modelo catalan de salud mental' (The myth of private management: the Catalan model of health), *Psiquiatria Publica*, 11, 94–101.

Editorial (1999) 'El 71.5 per cent de los españoles valora positivamente el sistema sanitario', *Jano*, 26 (3), 27.

Fisher, P. W. (1995) 'NHSCA in practice: the NHS market in the United Kingdom', *Journal of Public Health Policy*, 16, 452–91.

— (1999) 'La reforma del Servicio Nacional de Salud Britanico' (The reform of the British National Health Service), *Salud 2000*, 70, 13–18.

Gaviria, M. (1996) *La Séptima Potencia* (The Seventh Panel), Madrid: Ed. B.

Kutner, R. (1999) 'The American healthcare system. Health insurance coverage', *New England Journal of Medicine*, 340, 163–8.

Martín, M. (1997) 'Los cuestionables éxitos de la política sanitaria gallega' (The questionable success of Galician health policy), *Salud 2000*, 61, 8–15.

— (1998) 'La ruptura del aseguramiento unico, un paso definitivo' (The break up of individual insurance payments – a positive step), *El Pais*, 26 December.

— (1999) 'MEDTEC: el fracaso de la gestión empresarial en Sanidad' (The failure of private sector policies in health), *Salud 2000*, 71, 15–17.

— (2000) 'Falacias y miserias de la nueva gestion hospitalaria' (The falacies and miseries of new hospital management), *Salud 2000*, 76, 8–10.

Ministerio de Sanidad y Consumo (1998) *Acuerdo para la consolidación y modernización del Sistema Nacional de Salud* (Agreement for the Consolidation and Modernisation of the Spanish Health System), Madrid: Ministerio de Sanidad y Consumo.

OECD (1996) *OECD Report*, Paris: OECD.

Parlamento de Galicia (1987) 'Lei de Iniciativa Lexislativa Popular ante o Parlamento de Galicia (Bill of the Popular Legislative Initiative)', *Boletin Oficial do Parlamento de Galicia*, 2020.

Ponte, C. (2000) 'Fundación de Arriondas: Experiencia de un fracaso anunciado' (The experience of an unannounced failure), *Salud 2000*, 73, 12–13.

Reverte Cejudo, D. and Sanchez Bayle, M. (1999) 'Devolving health services to Spain's autonomous regions', *British Medical Journal*, 18, 1204–5.

Rey, J. (1999) *El futuro de la sanidad española. Un proyecto de reforma* (The Future of Public Health in Spain: A Reform Project), Madrid: Fundación Alternativas and Ex-Libris.

Sanchez Bayle, M. (1999a) 'Tareas ante la ofensiva privatizadora en sanidad' (Tax against privatisaiton in public health), *Salud 2000*, 73, 18–23.

— (1999b) 'The healthcare counter-reform in Spain', *Journal of Public Health Policy*, 20, 471–3.

— (1999c) *El estado del malestar* (The State of Ill Being), Madrid: Los libros de la Catarata.

— (2000) 'El caso español: la salud como negocio' (The case of Spanish health as business), *Le Monde Diplomatique* (edn español), 51, 3–4.

Sanchez Bayle, M. (ed.) (1996) *El sistema sanitario en España* (The Health System in Spain), Madrid: Los libros de la Catarata.

Spanish Government (1986) Ley General de Sanidad (The General Law of Health), *Boletin Oficial del Estado*, 29 April, 102, 15207–24.

Xunta de Galicia (1997) *Plan de Saude de Galicia* (The Galician Plan of Health), Santiago: Xunta de Galicia.

CHAPTER 12

The Sad Experience of Corporate Healthcare in the USA

STEFFIE WOOLHANDLER

Once, health policy pundits preached the gospel of market competition and managed care in the USA, promising efficient, consumer-responsive care. Today, market fundamentalism is less credible. After two decades of market-driven health policy, costs are once again soaring while at the same time coverage is contracting, and HMOs (Health Maintenance Organisations) have joined tobacco firms at the lowest ebb of public esteem. Yesterday's true believers have lapsed into cynicism. The *New York Times*, an early booster of market medicine, now warns that there may be no solution to healthcare's woes. Reality has swamped the arguments of the zealots for market solutions. Nihilism is their new defence: 'Things are bad. But there is no alternative (TINA).' The TINA claims come in two flavours: (i) extending coverage, bridling the power of HMOs, or improving quality would break the bank; (ii) though affordable, high-quality national health insurance is theoretically feasible, it is politically impossible; the opposition is too rich and American democracy too weak. This chapter confronts the first of these arguments directly.

Many of healthcare's worsening woes emanate from market medicine and its 'greed-is-good' business ethic. A widening circle of patients and carers suffer so that a narrow band of investors and executives profit. Non-profit national health insurance for the USA could expand coverage, improve care and limit costs by slashing healthcare bureaucracy and outrageous profits. Resources for care in the USA – hospitals, clinics, hi-tech machinery – are already plentiful, with personnel ready and willing, and with current spending levels that are sufficient.

The experience of many nations that spend less and get more proves that national health insurance works. Rebutting the second argument – that US democracy is too weak – requires direct political action.

More Americans lack health insurance today than at any time since the start of Medicare (the government-sponsored programme for elders) and Medicaid (the government-sponsored programme for some of the poor) in the mid-1960s.

Despite the economic boom of the 1990s, the number of uninsured continues to increase. Millions more will lose coverage as the economy flattens. Three-quarters of the uninsured are children or working adults. Although most Americans with private coverage have insurance through an employer, there is no inherent logic which links coverage to employment; other developed nations, such as those in Western Europe, provide health coverage as a right of citizenship. Even many full-time workers in the USA, especially minority workers, lack insurance. Several million poor women and children lost coverage when the Clinton administration slashed welfare in the mid-1990s, despite promises that former welfare recipients could continue their Medicaid coverage.

Meanwhile, workers are paying a higher share of premiums (and larger co-payments and deductibles) as firms shift costs on to employees (Sheils et al. 1999). Seniors have also faced rising out-of-pocket costs, and proposals to introduce market-based reforms in Medicare (for example, vouchers or premiums support programmes) would accelerate cost increases for Medicare recipients (American Association of Retired Persons 1995, 1998). While the uninsured face the gravest problems, what is important to note is that few Americans have adequate coverage; most who need long-term nursing home care pay out-of-pocket until

---

BOX 12.1 *Illness and Medical Costs: a Major Cause of Bankruptcy in the USA*

- 45.6% of all bankruptcies involve a medical reason or large medical debt
- 326,441 families identified illness/injury as the main reason for bankruptcy in 1999
- An additional 269,757 had large medical debts at time of bankruptcy
- 7 per 1,000 single women, and 5 per 1,000 men suffered medical-related bankruptcy in 1999

Source: *Norton's Bankruptcy Advisor*, May 2000

they are impoverished and qualify for Medicaid; while private insurance covers only 7 per cent of nursing home costs (Feder et al. 2000).

A study by a Harvard law professor, Elizabeth Warren, showed that nearly half of more than 1 million Americans who filed for bankruptcy did so because they could not cope with their medical bills or other financial consequences of illness or injury (*Norton's Bankruptcy Advisor*, May 2000). In many developing countries a major cause of indebtedness is related to medical expenditure. In the US health sector choice has also narrowed with the increasing intrusion of market forces in medicine. Forty-two per cent of privately insured adults were offered only one choice of health plan.

Consumer responsiveness and the notion of choice as trumpeted by market enthusiasts is thus rather illusory. Patients rarely switch health plans voluntarily; three-quarters of those changing plans are often forced to do so by their employer or because they have changed jobs.

Lack of coverage, insurance hassles, and other problems paying for care endanger the health of millions of people in the USA today. Many of those with either no coverage or minimal cover forgo care for potentially life-threatening symptoms such as chest pain or a breast

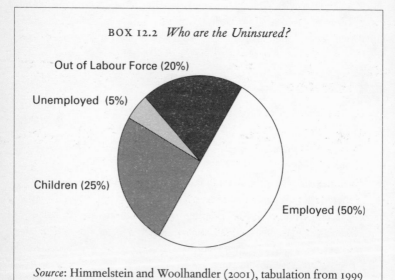

BOX 12.2 *Who are the Uninsured?*

Out of Labour Force (20%)

Unemployed (5%)

Children (25%)

Employed (50%)

Source: Himmelstein and Woolhandler (2001), tabulation from 1999 Centre for Public Services

lump. HMOs also often erect barriers to care, even in emergencies. For terminally ill patients and their families, financial suffering often compounds the burden of illness. Women frequently delay pre-natal care because they are uninsured or unable to pay. Many of the uninsured lack other necessities of life, forcing them to choose between medical care, food, rent and utilities.

Glaring inequalities in health and healthcare mirror a broader economic and social polarisation in the USA. The share of wealth held by the wealthiest 10 per cent of Americans grew from 49 to 69 per cent in the past two decades (Wolff 2000). While per capita income is higher in the USA than in Canada, all of the US advantage accrues to the wealthy; most Americans have less disposable income than their Canadian counterparts (US Department of Labor 1998). The USA has an exceptionally large gap between the rich and the poor, and the highest poverty rate among affluent, developed nations (Jesuit and Seeding 2002). Meanwhile, Americans work longer hours than workers in any other nation, even Japan. Rising inequality, the persistence of extreme poverty, and mandatory sentencing laws that substitute jail for drug treatment are packing US prisons.

Racial inequalities in infant death rates, which had shrunk in the late 1960s in the wake of civil rights successes, have expanded to historic

---

BOX 12.3 *Patients Refused Authorisation for ER Care*

- 8% to 12% of HMO patients presenting to two ERs were denied authorisation
- Authorisation delayed care by 20 to 150 minutes
- Of those denied:
- 47% had unstable vital signs or other high-risk indicators
- 40% of children were not seen in f/u by primary MD

Eventual diagnoses included: meningococcaemia (2), ruptured ectopic (2), shock due to haemorrhage (2), septic hip, PE, MI (2), ruptured AAA, pancreatitis, peritonsillar abscess, small bowel obstruction, unstable angina, pneumothorax, appendicitis, meningitis (3)

Sources: *Emerg Med* (1997), 15, 605; 1997; 15:605; *Acad Emerg Med* (1997); 4:1129; *Ann Emerg Med* (1990); 19:59

new heights. Overall death rates among African-Americans also remain far higher than among whites, mostly due to an excess of preventable diseases (Himmelstein and Woolhandler 2001: 43). When minorities get sick, they may be unable to find adequate treatment even when they can afford it; some 75 per cent of pharmacies in minority neighbourhoods in New York do not carry an adequate supply of narcotics for cancer pain relief (Morrison et al. 2000). Increasing the number of minority physicians is vital to improving access to care, for poor and minority patients. Yet the rollback of affirmative action portends a shortage of minority physicians for decades to come.

While millions of Americans are denied needed care, 300,000 hospital beds lie empty every day, and health policy leaders warn of an impending surplus of physicians. Meanwhile a growing army of health bureaucrats fights to keep sick patients away from idle healthcare resources and personnel (Himmelstein and Woolhandler 2001: 50).

Recent health policies have encouraged market-based strategies – an expanded role for investor-owned firms, reliance on competition to control costs and streamline care, and the emergence of managed care. While pro-market theorists often trumpet healthcare competition, only half of Americans live in regions with sufficient population density to support competition; a town's only hospital cannot compete with itself (Kronick et al. 1993).

HEALTH MAINTENANCE ORGANISATIONS (HMOS)

HMOs profit from healthy patients, and provide care for them on par with fee-for-service medicine. But sick lower-income patients face a 21 per cent higher risk of dying in HMOs than in fee-for-service (Ware et al. 1986) and elderly people with chronic conditions also fare poorly in HMOs (Ware et al. 1996). Sick HMO patients report substantial barriers to care. HMOs also impede access for Medicaid patients, and score poorly in consumer satisfaction surveys (Lillie-Blanton and Lyons 1998). Several studies demonstrate that HMOs provide poor-quality care to sick patients (Ware et al. 1996). Stroke patients covered by HMOs receive less specialist care than fee-for-service patients, get less rehabilitation care, and more often end up in nursing homes (Retchin et al. 1997). Medicare HMO patients needing home-care receive fewer home visits and have worse outcomes than similar patients covered by the traditional Medicare programme. HMOs in New York selectively refer heart surgery patients to the hospitals with the highest surgical death rates, presumably because those hospitals give HMOs a price break (Erickson et al. 2000). HMOs often under-treat people with mental illnesses. Depression, for example, is less likely to be recognised, appropriately treated or improved even in good HMOs, than in fee-for-service settings (Wells et al. 1989; Rogers et al. 1993). Many HMOs and employers subcontract mental health services to for-profit managed mental health-care firms that routinely provide substandard care. Less than one-third of primary care physicians report that they can always or almost always obtain high-quality mental healthcare for their patients (Center for Studying Health System Changes, *Newsletter*, 1997). Further, the share of psychiatric care in total health benefits has fallen by nearly one-half in the past decade (Hay Group 1999).

In areas where managed care predominates, charity care shrinks and research suffers (Hay Group 1999). Academic leaders attest to the damage that managed care has inflicted on research, teaching, care of the underserved and collegial relations (Simon et al. 1999). Nurses report being forced to care for more and sicker patients, and to neglect the human side of care (Shindul-Rothschild et al. 1996).

THE COST OF CARE

Contrary to widespread perceptions, Medicare's costs have risen less than those of private insurers (where managed care has predominated) (Himmelstein and Woolhandler 2001: 82–3). While market enthusiasts push Medicare to enrol seniors in HMOs, a study found that few seniors could make informed HMO choices (Hibbard et al. 1998); the sickest and frailest are the most vulnerable to being duped. Currently, Medicare HMOs receive a fixed premium from Medicare for each enrolee, regardless of their health. HMOs have recruited healthier-than-average Medicare patients, and encouraged sick enrolees to dis-enrol when they need expensive care (Morgan et al. 1997). Such strategies are highly profitable; by avoiding the sickest 4 per cent of Medicare enrolees, a plan could avoid 46 per cent of costs.

As managed care has come to dominate health insurance, for-profit HMOs have eclipsed non-profit plans (Interstudy 2001).[1] Yet the non-profit plans that are losing out in the marketplace rank higher on every quality measure collected by the National Committee for Quality Assurance (Himmelstein et al. 1999). Physicians who see more patients per hour (fast physicians) are favoured by managed care. Such physicians deliver worse care. They also omit tests needed and treatment for

patients covered by capitation contracts, which reward physicians for
doing less (Himmelstein and Woolhandler 2001: 97).

FOR-PROFIT AND QUALITY OF CARE

Primary care doctors are increasingly pushed to provide complex
speciality care that exceeds their knowledge or capabilities (St Peter et
al. 1999). What is most disturbing is that doctors face mounting pressure
to avoid sick (hence unprofitable) patients (Mason 1995). Even most
physicians who participate in capitation payment schemes believe they
are unethical. HMOs sometimes explicitly forbid doctors from criticising
the plan or telling their patients how they are paid (Woolhandler and
Himmelstein 1995). More often, HMOs use the threat of 'de-listing'
(effectively, firing) doctors who provide too much expensive care or
otherwise for failing to support the corporate line.

Some do well under managed care, notably the chief executive officers
(CEOs) of large healthcare firms (Himmelstein and Woolhandler 2001:
108). Their incomes ultimately derive from patients' premiums; overheads and profits consume as much as one-third of premiums in the
major for-profit plans. Misbehaviour in search of profit is predictable;
HMO/insurance executives owe first allegiance to their shareholders. In
the 1850s, Aetna profited from slavery, and now pleads that such
behaviour was perfectly legal. More recently, Cigna has deleted anti-
tobacco information from subscriber newsletters at the behest of Philip
Morris. And several major insurance firms hold large investments in
tobacco. Other firms that profit from care have also demonstrated a
flexible sense of morality (Himmelstein and Woolhandler 2001: 111).
The consulting firm, for example, whose guidelines are used by many
HMOs to dictate lengths of hospital stays, suggests dangerously brief
hospitalisation for seriously ill children (Benko 2000). The firm apparently demands little proof that its guidelines are safe, as long as they're
'efficient'. Meanwhile, for-profit ownership is spreading in many sectors
of healthcare and massive fraud has become routine. The two largest
investor-owned hospital chains (Columbia/HCA and NME/Tenet) have
admitted to illegal schemes to pad their incomes.

Even when not engaged in unlawful behaviour, for-profit hospitals
cost more and provide worse care. In communities whose medical
market is dominated by investor-owned hospitals, health costs are higher
and rising faster than in areas dominated by non-profits (Silverman et
al. 1999). Much of the excess costs of for-profit hospitals are due to

higher administrative costs; they actually spend less on clinical personnel than do non-profit hospitals (Woolhandler and Himmelstein 1997). Studies from the late 1990s have found higher death and complication rates at for-profit hospitals. Death rates at for-profit hospitals are 7 per cent higher than at comparable non-profit hospitals (Chen et al. 1999); this has been the case for at least a decade (Hartz et al. 1989). Studies have found more post-operative complications and more preventable adverse events at for-profit hospitals than at private non-profits. Among the sixty top-ranked hospitals in the USA shown to have lower death rates and better-quality care, only one is investor-owned. Other studies confirm this disturbing association between for-profit ownership and higher mortality (Yuan et al. 2000), and suggest that inadequate nurse staffing at investor-owned hospitals causes post-operative complications.

Poor quality has also become endemic among other types of for-profit health facilities. Low-quality care and chronically poor staffing have plagued nursing homes, most of which are investor-owned (Harrington et al. 2001). Professional staffing is scant and staff is poorly paid, for perhaps the most difficult work in healthcare. For-profit dialysis clinics have high death rates, low transplant rates, and less use of the optimal type of dialysis (peritoneal) for children (Garg et al. 1999). Canadian dialysis clinics, for example, virtually all of them non-profit, provide better care at lower cost. In sum, investor-owned health facilities provide inferior care at inflated prices.

Drug companies are the largest for-profit healthcare firms. In the past decade drug costs have soared (US Health Care Financing Administration, various years). In the USA, where firms have escaped the price regulations prevalent in other nations, drug prices are about 50 per cent higher than in other developed nations. For instance: Prilosec (medication for heartburn and ulcer) costs $3.30 a pill in the USA and $1.47 in Canada; the allergy drug Claritin is available for $2 per pill in the USA, for 48 cents in Australia and 41 cents in Britain. In Vermont a patient pays $95 a month for Tamoxifen (breast cancer medicine), but can get the same for $15 in Canada! One-third of seniors have no insurance for outpatient medications, and seniors in poor health who lacked drug coverage were spending, on average, $750 out-of-pocket in 1996. While HMOs and other large purchasers like the Defense Department often negotiate steep discounts, such concessions are unavailable to individual buyers. Meanwhile, pharmaceutical firms have recorded the highest profits among all Fortune 500 industry groups for 1995 to 1999 ($27.3 bn in 1999) (Fortune 500 rankings), and wielded their political might to minimise their taxes (Himmelstein and Woolhandler 2001: 145). While the firms tout their high research spending (much of it squandered on developing useless minor modifications of existing bestsellers) they spend far more on marketing and profits than on research and development. The billions spent on marketing not only waste money but also mislead physicians, worsen their prescribing and distort research (see www.nofreelunch.org). Drug firms also oppose any policy that might hold down their prices. They have fought any proposal to expand Medicare coverage of outpatient medications which might allow Medicare to negotiate prices.

UNIVERSAL COVERAGE VERSUS SELECTIVE SURVIVAL: THE COSTS

International experience proves that universal coverage is feasible and improves health. Every other developed nation assures health coverage for the entire population (OECD 1999). The US infant mortality rate, among the lowest in the world in 1950, is now disturbingly high (OECD 1999). We trail other nations on life expectancy for both women and men and score poorly on measures of premature death. Meanwhile, our health costs per capita are nearly double those of any other nation, and rising more rapidly. For example, in 1998 the USA was spending $4,270 per capita as compared to $2,400 in Germany, $2,250 in Canada and $1,450 in the UK (Andersen et al. 2000). Indeed, government spending on healthcare in the USA exceeds total health spending in any other nation.

Government spending includes not only Medicare and Medicaid, but also public expenditures to purchase private insurance for government workers and tax subsidies for private insurance (Shiels and Hogan 1999). These massive tax subsidies are sharply regressive, offering little to a poor family but thousands to a wealthy one.

High medical costs in the USA cannot be blamed on the elderly since other nations have older populations. Nor are Americans voracious consumers of care. The USA has fewer physician visits and lower hospital use per capita than other nations. Surveys of English-speaking countries show that Americans face the greatest barriers to care (Himmelstein and Woolhandler 2001: 166). Moreover, the managed care-dominated system in the USA frequently forces people to switch doctors, disrupting the continuity of care.

CONTRASTING SOME EXPERIENCES: CANADA AND THE USA

As the USA was implementing Medicare and Medicaid in the mid-1960s, Canada was putting in place national health insurance. The Canadian government offered the provinces substantial funding for universal, comprehensive, publicly administered coverage. Within one year of the programme's start-up, the proportion of patients with serious symptoms who saw a doctor increased sharply. Infant mortality, which had long been higher than in the USA, fell rapidly, and has remained below the US level (OECD 1999). While universal healthcare has not erased inequalities in health, it has ameliorated them. Even poor infants in Canada have death rates below the US average (Anon. 1999). While homeless men in Toronto have higher death rates than the non-homeless, they fare far better than homeless men in US cities (Hwang 2000).

Despite waits for some specialised care, peer-reviewed studies continue to find that quality of care for Canadians is at least as good as the care received by insured Americans (though Canada spends far less). Depressed Canadians receive more professional help, and more appropriate treatment than their American counterparts (Katz et al. 1998). Canada has lower surgical death rates than the USA, and lower cancer death rates for potentially curable tumours.

Waits for cataract surgery are decreasing, though surgeons who have private practices (and can presumably increase their private referrals by maximising waits in the public system) appear to inflate the waiting times (DeCoster et al. 1999). Seniors in Canada actually get more of most types of physician care than do American seniors (Welch et al. 1996). Meanwhile, medicine has remained a highly respected and desirable career in Canada, attracting twice as many applicants per medical school place than in the USA. In sum, despite spending roughly half of what the Americans do, Canadians enjoy better health, the security of universal coverage, and a system that is relatively free of bureaucracy and constraints on patient choice.

Yet Canada also has problems. Wealthy Canadians, whose taxes help subsidise the coverage of the less affluent, have pushed conservative governments to cut health spending, particularly hospital budgets. (In contrast, in the USA healthcare financing is highly regressive; the rich pay less.) In addition, as care has shifted from hospitals to home, and medication costs have risen, Canada's insurance has not kept pace;

coverage of home-care and outpatient drugs is patchy. These problems are amplified by US and Canadian business groups anxious to undermine the public system and increase pressure for the expansion of private, for-profit medicine. In addition to media campaigns and lobbying in Canada, these firms have used the World Trade Organisation to press their case against publicly funded, non-profit healthcare.

National health insurance has effectively contained costs in Canada, perhaps too effectively. Canada's healthcare costs have been flat since the mid-1990s. Canada's single payer system greatly simplifies administration, cutting insurance overheads to about 1 per cent (vs. 15 per cent of premiums in the USA) and reducing bureaucratic costs for hospitals and doctors (Woolhandler et al. 1993). Overall, Canada saves about $857 per capita annually on bureaucracy alone. Additionally, Canada saves through improved health planning (for example, minimising the duplication of expensive services) and an emphasis on primary care.

Americans pay a great deal more for their healthcare – funding extraordinary incomes for executives and investors. Yet patients are denied care or forced to struggle to get what they need while market values increasingly intrude in the examining room. Like people in other nations, Americans want a system that assures care at an affordable price, that engenders trust and respect, and affords patient choice. A universal, tax-funded, non-profit national health programme organised like Canada's – though better funded – could achieve these goals.

Under such a system all Americans would receive a card entitling them to care at any doctor's office, hospital, clinic of their choice. Hospitals, clinics and other institutional providers would negotiate global budgets with the programme, and receive a single monthly payment to cover all costs – eliminating most billing bureaucracy. Physicians in private practice would be paid based on a single negotiated fee schedule, greatly simplifying billing. For most Americans, savings from eliminating private insurance premiums would more than offset tax increases to pay for the programme. The General Accounting Office and many private-sector studies have concluded that bureaucratic savings would offset the costs of expanding coverage (Woolhandler et al. 1993). Some of the resources saved on bureaucracy should be devoted to upgrading long-term care, the poorest sector of our healthcare system. Projections that national health insurance is affordable gain credibility because every other developed nation has universal coverage while spending far less. The facilities and human resources needed to provide care to all Americans are already in place.

Surveys have consistently shown wide popular support for universal coverage, though views of political leaders reflect the more conservative convictions of the business community ('Results of Harris Poll', *USA Today*, 23 November 1998). The massive donations that come largely from the wealthiest Americans sway Congress as well as state legislators. As a result, policy debate is dominated by options such as medical savings accounts (MSAs) and voucher programmes that would undermine government oversight, raise costs, open new profit opportunities, and allow the wealthy and healthy to minimise their subsidy to working families, the sick and the poor. Both voucher programmes and MSAs would greatly increase bureaucratic overheads and the costs of health insurance by replacing group coverage with millions of individual policies.

The medical profession has, in the past, been a bulwark against national health insurance. However, many physicians have now concluded that only national health insurance can rescue the patients, and the profession. Over 9,000 US physicians have joined the Physicians for a National Health Programme, a group that advocates national health insurance for the USA. A majority of medical school faculty, students and residents – including most medical school deans in the USA – support a single payer national health programme. Once such views could be dismissed with the cold war epithet of 'socialised medicine', but even an iron curtain cannot for ever conceal a system's failure or a solution that lies just across the border.

NOTE

1. Interstudy Publications, founded by a doctor in 1973, is a leading researcher and publisher in the US of data, directories and analyses for HMOs. Among others it publishes a regular series of updates called Competitive Edge updates that provide an overview of current industry trends in HMO services, enrolment, changes and profitability. (For more information see www.interstudypublications.com).

REFERENCES

American Association of Retired Persons (1995, 1998) US Select Committee on Ageing, AARP 4/95 and 3/98; and Commonwealth Fund (New York City).

Andersen, G. F., Hurst, J., Hussey, P. S. and Jee-Hughes, M. (2000) 'Health spending and outcomes: trends in OECD countries, 1960–1998', *Health Affairs* (Millwood), 19 (3), 150–7.

Anon. (1999) 'Health status of children', *Health Reports*, 11 (3), 25–34.

Benko, L. B. (2000) 'Not by the numbers, please', *Modern Healthcare*, 30 (19), 34.

Chen, J., Radford, M. J., Wang, Y., Marciniak, T. A. and Krumholz, H. M. (1999) 'Do "America's Best Hospitals" perform better for acute myocardial infarction?', *New England Journal of Medicine*, 340 (4), 286–92.

DeCoster, C., Carriere, K. C., Peterson, S., Walld, R. and MacWilliam, L. (1999) 'Waiting times for surgical procedures', *Medical Care*, 37 (6 Suppl.), JS 187–205.

Erickson, L. C., Torchiana, D. F., Schneider, E. C., Newburger, J. W. and Hannan, E. L. (2000) 'The relationship between managed care insurance and use of lower-mortality hospitals for CABG surgery', *Journal of the American Medical Association*, 283 (15), 1976–82.

Feder, J., Komisar, H. L. and Niefeld, M. (2000) 'Long-term care in the United States: an overview', *Health Affairs* (Millwood), 19 (3), 40–56.

Garg, P. P., Frick, K. D., Dioner-West, M. and Powe, N. R. (1999) 'Effect of ownership of dialysis facilities on patients' survival and referral for transplantation', *New England Journal of Medicine*, 341, 1653–60.

Harrington, C., Woolhandler, S., Mullan, J., Carrillo, H. and Himmelstein, D. U. (2001) 'Does investor owership of nursing homes compromise the quality of care?', *American Journal of Public Health*, 91: 1452–55.

Hartz, A. J., Krakauer, H., Kuhn, E. M., Young, M., Jacobsen, S. J., Gay, G., Muenz, L., Katzoff, M., Bailey, R. C. and Rimm, A. A. (1989) 'Hospital characteristics and mortality rates', *New England Journal of Medicine*, 321 (25), 1720–5.

Hibbard, J. H., Jewett, J. J., Engelmann, S. and Tusler, M. (1998) 'Can Medicare beneficiaries make informed choices?' *Health Affairs* (Millwood), 17 (6), 181–93.

Himmelstein, D. U. and Woolhandler, S. (with Ida Hellander) (2001) *Bleeding the Patient: The Consequences of Corporate Health Care*, Monroe, ME: Common Courage Press.

Himmelstein, D. U., Woolhandler, S., Hellander, I., Wolfe, S. M. (1999) 'Quality of care in investor-owned vs not-for-profit HMOs', *Journal of the American Medical Association*, 282 (2), 159–63.

Hwang, S. W. (2000) 'Mortality among men using homeless shelters in Toronto, Ontario', *Journal of the American Medical Association*, 283, 2152–7.

Interstudy (2001) *Competitive Edge*, St Paul, MN: Interstudy Publications.

Jesuit, D. and Seeding, T. (2002) 'Poverty and income distribution' (Income Study Working Papers No. 293), Luxembourg, January.

Katz, S. J., Kessler, R. C., Lin, E. and Wells, K. B. (1998) 'Medication management of depression in the United States and Ontario', *Journal of General and Internal Medicine*, 13 (2), 77–85.

Kronick, R., Goodman, D. C., Wennberg, J. and Wagner, E. (1993) 'The marketplace in healthcare reform. The demographic limits of managed competition', *New England Journal of Medicine*, 328, 148–52.

Lillie-Blanton, M. and Lyons, B. (1998) 'Managed care and low-income populations: recent state experiences', *Health Affairs* (Millwood), 17 (3), 238–47.

Mason, S. A. (1995) 'Consultants must keep their act clean', *Modern Healthcare*, 25 (38), 28.

Morgan, R. O., Virnig, B. A., DeVito, C. A. and Persily, N. A. (1997) 'The Medicare-HMO revolving door: the healthy go in and the sick go out', *New England Journal of Medicine*, 337 (3), 169–75.

Morrison, R. S., Wallenstein, S., Natale, D. K., Senzel, R. S. and Huang, L. L. (2000) '"We don't carry that" – failure of pharmacies in predominantly non-white neighborhoods to stock opioid analgesics', *New England Journal of Medicine*, 342 (14), 1023–6.

OECD (Organisation for Economic Co-operation and Development) (1999) *Computerised HealthCare Database*, Paris: OECD.

Retchin, S. M., Brown, R. S., Yeh, S. C., Chu, D. and Moreno, L. (1997) 'Outcomes of stroke patients in Medicare fee for service and managed care', *Journal of the American Medical Association*, 278 (2), 119–24.

Rogers, W. H., Wells, K. B., Meredith, L. S., Sturm, R. and Burnam, M. A. (1993) 'Outcomes for adult outpatients with depression under prepaid or fee-for-service financing', *Archives of General Psychiatry*, 50 (7), 517–25.

Shiels, J. and Hogan, P. (1999) 'Cost of tax exempt health benefits in 1998', *Health Affairs*, 18 (2), 176.

Sheils, J. F., Hogan, P. and Manolov, N. (1999) 'Paying more and losing ground', *International Journal of Health Services*, 29, 485–518.

Shindul-Rothschild, J., Berry, D. and Long-Middleton, E. (1996) 'Where have all the nurses gone? Final results of our Patient Care Survey', *American Journal of Nursing*, 96 (11), 25–39.

Silverman, M., Fisher, E. and Skinner, J. S. (1999) 'The association between for-profit hospital ownership and increased medicare spending', *New England Journal of Medicine*, 341, 420–6.

Simon, S. R., Pan, R. J., Sullivan, A. M., Clark-Chiarelli, N., Connelly, M. T., Peters, A. S., Singer, J. D., Inui, T. S. and Block, S. D. (1999) 'Views of managed care – a survey of students, residents, faculty, and deans at medical schools in the United States', *New England Journal of Medicine*, 340 (12), 928–36.

St Peter, R. F., Reed, M. C., Kemper, P. and Blumenthal, D. (1999) 'Changes in the scope of care provided by primary care physicians' *New England Journal of Medicine*, 341 (26), 1980–5.

US Department of Labor (1998) *Monthly Labour Review*, Washington, DC, US Dept of Labor, April.

US HealthCare Financing Administration (various years) *National Health Accounts*, Office of the Actuary, Vol. 22, 35–78.

Ware, J. E. Jr, Bayliss, M. S., Rogers, W. H., Kosinski, M. and Tarlov, A. R. (1996) 'Differences in 4-year health outcomes for elderly and poor, chronically ill patients treated in HMO and fee-for-service systems. Results from the Medical Outcomes Study', *Journal of the American Medical Association*, 276 (13), 1039–47.

Ware, J. E. Jr, Brook, R. H., Rogers, W. H., Keeler, E. B., Davies, A. R., Sherbourne, C. D., Goldberg, G. A., Camp, P. and Newhouse, J. P. (1986) 'Comparison of health outcomes at a health maintenance organisation with those of fee-for-service care', *The Lancet*, 1 (8488), 1017–22.

Welch, W. P., Verrilli, D., Katz, S. J. and Latimer, E. (1996) 'A detailed comparison of physician services for the elderly in the United States and Canada', *Journal of the American Medical Association*, 275 (18), 1410–16.

Wells, K. B., Hays, R. D., Burnam, M. A., Rogers, W., Greenfield, S. and Ware, J. E. Jr. (1989) 'Detection of depressive disorder for patients receiving prepaid or fee-for-service care: Results from the Medical Outcomes Study', *Journal of the American Medical Association*, 262 (23), 3298–302.

Wolff, E. (2000) 'Top heavy', *Left Business Observer*, 94 (3).

Woolhandler, S. and Himmelstein, D. U. (1995) 'Extreme risk: the new corporate proposition for physicians', *New England Journal of Medicine*, 333, 1706–8.

— (1997) 'Costs of care and administration at for-profit and other hospitals', *New England Journal of Medicine*, 336 (11), 769–84.

Woolhandler, S., Himmelstein, D. U. and Lewontin, J. P. (1993) 'Administrative costs in US hospitals', *New England Journal of Medicine*, 329 (6), 400–3.

Yuan, Z., Cooper, G. S., Einstadter, D., Cebul, R. D. and Rimm, A. A. (2000) 'The association between hospital type and mortality and length of stay: A study of 16.9 million hospitalized Medicare beneficiaries', *Medical Care*, 38 (2), 231–45.

CHAPTER 13

Transformation of the Cuban Health Sector: the Past Forty Years

FÉLIX J. SANSÓ SOBERATS

This chapter outlines the changes that have taken place in the Cuban health system over the past forty years. It focuses on reforms that have enabled the health system to widen participation and coverage at a time of considerable economic and political turmoil that was largely beyond the control of the Cuban government.

No matter how much of a physician's time is consumed by medical practice, still it is essential that he/she study the background to public health and medicine, not only to increase knowledge, but also because it is an indispensable source of learning. It reveals the experiences gained from intervention undertaken to preserve and promote health within a social environment. The history of public health in Cuba is a rich source of knowledge, experience and historical lessons learned.

The evolution of public health in Cuba during the twentieth century has three clearly distinguishable stages: the first from 1902 to 1958; the second, following the establishment of the revolutionary government, from 1959 to 1989; and the third from 1989 to the present day (Delgado García 1998).

THE CUBAN PUBLIC HEALTH SYSTEM: HISTORICAL BACKGROUND (1902–58)

Since the establishment of the Republic at the beginning of the twentieth century, the Cuban public health system (which until then had focused mainly on sanitation measures) underwent a process of centralisation. Its array of diverse sanitary institutions were largely uncoordinated and operated independently of each other. The Secretariat of Sanitation and Charity was established in 1909, and, for the first time, this sector became a branch of the central government (Delgado García 1996).

Both the international economic crisis, which resulted in the First World War, and the dictatorial and corrupt governments existing in Cuba at the time led to a rapid deterioration in the organisation and function of this fledgling public health system. This not only increased instability among the medical work-force, but also encouraged administrative corruption, which allowed the illicit enrichment of many politicians of the young Republic. However, with the establishment of a new and progressive constitution in 1940, popular expectations regarding improved public health facilities grew. But frequent changes in leadership at the ministerial level (some twenty-three ministers came in and out of office over an eighteen-year period) prevented the establishment of effective long-term plans in public health (Arocha Mariño 2000a). Another factor that contributed to the weakening of public health activity, from as early as 1940, was the proliferation of autonomous organisations which tended to act independently of the Ministry (Delgado García 1995).

The consolidation of the social forces that formed the dominant national oligarchy during this period reinforced the need for better-quality medical care, as well as for improving access to existing facilities. These factors, together with the rapid development of medical technology, determined to some degree the increase in mutual cooperative medical centres and private practice clinics in the country during the 1950s. By the early 1960s the majority of the population, including those in rural areas, were supported by the state system. However, under this system hospitals, about ninety-seven of them, were poorly equipped and had very limited budgets to provide both medical and preventive care. Limited resources were further depleted by dishonest administrators. Lastly, the rural population who lived in the remotest regions of the country spent most of their lives without ever seeing a doctor. During the politically turbulent years of the 1950s in particular, they had often to make do with the assistance of traditional practitioners. Not surprisingly during this period, the public health situation was so poor that death rates from infectious diseases were high, worsened by a lack of understanding of the factors affecting morbidity. The high levels of morbidity were in large part due to the absence of any medical or preventive care, as well as the absence of an appropriate clinical infrastructure (Arocha Mariño 2000b).

TRANSFORMATION OF THE CUBAN HEALTH SECTOR (1959–89)

Since its establishment in the 1960s, the Cuban National System of Health (SNS) has carried out substantial as well as long-standing reforms. During the initial stages (from 1959 to 1989), the reforms were the logical consequence of the social and economic development of the country. Their content and formulation were also a reflection of the attention paid to public health and the belief that access to health services is a human right for every citizen (Gusmán and Mariño 2000).

The SNS was based on the following principles:

- prophylactic
- socialist and public
- accessibility and coverage
- integrity and planned development
- unity of medical science, teaching and practice
- active participation by the population
- internationalism

By 1964, polyclinics had been established in order to provide the widest possible access to medical care. With the introduction of basic health services in 1965, Health and Integrated (poly) clinics were organised with a focus on primary care and prevention. In 1968 Health Areas were created and subdivided into population/geographical sectors of between 3,000 and 5,000 inhabitants. The idea was to initiate actions at the community level through the use of nurses as well as doctors. Community polyclinics were also established in 1974, bringing the basic medical specialities closer to the community. The main emphasis was always on preventive care despite the varied organisation of the public health system by sectors.

Within a decade, primary healthcare programmes based on family physicians and nurses were established. These operated on the basis of having community-based medical teams. The service aimed at providing primary health and preventive services to cover up to 600 inhabitants in particular geographical areas.

In order to improve basic health, state primary health programmes aimed at expanding medical and technical education were drawn up simultaneously in order to create human resources. The emphasis of the educational programme was also on prevention, so that it could respond to the requirements and growing demand for healthcare as well as focus upon building capacity. Within this strategy, the introduction of new technologies was prioritised together with the creation and development of centres of research. All these factors contributed to the overall strengthening of the SNS. This strategy was implemented in such a way that, by the end of the 1980s, the public health situation in Cuba had been radically transformed. This meant, for example, that before 1990:

- all Cubans had full and free access to health services
- the number of doctors increased from 1 per 1,000 to 1 per 396
- the number of dentists increased 30 times from 200 to 6,500
- the number of nurses increased 22 times from 2,500 to 53,595
- the number of lowest level nurses (auxiliaries) decreased, from 60 per cent of the total number of nurses in 1967, to just 2 per cent in 1987, highlighting the success of training programmes
- the number of health institutions (private, cooperative and state) increased from 344 in 1958 to 1,430 units at present; also, these were diversified in type and services offered
- the infant mortality rate fell from 60 deaths per 1,000 live births to 11.1 in 1989
- the rate of mortality due to infectious diseases decreased from 62.7 to 9.3 per 100,000 inhabitants and its percentage in the general mortality went down from 11.6 per cent to 1.4 per cent (Cuban Ministry of Public Health 1999)

THE PAST DECADE: 1989–2001

The demise of the Soviet Union and the rest of the European Socialist bloc, the market for more than 80 per cent of Cuban imports, drastically deprived Cuba of guaranteed income. Among this was included 63 per cent of food imports, 98 per cent of oil imports, 86 per cent of raw materials and 80 per cent of machinery and equipment imports. This had a dramatic impact on the Cuban economy during the 1990s. This was exacerbated by the continuing economic blockade first imposed on Cuba by the government of the United States in 1962. The blockade was worsened by the Torricelli Bill and, more recently, by the Helms–Burton Law, which increased punitive measures with regard to imports into Cuba. As a result there has been increasing economic hardship, which has inevitably had a negative impact on the public health system. The economic crisis generated by the US blockade does not make concessions for exceptional circumstances such as epidemics or emergencies. It has been difficult, if not impossible, to buy materials, equipment and drugs produced in the United States. The systematic harassment arising out of the blockade is also felt on a daily basis in the actions of the US government and its representatives banning as well as preventing the export of Cuban goods and services to anywhere in the world. This has acted as a major obstacle to the economic development of Cuba and is detrimental to its progress.

In the midst of this difficult economic situation, a number of political decisions were made to sustain the achievements already gained by the Cuban public health system, without the need to adopt 'neo-liberal measures'. A testimony to this is the fact that during the most difficult period of economic sanctions against Cuba, no public health institutions were closed nor any public health workers removed from their jobs. Instead, economic measures were adopted to increase health benefits for every citizen, with special emphasis upon the needs of vulnerable groups such as older people, children and women. Paradoxically, rather than worsening, most health indicators began to improve. Thus, maintaining the level of public health as a priority became a challenge for health workers and government alike, and its promotion became a strategic aim for the whole of Cuban society (Cardona Osorio 1998). During the most difficult period of sanctions against Cuba two main principles of the Cuban public health system were reinforced: first, that the whole of the Cuban health system would continue to be totally financed by the state budget; second, it was agreed to maintain all health services free of charge, thereby ensuring universal coverage.

However, owing to years of economic blockade, and despite all the achievements in public health, there are grounds for a complete overhaul of the existing system since the health sector continues to face shortages and problems. These relate mainly to the physical decay of actual buildings and increasingly poor management capability. All these factors result in disappointment among the population, thereby increasing the need for an evaluation of the whole system.

EXPENDITURE ON THE HEALTH SECTOR

During the 1990s, the health sector was given priority for access to public funds. Thus, the percentage of GDP spent on public health provision and of the state budget on expenditure on this sector increased dramatically. This illustrates that the public health system remained a political priority at a time when many other activities and sectors were being run on meagre budgets.

However, between 1990 and 1994, while expenditure on hospitals decreased, it was increased for primary care. But there was a significant drop in overall new investments such that by 1994, the health sector received only 3.1 per cent of total expenditure (see Table 13.1). The amount of hard currency for the import of critical medical supplies was also affected by the inability to import. This reduced even further the availability of much-needed medicines and supplies by 20 to 30 per cent, due to the need to acquire them under market conditions imposed by the blockade (Cardona Osorio 1998). This has led to a shortage of drugs, raw materials for the pharmaceutical industry, medical supplies, spare parts for medical and non-medical equipment, as well as the lack of any new equipment. This situation has not only imposed constraints upon the whole system, but also led to the deterioration of the overall service.

The Cuban health system requires a substantial increase in resources, to allow it to guarantee much-needed supplies and also to begin a process of capital improvement of institutions and of much-needed medical equipment. A significant effort is being made to increase the sources of revenue in hard currency within the system itself, which has risen from a mere 4 per cent of GDP in 1994 to 6 per cent in 2002.

Table 13.1 shows the trends in total investment available to the health sector from 1989 to 1997. The donation of equipment and cash by governments, agencies, non-governmental organisations, solidarity movements as well as individual friends of Cuba has helped considerably

TABLE 13.1 Resources in hard currency in the health sector, 1989–97

Year	Real expenditure (US $ million)
1989	227.3
1990	127.3
1991	98.0
1992	70.7
1993	66.9
1994	90.1
1995	108.0
1996	126.6
1997	112.3

Source: Dirección de Planificación y Economía, MINSAP

to ameliorate the critical situation that Cuba faced. This help has been a powerful expression of international solidarity and friendship, and an acknowledgement of Cuban advances in public health. These donations have also been undertaken voluntarily and through personal commitment. The Cuban population is aware of this international support, despite the trade sanctions imposed by the US government, and appreciates and respects the enormous solidarity shown and assistance extended to the country, especially in the public health sector, during its worst moments of hardship.

STRATEGIC PRIORITIES OF THE CUBAN HEALTH SYSTEM

Cuba formulated the strategies and priorities of its health service for the period 1995–2000 with the aim of continuing the sustainable development of the health system, and improving health indicators for the whole population. The strategies and programmes of the SNS are contained in a document known as the 'Methodological Brief of the Ministry of Public Health'. A broad programme for decentralisation of management was carried out, for example, in order to increase the efficiency of activities and in the context of encouraging greater community as well as intersectoral participation.

An important development in the current strategic plan has been the formation of participative forums. The participative forums have been adopted as health councils at national, provincial, municipal as well as local levels to undertake intersectoral coordination and to achieve true decentralisation. It has been acknowledged by the government that, at the local level, social participation complemented by mobilisation of resources is a key to overall improvements in the medical, economic and social impact of the health system; and that improvements in health status can be made only through an analysis of the local situation regarding healthcare, supported by resources and ongoing discussions within those communities about issues of health and well-being. These evaluations resulted in the following strategies and programmes being adopted.

Strategies

1. Reorientation of the health system towards primary care, and to ensure that at its core are the family physician and nurse.

2. Reinforcement of secondary services through improvement in hospital care.

3. Revitalisation of hi-tech programmes and research institutions within the system.

4. Development of the Programme of Natural and Traditional Drugs and Medicine.

5. Prioritisation of some vital areas of the system such as dentistry and eye-care.

6. The provision of an integrated system for urgent cases and medical emergencies.

Programmes

1. Mother/child programme.
2. Chronic non-transferable diseases programmes.
3. Transferable diseases programmes.
4. Geriatrics programme.

The Ministry of Public Health has declared as its core strategy the consolidation of the municipal health system. This is related to the fact

TABLE 13.2 Indicators of health status and availability of health services in Cuba, 2000

Infant mortality rate per 1,000 live births	7.2
Mortality rate of children under 5 years of age per 1,000 live births	9.1
Percentage of surviving children at 5 years of age	98.9
Perinatal mortality rate	12.7
Infant mortality rate from acute respiratory infections per 1,000 live births	0.3
Percentage of infectious and parasitic diseases from the total number of deaths	0.8
Physicians per 10,000 population (1999)	58.2
Dentists per 10,000 population (1999)	8.9
Number of family physicians	30,133
Population cared for by family physicians (%)	99.1
Nursing personnel per 10,000 population	74.3
Medical care beds per 1,000 population	5.2
Social service beds per 1,000 population	1.3
Average educational level of the population	9th grade
Literacy rate % (National Statistics Bureau)	96.2
Percentage of population with safe drinking water supply (1999)	95.0

Source: Cuban Ministry of Public Health (2000)

that this sector acts as a key component of the overall public health system and such support will help to strengthen overall social development.

The space allocated to social medicine within the municipality provides for intersectoral activity and community participation under the aegis of the municipal and local health councils. This encourages the sustenance of healthy communities through greater involvement in local affairs. It also includes the system of primary care, consolidation of the public health systems, building up the epidemiological profile of the community, supporting a network of essential drugs and medication, prioritisation of treatment based on availability of drugs, development of natural and traditional medicine, optimisation of services within the community, projections of service availability for the community through focused research in public health and medical specialities, programmes for continuing studies by professionals and technicians, and organisation of services by other units of the health system. The municipal health system encompasses all the above activities and, hence, is the sector where sustainable development of a healthy population is most feasible and relevant.

Despite the past decade of economic crisis, Cuba has achieved the best possible health indicators in all of its history. Table 13.2 shows the main health status and some other indicators for the year 2000.

THE SOCIAL SECURITY SYSTEM

At the end of 1958 there were in all about fifty-two social security institutions in Cuba. They were classified under the broad umbrella of those dealing with 'state pensions', 'professional insurance' and 'workers' insurance'. In spite of the high number of services, social security provision covered only between 40 and 50 per cent of all paid workers. There is no health insurance in Cuba.

Despite regular contributions from ordinary people, by the 1950s most of the social security institutions had been made bankrupt through systematic embezzlement, which led to reduced quotas as well as worthless pension accounts. When the infamous Cuban dictator Fulgencio Batista fled the country at the end of 1958, most of the so-called union officials stole all remaining funds. In the aftermath of dictatorial rule, the ___ government worked out a plan that covered most of the ___ of the bankrupt institutions. This was undertaken ___ guarantee the flow of its short- and long-term commitments. It drafted a law to cover all risks, to expand workers' protection, to provide regular pensions, to set up a rational and unified administration as well as creating health insurance, and, most significantly, it agreed to supply all these free of cost (Gutierrez and Peñate 2000). After much discussion on the Bill by workers, who had been allowed to express their needs, the Social Security Law No. 1100 was passed. This provided all workers and their families with social assistance in case of illness, maternity benefits, accident and professional illness cover, age-related illness and death cover. The main emphasis of the state was to support the creation of employment rather than to support the unemployed through special funding.

The Law 1100 in the social sector was a major complement to commitments made in the health sector. It covered the following areas:

- it widened the coverage to 100 per cent of wage-earners, including field workers and their families
- it established a coherent system of services, providing a guarantee for usage without interruption
- it included among its contingencies accidents while working and professional diseases including a social approach to prevention, care and rehabilitation
- it included maternity benefits (in Cuba today, a working pregnant woman has her job secured for one year after the birth of a child and receives paid leave of 100 per cent of her salary six weeks before delivery and for a year following the birth)
- the framework of services included common diseases and accidents of common origin, that were not insured previously in Cuba
- for social security, the law would cover all time worked at any job by the insured person

Under this law the costs covered by the family in matters of healthcare are only those for drugs specially prescribed to ambulatory patients, hearing aids, orthopaedic and dental prostheses, wheelchairs, crutches and similar equipment, and spectacles. Irrespective of the costs incurred, in all cases the prices paid are heavily subsidised by the state. Low-income patients in particular receive monetary help, as well as free supplies of these drugs and prostheses.

This law was amended in 1973, 1979 and in 2001. Since 1979, a system of social care has been established that provides protection to practically every household where there are no income-earners, normally legally bound to provide for their families, or to households where there

are persons who are unable to cover all the requirements. This is valid also for persons who are unable to work or those who are orphans and do not have a family to provide them with food, shoes, clothes, linen and domestic care as is the case with some visually impaired and disabled elderly people. Such groups are granted domestic help or a carer, who is paid by the state.

The main programmes of social care may be described as follows:

- National Programme for Social Community Services to the Elderly
- Programme of Social Work for Single Mothers
- Programme for Social Care to Socially Disadvantaged Minors
- Programme for Social Care and Rehabilitation of Disabled Persons
- Programme of care for other vulnerable groups

The Cuban health system as it exists today would not have been able to achieve the results that it has without the comprehensive Social Security and Care Law. The care laws have generated major results and, in particular, these three systems have become one unit aimed at the improvement of the health of the entire population.

CONCLUDING REMARKS

This is a general outline of the main changes that have taken place in the Cuban health system over the past four decades. In this author's opinion, the government's will to give this system priority and to provide the funds for the development of the people's health have been decisive in achieving such results. Likewise, the unity of society as a whole, not just of the health system, has been important.

Thousands of Cuban health workers have given their cooperation to more than sixty countries throughout the world. Currently, about 6,114 Cuban doctors and paramedical personnel work in other countries. A Latin American School of Medicine was founded in Cuba in which young people from all over Latin America come to study free of charge, having committed themselves to practising in their countries and in the most remote areas. This is no doubt an example of the humanism and solidarity that has sustained the modern state of Cuba; it is not a sign that a surplus of resources needs to be shifted.

REFERENCES

Note: all original references in Spanish, translated for this chapter only.

Arocha Mariño, C. (2000a) 'Economy and public health in Cuba in the 1940s', *Rev Cubana Salud Pública*, 24 (2), 128–33.

— (2000b) 'Economy and public health in Cuba in the 1960s', *Rev Cubana Salud Pública*, 24 (2), 141–7.

Cardona Osorio, J. (1998) 'Public health during the crisis', *Rev Cubana Med Gen Integr*, 14 (3), 286–94.

Castillo Guzmán, T. O. and Arocha Mariño, C. (2000) 'Cuban people's health in the revolutionary period', *Rev Cubana Salud Pública*, 26 (1), 57–62.

Cuban Ministry of Public Health (2000) *Annual Statistics of Health*, Havana, Cuba.

Delgado García, G. (1995) 'Cuban presence at the origins of international of public health organizations', *Cuaderno de Historia*, 80.

— (1996) *Conference on History of the Administration of Public Health*, Havana: Ciencias Médicas.

— (1998) 'Historical development of Cuba's public health', *Rev Cubana Salud Pública*, 24 (2), 110–18.

— (2000) 'On the 90th anniversary of the foundation in Cuba of the world's first Ministry of Health', *ACIMED*, 8 (1), 60–3.

Gutierrez Urdaneta, L. and Peñate Rivero, O. (2000) *Changes in the Latin American Pension Systems. The Cuban Alternative*, Havana: Ciencias Sociales.

Rodríguez Justiz, F., Toledo Romaní, M. E., Pérez Chacón, D. and Sánchez Ramírez, E. (2000) 'The globalization and pattern of Cuban Comprehensive General Medicine. Challenges and opportunities', *Rev Cubana Med Gen Integr*, 16 (1), 73–9.

CHAPTER 14

The Political Economy of Healthcare Reforms in Malaysia

CHAN CHEE KHOON

As profitability in manufacturing has declined because of international competition, corporations have turned to services as an alternative source of profit. According to the European Commission 'The service sector accounts for two thirds of the [European] Union's economy and jobs, almost a quarter of the EU's total exports and a half of all foreign investment flowing from the Union to other parts of the world'. In the USA, more than a third of economic growth over the past five years has been because of service exports. The World Bank has calculated that in less-developed countries alone, infrastructure development involving some private backing rose from US$15·6 billion in 1990 to $120·0 billion in 1997 ... With the backing of powerful coalitions of trans-national and multinational corporations, the race is on to capture the share of gross domestic product governments currently spend on public services. (Price et al. 1999)

REINVENTING THE MALAYSIAN STATE

In Malaysia, the shifting balance between market and state has many nuances. Never a significant welfare state in the usual mould, the Malaysian state has none the less been a dominant social and economic presence, dictated by its affirmative-action-type policies, which eventually metamorphosed into state-led indigenous capitalism. Privatisation in Malaysia is intimately linked with the emergence of an indigenous bourgeoisie, with continuing, favoured access to state assets and prerogatives. Internationally, it is also conditioned by its fluid relationships of converging alliances and contested compromise with international business, including the trans-national health service industries.

From a conventional, technocratic perspective, the Malaysian government's involvement in the healthcare sector can be said to have rested on the following premises:

1. The government, as the mandated guardian of the welfare of the public, was responsible for its health. Until recently, this was taken to mean a direct role for the government in the provision of healthcare services. As a national development goal, satisfactory health for the population at large was a desirable end in itself and the government enhanced its legitimacy and standing to the extent that this social contract was fulfilled.

2. Satisfactory health status, in the form of a healthy and productive work-force, was also a means towards the goal of rapid economic growth and development (Zainab 1996). In line with the emphasis on productivity-driven growth in the Seventh Malaysia Plan, the Economic Planning Unit considered that investment in human capital (health, education, skills, organisational restructuring and suchlike) would improve human productive capacity, and thereby accelerate the process of economic growth (Economic Planning Unit 1996).

3. On account of periodic outbreaks of familiar as well as novel infectious diseases (cholera, viral myocarditis, Nipah encephalitis, malaria, dengue fevers), the government is also concerned that disease outbreaks capable of disrupting the normal conduct of business and economic life should at least be kept within tolerable limits, if not eradicated. We might make the same point about environmental health threats in general, in particular, disruptive pollution episodes such as the recurrent, seasonal smogs in South-East Asia.[1]

As part of its vision of a maturing, diversified economy, the Malaysian government has now added a further dimension to its health development policy, that of the encouragement of an advanced healthcare industry in Malaysia, relying upon the private sector as the engine for what is intended to be an important growth industry in the services sector. Beyond catering for domestic demand, it would also be promoted as an export service industry targeted at regional as well as an international clientele.[2]

The underlying assumption is that the populace is becoming more affluent, and that, as disposable incomes rise beyond the requirements of other consumption essentials, a market for healthcare services is emerging and citizens can be expected increasingly to shoulder their own healthcare expenditures (Chan 1997). The government would remain the provider of last resort for the destitute, whether through some kind of means test or other rationing device to discourage excessive demand, and, of late, through the encouragement of social safety-nets (targeted programmes) such as medical welfare trust funds.[3] However, the key assumption is that as poorer countries attain developmental take-off, the growth trajectory will see the emergence of sizeable markets for service industries, 'sunrise' industries like healthcare, education, and leisure and tourism-related ventures for an increasingly affluent middle class. Most importantly, the market for healthcare and social services would be dramatically expanded as the downsizing of public sector healthcare proceeds, amid a general retreat of government from its role as provider, and, to an extent, even its role in financing healthcare.

EMERGING HEALTHCARE MARKETS

A quick perusal of the websites of foreign missions in Kuala Lumpur is instructive; their economic intelligence units suggest to us the stakes involved in these emerging markets, for local would-be healthcare entrepreneurs as well as for their potential foreign partners. For example, for the fiscal year 2000, the designated 'best prospect' markets listed by the Commercial Service of the US Embassy in Kuala Lumpur were, by priority ranking:

- medical equipment and healthcare
- health and food supplements
- industrial automation and process control equipment
- industrial chemicals
- water and wastewater
- furniture-design services, components, machinery and equipment
- education, human resource development training and distance learning
- e-commerce

This list of priorities highlights the primary interest of trans-national corportations, as well that of their national partners, in trade in a diverse range of sectors, but dominated by the services sector. Similarly, the Australian Trade Commission (Austrade, the Australian federal government's export and investment promotion agency) projected in early 2000 that

the demand for quality healthcare continues to grow in Malaysia ... There is strong potential for Australian involvement in many aspects of healthcare development and delivery. Opportunities include: planning, design & management of specialised healthcare facilities; training and provision of continuing and specialised medical education; medical equipment; telemedicine and digitalised imaging systems; manufacture of medical disposables and equipment in Malaysia.

According to the Trade and Investment Department of the British High Commission in Malaysia:

> although the public hospital corporatisation has been [put on hold], it is also important to monitor progress on the shift on procurement decision making from central government to individual hospitals within the expanding corporatisation programme ... This is likely to witness the emergence of a new group of buyers on to the market ... British equipment suppliers should also seriously contemplate establishing Joint Ventures and/or Technology Transfer arrangements to manufacture their products locally. Local companies are also now actively seeking such opportunities ... Another area of interest is medical training and education (including distance learning) ... The pharmaceutical industry may also be a potential growth area. Here again, the emphasis will be on local manufacturing as the Government wishes to reduce dependence on imported pharmaceuticals from 70 per cent to 50 per cent. For British pharmaceutical companies therefore, it may come down to a choice of manufacturing locally or losing the market entirely. (www.britain.org. my/trade/sector_summary/healthcare.htm)

Private sector expansion into healthcare in Malaysia therefore builds on a vastly expanded market, or expectations of such, brought about by the Malaysian government's privatisation policy. How vast is this market, in more precise terms?

PRIVATISATION IN PRACTICE

In 1996, the hospital support services of the Ministry of Health were privatised. Cleaning services, linen and laundry, clinical waste management, biomedical engineering maintenance, and facilities engineering maintenance for the Ministry of Health's general, district and nucleus hospitals and other facilities (accounting for 14 per cent of the Ministry of Health budget) were contracted out in what was then described as the largest privatisation exercise ever in hospital support services. This was a concession worth US $2.8 billion over fifteen years, and it was awarded to three local consortia in joint venture with their foreign partners, in an exercise with little transparency, accountability or competitive tendering (*New Straits Times*, 29 October 1996).

According to figures from the Finance Division of the Ministry of Health, expenditure on hospital support services went up from RM 143 million (US $54 million in 1996) to RM 468.5 million (US $174 million, 1997), a 3.2-fold increase with little evidence of commensurate expansion of services or improvements in quality. It has since steadily increased to RM 507.9 million (US $188 million, 1999) (Chan et al. 2000). Added to these are the costs of monitoring to ensure that the concessionaires comply with the performance standards stipulated in the contractual agreements, amounting to RM 60 million over the five-year period (1997–2001).

This concession followed the privatisation of the Government Medical Stores (GMS) in 1994. A fifteen-year concession to procure, store and distribute pharmaceuticals and medical supplies to government healthcare facilities (annual volume US $100 million, 8 per cent of the Ministry of Health budget) was awarded to Remedi Pharmaceuticals (M) Sdn Bhd, a company closely linked to the ruling party. Researchers at Universiti Sains Malaysia conducted a study in 1997 which compared the price lists for GMS and Remedi overlapping items, and reported a 3.3-fold (weighted) increase in prices after privatisation, again with little evidence of improvement in quality of products or services provided (Ibrahim et al. 1997).

All this needs to be compared with the previous performance measures and track record of public sector healthcare. Government-provided healthcare in Malaysia has been internationally recognised (Heller 1982). While there are many areas in need of much improvement, the aggregate performance is quite remarkable. With expenditures of less than 2 per cent of GDP, public sector healthcare has been instrumental in delivering impressive value-for-money improvement in health status: an infant mortality rate of 7.9 per 1,000 live births in 1999, life expectancies at birth approaching the mid-70s (females 74.9; males 69.9), 90 per cent of the population living within 5 km or one hour's travelling distance of a primary healthcare facility, immunisation rates which exceed 90 per cent for most vaccine preventable childhood illnesses.[4] So, in Malaysia, it is hard to justify privatisation of healthcare on the basis of it being a financial burden on the public purse (despite a 95 per cent subsidy), or on grounds of cost-efficiency.

IS THERE AN EFFICIENT PRIVATE SECTOR IN MALAYSIA?

It may be suggested that market forces in Malaysia were distorted by a lack of competitive tendering, such that if you left it to the free market without meddlesome government and political interference, the outcomes would have been far different. At an eighth APHM Health Conference in Kuala Lumpur (19–21 June 2000), the president of the Association of Private Hospitals of Malaysia (APHM) called for government intervention to restrict the number of private hospitals in the Kuala Lumpur (KL) metropolitan area, to overcome the glut of hospital beds resulting from a building frenzy over the last decade. It needs to be pointed out that this problem pre-dated the economic crisis, which began in 1997, although the crisis-related drop in demand exacerbated it. Until the late 1990s, there were as many MRI (magnetic resonance imaging) scanners in metropolitan KL as there were in the whole of Australia, and the APHM president was appealing for regulatory measures such as licensing approvals to limit the acquisition of expensive medical equipment by private hospitals (*The Sun*, 20 June 2000). Meanwhile, the Malaysian Society of Radiographers has publicly expressed its concern over the inadequately trained personnel hired by private hospitals to operate imaging equipment (*The Sun*, 28 May 2001). To minimise their losses from under-utilised, expensive equipment, private hospitals were also shifting the sunk costs on to patients' drug charges[5] and other inpatient services (*The Star*, 10 February 2001), while simultaneously trying to capture a larger share of the regional health tourism market (*The Star*, 9 May 2001). In early 2001, there were five cardiac catheterisation laboratories in the state of Penang, as against four in all of Singapore, a city-state with more than three times the population of Penang and a per capita income three times the Malaysian national average (1999 purchasing power parity).

In 1993, the Ministry of Health and the Academy of Medicine released the findings of a collaborative study on the utilisation of specialist medical services, which reported that:

> about 70 per cent of the patients managed by the public sector specialists and about 25 per cent of those managed by the private sector specialists were complex cases that required the expertise of a specialist ... This difference in the utilisation of specialist expertise is not unexpected. This is because in the present system, private specialists manage

mainly unscreened, walk-in patients whereas the public specialists manage mainly referred patients ... The under-utilisation of specialists in the private sector is most marked in obstetrics and gynaecology, and in paediatrics. (Suleiman et al. 1993)

The few systematic studies and investigative media reports together provide no evidence of a more efficient allocation of resources or superior cost-efficiency in the private healthcare sector.

Interestingly, there appears to be no monolithic attitude within the private sector towards government intervention and regulation, towards questions of market and state. It seems to depend on whether one is a would-be entrepreneur, or an existing enterprise wary of more competition and threats to market share. If anything, the recent track record of market-driven medicine is a salutary reminder of how the private sector can be terribly wrong in projecting market demand and business volumes, to the extent that they need to ask for government intervention to regulate the market, if not public subsidies and handouts to prevent its outright collapse. Noam Chomsky summed it up well: 'privatisation? that's "socialism" for the rich (i.e. corporate welfare and bailouts for cronies), market discipline for the poor' (Chomsky 1996).

This poor track record is not confined to Malaysia. The aggregate performance of the market-driven US healthcare sector is deplorable. Despite consuming 14 per cent of GDP (double the Western European/ Japanese average), it leaves 43 million residents without health insurance cover, including 10 million uninsured children (one in seven) (Children's Defense Fund 1997). Many more have inadequate cover for catastrophic illness. The USA has state-of-the-art medical technology, but its infant mortality rate in 1997 was exceeded only by Poland, Hungary, Mexico, Korea and Turkey among the twenty-nine OECD countries (OECD 2000). At the level of institutional performance, it has been shown that for-profit hospitals in the USA are 3–11 per cent more expensive than not-for-profit hospitals, that they spend more on overheads and administration while hiring fewer nurses, they provide less charity care, and provide patients with fewer hospital days (Woolhandler and Himmelstein 1999). A set of comparative case studies from the UK, the Netherlands, Sweden, Southern Europe (Greece, Italy, Portugal, Spain), Israel, New Zealand and Latin America (Argentina, Brazil, Chile, Ecuador) reveal how governments and institutions responded to pro-competition healthcare policies during the 1990s. Most began with enthusiasm and then drew back as they realised the danger of greater costs (rather than less), more inequality, dislocations and back-door reductions in coverage. The few that carried out competition reforms experienced a political backlash and defeat at the next election (Light 2001).

Public sector healthcare may not always outperform the private sector. The reverse, however, is demonstrably false, and to continue dismantling public healthcare out of an obsessive faith that market-based solutions will invariably deliver higher efficiency and lower unit costs is clearly unwarranted. It is, therefore, dismaying to note that influential agencies like the World Health Organisation grant undue concessions to neo-liberal policies even while acknowledging that not only do market-oriented approaches lead to intolerable inequity with respect to a fundamental human right, but growing bodies of theory and evidence indicate markets in healthcare to be inefficient as well (WHO 1999).

HEALTHCARE FINANCING: THE PRIVATISATION OF SOCIAL INSURANCE

Of late, the attention in Malaysia has shifted to reforms in healthcare financing. The official government stance for many years has been that corporatisation and privatisation of the public hospitals,[6] as mandated in the seventh Malaysia Plan,[7] would only proceed in parallel with the introduction of national health insurance. Since 1992, these corporatisation exercises, involving the National Heart Institute, University of Malaya Medical Centre, Hospital Universiti Sains Malaysia and Hospital Universiti Kebangsaan Malaysia have been accompanied by steadily rising patient charges. The public remains uneasy about the future status of the remaining Ministry of Health hospitals,[8] their anxiety not relieved by the Health Minister's conspicuous silence over the promised national health insurance scheme. On 3 March 2001 the Health Minister finally announced that a National Health Financing Authority (NHFA) would be established over the next five years, to oversee a national health financing scheme. No operational details were available, but the eighth Malaysia Plan (2001–2005) briefly notes that this would not preclude a continuing, complementary role for private health insurance. Most importantly, it was left ambiguous whether the national health financing scheme would allow those who preferred private health insurance to opt out.

Judging by the multitude of private medical insurance schemes that have emerged in the interim, it appears that the Malaysian government has adopted a de facto policy in healthcare financing which will rely heavily on a patchwork of profit-driven health insurance and managed care schemes as a supplement to the NHFA. Significantly, there has been no clear-cut statement from the Health Minister that the NHFA would not be privatised. In the meantime, the insurance industry, local as well as foreign, has been discreetly but systematically lobbying against proposals[9] for publicly-operated universal health insurance put forward by healthcare professionals[10] (Malaysian Medical Association 1999) and the lay public (Chan 2000). Foreign insurers (such as Prudential plc, UK) who brought in funds and acquired local equity during the East Asian currency crisis as a supportive (not altruistic) gesture to help stabilise a volatile financial situation,[11] are reportedly now looking forward to a business-friendly environment in which to develop markets for healthcare and other insurance products. For-profit managed care and health maintenance organisations, modern incarnations of the health insurance industry, have also emerged amid much recrimination from healthcare providers (*The Sun*, 25 September 2000; *The Star*, 14 April 2000). For the moment they are mostly locally-led initiatives, with foreigners waiting in the wings while the market is being tested.[12]

MANAGED CARE WRIT LARGE?

On 15 December 2000, *The Edge Daily* (online business journal) reported that Aetna-ING, one of the largest health insurers in Malaysia, had linked up with WorldCare Health (Malaysia) Sdn Bhd, the Malaysian subsidiary of US-based WorldCare Consortium. WorldCare Consortium is a leading international player in tele-medicine, operating a globally distributed referral network with links to the Johns Hopkins Medical Institutions, the London Clinic, Duke University Medical Center, Cleveland Clinic Foundation, Massachusetts General Hospital, Brigham and Women's Hospital (Boston), Spaulding Rehabilitation Center and the Dana-Farber Cancer Institute (Harvard Medical School), among others. This fusion of bulk purchasing power (insurers' patient pools) with electronic referrals (tele-consultations, tele-imaging and so on) to designated healthcare providers locally and globally – namely, an electronically-enabled feeder network for patient referrals for those who are enrolled in healthcare plans – is for-profit managed care in the making, globalised with the aid of information technologies. Affluent healthcare consumers would appreciate the easier access to state-of-the-art healthcare and consultations, but poorer patients faced with cutbacks in social supports and a deteriorating public sector would inevitably end up on the bottom rungs of a multi-tier system.

CONCLUSION

While the Malaysian case study has been presented in some detail, it is evident that this is merely one instance of a worldwide phenomenon. In the last decade, the California-based Academy for International Health Studies (AIHS) has emerged as a significant forum for multinational health industries, for business networking and market intelligence, and for setting industry-wide strategies and agenda. At its International Summit on the Private Health Sector (Miami) in December 2000, over 600 delegates from fifty-two countries and seventy international organisations – health plan chief executive officers and senior management teams, top-ranking government officials, medical equipment manufacturers, pharmaceutical research companies, informatics vendors, academicians and consultants, media analysts and international agencies – gathered to update themselves on 'market trends and global opportunities for healthcare companies, health plans, collaborating sickness funds, mutualities, medical schemes, private insurers and social security funds. Delegates were exposed to a wide variety of managed care and health policy expertise, partnership opportunities, speakers, technology, conferences, data, market research, educational programs and other goods and services of import to the global healthcare industry' (Buse and Walt 2000).

Set against this backdrop, healthcare privatisation in Malaysia emerges as an evolving, negotiated interaction between politically well-connected Malaysian entities, often in junior partnership with their foreign collaborators, who see vast business opportunities opening up with further receding of the state. It has little to do with burdensome public expenditures, cost-efficiency, client responsiveness or greater consumer satisfaction.

NOTES

Research funding from GESEAS (Goteborg–USM) and STINT (Uppsala–USM) collaborative projects and from the Sumitomo Foundation is gratefully acknowledged.

1. In a bizarre effort to reverse the negative impact of these infectious and environmental health threats on tourist arrivals, the Barisan National Legislative Assembly representative for Lukut proposed that Bukit Pelanduk (the southern

epicentre of the 1998–99 Nipah virus outbreak which claimed 105 lives) be promoted for its ghoulish potential to 'attract foreign tourists from the region, including
China, India and Japan (as well as) the US and Britain' (*The Star*, 4 September
2000).

2. Mohamed Isa, the Chief Minister of Negri Sembilan state, while launching
the ambitious Nilai Health Care Valley project, declared: 'we want to reverse the
process of Malaysians going overseas to seek advanced medical treatment. With
the setting up of the valley, we want foreigners to come here to seek treatment
instead. There is no reason why we cannot succeed because of the facilities available
here and the expertise to be brought in ... [the complex] ... will not only serve as
a magnet for patients in this region, but will also serve as a nucleus for new
business enterprises and offshore investment here' (*The Star*, 22 January 1994).

3. 'the [Malaysian] government is establishing a national welfare trust fund
[relying on philanthropic] contributions from individuals and private organizations
to finance healthcare and medical treatment costs for the poor' (*The Star*, 11 April
2000).

4. Childhood immunisation rates in 1999 were 100 per cent for BCG, 94.1 per
cent for DPT (third dose), 91.1 per cent for hepatitis B, 93.4 per cent for polio and
86.2 per cent for measles. Malaysia was declared to be polio-free in October 2000
(eighth Malaysia Plan, Economic Planning Unit, Prime Minister's Department
2001).

5. The Consumers' Association of Penang reported that drug prices at private
hospital pharmacies were up to 55 per cent higher (on average 29 per cent higher)
than at free-standing private pharmacies (*Utusan Konsumer*, February 2001).

6. In the Malaysian context, 'corporatisation' refers to a change in status of a
governmental department to a free-standing corporate entity, with substantial
operational and financial autonomy (an example is the National Heart Institute).
'Privatisation' covers a range of scenarios, including contracting out to private
sector concessionaires, build-operate-transfer, build and transfer, management buy-
out, conversion to publicly listed companies in which the government may still be
the substantial or majority shareholder (examples are Tenaga Nasional Bhd and
Telekom Malaysia Bhd). Public anxiety over corporatisation derives from fears
that it is a wayside station along the route to fully privatised social services and
utilities. (For an extended discussion see Jomo 1995.)

7. 'To increase the efficiency of services and to retain qualified and experienced
manpower (in the public sector), the corporatisation and privatisations of hospitals
as well as medical services will be undertaken during the Plan period. The government will gradually reduce its role in the provision of health services and increase
its regulatory and enforcement functions. A health financing scheme to meet
healthcare costs will also be implemented. However, for the low-income group,
access to health services will be assured through assistance from the government'
(Economic Planning Unit 1996). The Malaysian 7th Plan (1996–2000), Econonomic
Planning Unit, Prime Minister's Department.

8. With firm support from organised labour, a mass campaign coordinated by
the Citizen's Health Initiative managed to force a moratorium on the pending
corporatisation of the remaining public hospitals. In less than two weeks of

mobilisation, in July 1999, the Malaysian Trade Union Congress (MTUC) delivered 10,000 signatures from union members to the Health Minister, demanding a halt to the corporatisation of public hospitals and a review of the privatisation of ancillary services. The various state branches of the FELDA Employees Union were among the most active in this effort, and played a key role in disseminating these concerns to the rural hinterlands as well. This temporary victory was well received by the Malaysian public, but was also perceived as pre-election expediency in the run-up to the November 1999 general elections, a sad testimony to the widespread cynicism then prevailing.

9. Malaysian Medical Association National Health Care Plan, prepared for the second National Economic Consultative Council (MAPEN II) 2000.

10. Resolution from the Primary Care Doctors Organisation of Malaysia (PCDOM) public forum on 'Financing for Healthcare: How will it affect you?' (21 May 2000, Univeristi Malaya) www2.jarring.my/pcdom/finance.htm

11. Prudential Plc (UK), hitherto a minority shareholder in Berjaya-Prudential, made major inroads into the financially troubled joint venture during the East Asian currency crisis. In return for raising its equity to 51 per cent in the joint venture, it won major concessions allowing it to market investment-linked insurance products, a privilege so far restricted to local insurers. This paved the way for other foreign insurers to negotiate for wide-ranging concessions as well. The implications of these developments for healthcare financing and national health insurance bear watching. Prudential has recently entered the market for healthcare insurance.

12. Telekom Malaysia Bhd, one of the largest private sector employers in Malaysia, signed up with Pantai Medicare Sdn Bhd, an HMO/managed care subsidiary of the Pantai Holdings Bhd healthcare conglomerate, for management of health benefits of Telekom staff and their dependants. The CEO of Pantai indicated that the HMO was in advanced negotiations with ten other companies and aimed to enrol 200,000 members by the year-end (*The Edge Online*, 20 October 2000).

REFERENCES

Buse, K. and Walt, G. (2000) 'Global public–private partnerships: part I – a new development in health?', *Bulletin of the World Health Organization*, 78 (4), 549–61.

Chan, C. K. (1997) 'Health and Development towards the millennium: reinventing the government, or the demise of community?', Paper presented at the USM-MMA-CAP National Conference on 'Privatisation and Healthcare Financing in Malaysia: Emerging Issues and Concerns', 5–6 April, Univeristi Sains Malaysia.

— (2000) 'Towards a citizens' proposal for health care reforms', *Ekonomika*, 12 (3), 10–12.

Chan, C. K., Noorul, A. M. and Dzulkifli, A. (2000) 'A sunrise industry: the emergence of investor-led, corporate healthcare', Paper presented at the National Seminar on 'Health and Health Care in Changing Environments: the Malaysian Experience', 22–23 April, Kuala Lumpur.

Children's Defense Fund (1997) Child Health Fact Sheet (17 January), Washington, DC: Children's Defense Fund.

Chomsky, N. (1996) 'Free market fantasies: capitalism in the real world', San Francisco: AK Press Audio (CD recording, 13 April).

Economic Planning Unit (1996) *Seventh Malaysia Plan*, Kuala Lumpur: Prime Minister's Department.

Heller, P. S. (1982) 'A model of the demand for medical and health services in Peninsular Malaysia', *Social Science and Medicine*, 16, 267–84.

Ibrahim, M. I., Zubaidah, C. E. and Dzulkifli, A. (1997) 'Drug distribution systems in Malaysia: the privatization of the General Medical Store', Paper presented at the National Conference on 'Privatisation and Healthcare Financing in Malaysia', 5–6 April, Penang: Universiti Sains Malaysia.

Jomo, K. S. (1995) *Privatising Malaysia: Rents, Rhetoric, Realities*, Boulder, CO: Westview Press.

Light, D. (2001) 'Comparative studies of competition policy', *Social Science and Medicine*, Special Issue on Comparative Studies of Competition Policy, 52 (8).

Malaysian Medical Association (1999) *Health for All: Reforming Health Care in Malaysia*, Kuala Lumpur: MMA.

OECD (2000) www.oecd.org/publications/figures/2000/english/Health status. pdf

Price, D., Pollock, A. and Shaoul, J. (1999) 'How the World Trade Organisation is shaping domestic policies in healthcare', *The Lancet*, 354 (27), 1889–92.

Suleiman, A. B., Wong, S. L., Jai Mohan, A., et al. (1993) *Utilisation of Specialist Medical Manpower*, Report of a collaborative study by the Ministry of Health and the Academy of Medicine, 1992–93, Kuala Lumpur: Ministry of Health.

WHO (1999) *World Health Report 1999*, Geneva: WHO.

Woolhandler, S. and Himmelstein, D. (1999)'When money is the mission – the high costs of investor-owned health care', *New England Journal of Medicine*, 341 (6), 444–6.

Zainab, A. K. (1996) 'Policies and objectives under the Seventh Malaysia Plan', paper presented at the APHM National Health Care Conference, Kuala Lumpur.

CHAPTER 15

Implementing Universal Healthcare Coverage in Thailand

SANGUANN NITAYARUMPHONG

SUPASIT PANNARUNOTHAI

Thailand is a constitutional monarchy with a population of 62 million in 2000. Its population size is similar to that of the United Kingdom (1991), yet the population density is one-half that of the UK. It has seventy-six provinces including Bangkok, with 31 per cent of the population living in urban areas.

Thailand's economic growth in the last few decades has been remarkable, with the average of 8 per cent per year up to 1996. This has allowed the country to achieve much higher per capita incomes than other countries in the region. Even though its macro-economic policies have promoted high rates of economic growth, its policies and interventions to improve the status of the poor have been uneven. This spectacular economic growth has allowed Thailand to examine the quality of the growth. As the country's economy strengthens, both income disparities and inequalities within the healthcare system have become more obvious. Health resources of all kinds – personnel, facilities and medical technology, for example – remain concentrated in Bangkok and other large cities.

Thailand was the first country to be affected by the economic crisis in Asia in July of 1997. Its relatively late start in developing social security systems means that a large proportion of the population suffered as a result of not having adequate access to healthcare. The recent economic downturn also seems to have placed policy measures aimed at addressing those inequalities on hold.

This chapter considers the background to Thailand's healthcare system, the existing health benefits coverage, and provides information on health-related inequalities, in order to show an overview of the current situation in Thailand. It suggests that, given the current situation of growing inequalities in access to healthcare, Thailand should work towards universal coverage, outlining a plan of how such a policy might be financed. It will also show how, by providing a specified basic health package, the country would be able to assure the quality of the services provided to a larger group of the population.

THE HEALTHCARE SYSTEM

It has been Thai government policy for many years to extend health services to remote areas, especially during the era of Health for All (since 1983). Table 15.1 shows that between 1979 and 1995 the population per bed ratio increased from 1:752 to 1:501. However, the relative distribution did not change when comparing the discrepancy between Bangkok and the poorest region in the north-east. The explanation for this is that although the government may intervene by expanding public hospital bed capacity in the poorest areas, the private sector does not expand where people are unable to pay for care and instead increases capacity in the richer areas, notably Bangkok alone (Table 15.2). Between

TABLE 15.1 Number of hospital beds (and population to bed ratio) by region, 1979–95

Region	1979	1983	1987	1991	1995
Bangkok	14,585	18,486	24,376	21,704	25,226
	(337)	(310)	(257)	(257)	(221)
Central	17,481	21,954	24,628	25,519	34,248
	(543)	(454)	(483)	(507)	(395)
North	9,917	12,751	14,252	16,181	20,943
	(980)	(797)	(756)	(682)	(568)
South	8,515	10,258	11,153	11,888	14,449
	(665)	(596)	(659)	(603)	(530)
North-east	10,776	14,989	15,887	18,560	23,541
	(1,511)	(1,167)	(1,208)	(1,075)	(875)
Bangkok: North-east	1:4.5	1:3.8	1:4.7	1:4.2	1:4.3
Total	61,274	78,438	87,554	93,852	118,417
	(752)	(631)	(633)	(604)	(501)

Note: The figures in brackets are the population to bed ratios.
Source: Report on Health Resources, Bureau of Health Policy and Plan, Ministry of Public Health (1996)

1970 and 1988 the proportion of private hospitals rose and this is a result
of a rapid increase in the number of large hospitals, consistent with the
economic boom of the past decade.

The growth of such private hospitals has encouraged doctors to stay
in urban areas (Nitayarumphong and Tangcharoensathien 1994). Hospital beds serve as the basis for other health resources to accumulate.
However, the distribution of health personnel varies in accordance with
the number of beds. There are more doctors in Bangkok; thus each
doctor looks after only half the number of inpatients that doctors in the
provinces look after, sharing a skewed distribution of health resources
(see Table 15.3).

THE COVERAGE OF HEALTH BENEFIT

The first national survey on health benefit coverage was carried out
at the household level by the National Statistical Office in 1991. At that
time, only one-third of the population was covered by any kind of
health benefit schemes. The total coverage rates were no different among

TABLE 15.2 Number and proportion of hospital beds by sector, 1979–97

Year	Ministry of Public Health	Other ministries	State enter-prises	Local adm. agencies	Private sector	Total
1979	44,964 (66.0)	14,672 (21.5)	843 (1.2)	1,387 (2.0)	6,210 (9.1)	68,076
1985	53,286 (69.5)	13,773 (17.0)	951 (1.2)	1,687 (2.1)	8,275 (10.2)	80,972
1989	58,927 (65.5)	17,118 (19.0)	2,335 (2.6)	2,057 (2.3)	9,545 (10.6)	89,982
1993	65,558 (64.8)	15,784 (15.6)	2,229 (2.2)	2,232 (2.2)	15,363 (15.2)	101,166
1995	73,191 (61.8)	15,430 (13.0)	365 (0.3)	2,165 (1.8)	27,266 (23.1)	118,417
1997	79,818 (60.3)	18,074 (13.6)	2,360 (1.8)	2,208 (1.7)	29,945 (22.6)	132,405

Notes: The figures for the private sector might be 10 per cent lower than reality.
The 1985 data is incomplete, so the 1984 data is used instead.

Source: *Health in Thailand*, Ministry of Public Health, 1995–96

people in urban and rural areas, but the types of benefits differed (see Table 15.4). The main benefit scheme for urban people was the Civil Servant Medical Benefit Scheme (CSMBS), but the main protection for rural people was provided by the low income and public welfare schemes (NSO 1993). Additional protection in rural areas was provided by the health card scheme, acting as an insurance scheme. In 1993 (two years after the enactment of the Social Security Act) only 7 per cent of the population were protected by the compulsory insurance scheme.

The government's policy of expanding health benefit coverage has grown to cover elderly people and children up to twelve years of age. According to the Health Insurance Office of the Ministry of Public Health, 1995 saw the highest coverage rate of 72 per cent of the population, as the result of targeting 44 per cent of the population under the low income and public welfare schemes. The second national survey on health benefit coverage in 1996 revealed that the coverage was not as high as the MoPH's figures, after adjusting for the public welfare coverage which provides benefit to the aged and children under twelve years. By 1996, the coverage rates were different in urban and rural

TABLE 15.3 Number of doctors (and population to doctor ratio) by region, 1979–95

Region	1979	1985	1989	1993	1995
Bangkok	4,069	3,917	5,888	6,191	5,582
	(1,210)	(1,512)	(1,063)	(905)	(999)
Central	1,814	1,444	2,008	2,499	3,309
	(11,652)	(7,010)	(5,920)	(5,224)	(4,042)
North	741	777	2,021	1,822	2,037
	(13,112)	(13,269)	(5,331)	(6,243)	(5,824)
South	362	786	1,165	1,274	1,369
	(15,641)	(7,822)	(6,306)	(5,737)	(5,510)
North-east	633	1,134	1,631	1,848	1,884
	(25,716)	(15,709)	(11,762)	(10,848)	(10,805)
Bangkok: North-east	1:21	1:10	1:11	1:12	1:11
Total	6,619	8,058	12,713	13,634	14,181
	(6,956)	(6,254)	(4,361)	(4,207)	(4,180)

Notes: The figures here are population per one doctor.

Source: *Report on Health Resources*, Bureau of Health Policy and Plan, Minstry of Public Health (1995–96)

TABLE 15.4 Health benefit coverage (% of total population), 1991–97

| Schemes | 1991 | | | 1993 | 1995 | 1996 | | | 1997 |
	Total	Urban	Rural	Total	Total	Total	Urban	Rural	Total
CSMBS and state enterprise	10	23	7	11	11	10	18	8	11
Social security	*	*	*	7	7	6	13	4	7
Low income and public welfare	17	2	20	27	44	30	19	32	41
Health Card scheme	2	0	2	5	8	15	2	19	9**
Private employee benefits	2	7	1	na	na	–	–	–	na
Private insurance and others	1	0	1	1	2	2	3	2	na
Not covered	68	68	68	49	28	37	45	35	32
Total	100	100	100	100	100	100	100	100	100

Notes: * The social security scheme was established in 1991.   ** In 1997, the Health Insurance Office reported that 16 per cent of the population purchased the card.   na: not available or not taken into account.

Sources: 1991 – NSO (1993); 1993 – Pannarunothai and Tangcharoensathien (1993); 1995 – Health Insurance Office (MoPH 1995); 1996 – adapted from NSO (1998); 1997 – Budget Bureau (1997) calculations at the beginning of the year for budget allocation areas. High coverage of the low income and public welfare schemes and the voluntary health card among rural people made the total coverage in rural areas 10 per cent higher than in urban areas, even though the urban population was protected by better schemes such as the CSMBS and the social security scheme.

However, the Budget Bureau argued that many people were counted twice; after removing this double-counting, the Budget Bureau accepted that, in 1997, the public welfare schemes would cover 41 per cent of the total population. This caused a slight drop in the coverage rate in 1997, but if the latest figures of the Health Insurance Office were taken into account, 16 per cent of the population bought Health Cards (confirmed by the NSO survey in 1996). This would mean that by 1977 only about 25 per cent of the population was not covered by any health benefit schemes.

In terms of ambulatory care, the MoPH has successfully expanded health centres and community hospitals to all villages and districts. Visits to health centres, for example, increased by 23 per cent per year from 1977 to 1985, and 26 per cent per year from 1985 to 1995, while the visits to community hospitals increased faster in the first period (35 per cent per year) and then slowed down to 15 per cent per year. This increased the share of ambulatory visits made by rural people to health centres and district hospitals from 54 per cent of the total visits at all public health services outside Bangkok in 1977 to 81 per cent in 1998 (Bureau of Health Policy and Planning 1997) (see Table 15.5).

TABLE 15.5 Proportion of outpatients at various levels of health facilities, 1977–98 (percentages)

Date	Health centres	District hospitals	Community hospitals
1977	5.5 (46.2)	2.9 (24.4)	3.5 (29.4)
1981	7.5 (33.1)	6.0 (26.4)	9.2 (40.5)
1985	10.0 (32.4)	11.1 (35.9)	9.8 (31.7)
1989	10.9 (27.7)	12.9 (32.8)	15.5 (39.4)
1993	12.0 (21.2)	21.1 (37.2)	23.6 (41.6)
1995	14.6 (20.0)	26.1 (35.7)	32.4 (44.3)
1996	15.5 (19.6)	28.0 (35.5)	35.4 (44.9)
1997	12.0 (21.2)	21.1 (37.2)	41.5 (47.2)
1998	14.6 (20.0)	33.9 (35.1)	44.5 (46.1)

Source: National Statistical Office (1998)

TABLE 15.6 Benefit schemes and their characteristics

Scheme characteristics	Low income & public welfare	CSMBS	SSS	WCS	Health Card	Private insurance
Benefit package						
Ambulatory services	Only public designated	Public only	Public & private	Public & private	Public (MoPH)	Public & private
Inpatient services	Public only	Public & private	Public & private	Public & private	Public (MoPH)	Public & private
Choice of provider	Referral line	Free	Contractual basis	Free	Referral line	Free
Cash benefits	No	No	Yes	Yes	No	Usually no
Inclusive conditions	All	All	Non-work-related illness, injuries, except 15 conditions	Work-related illness and injuries	All	As stated in the contracts
Maternity benefit	Yes	Yes	Yes	No	Yes	Varies
Annual physical checkup	No	Yes	No	No	Possible	Varies
Promotion and prevention	Very limited	Yes	Health education and immunisation	No	Possible	Varies
Services not covered	Private bed, special nurse, eye glasses	Special nurse	Private bed, special nurse	No	Private bed	Varies

Financing

Source of funds	General tax	General tax	Tripartite contributions, 1.5 per cent of payroll	Employer, 0.2–2 per cent of payroll with experience rating	Household purchase 500 baht + tax subsidy 500	Premium
Financing body	MoPH	Ministry of Finance	Ministry of Labour	Ministry of Labour	MoPH	Competitive companies
Payment mechanism	Global budget	Fee-for-service reimburse	Prospective capitation	Fee-for-service reimburse	Limited fee-for-service	Fee-for-service reimburse
Co-payment	No	Yes, for IP at private hospital	Maternity and emergency services	Yes, if beyond the ceiling of 30,000 baht	No	Almost none

CSMBS: Civil Servants Benefits Scheme
SSS: Social Security Scheme
WCS: Workmen's Compensation Scheme

Sources: Pannarunothai and Tangcharoensathien (1993); Supachutikul (1996); Tangcharoensathien and Supachutikul (1997)

HEALTH-RELATED INEQUALITIES

Different health benefit schemes have tended to target different groups of the population and provide different benefit packages (see Table 15.6). The low income and public welfare schemes provide free care at public designated facilities for nearly all conditions, with no co-payment. The CSMBS, the fringe benefit for civil servants and their dependants, provides greater choice of health facilities with access to inpatient services at private hospitals and with some co-payments for treatments in private hospitals, although not in public hospitals. The Social Security Scheme (SSS), comprehensive compulsory health insurance, limits the choice of healthcare to a contracted hospital (public or private) with no co-payments, while the Workmen's Compensation Scheme (WCS), a work-related compulsory insurance scheme, provides better access, but with co-payments (if the total charge is higher than the set ceiling). The Health Card (HC), a voluntary scheme managed by the MoPH, provides access only to MoPH facilities with referral networks, has no co-payments and targets vulnerable groups.

TABLE 15.7 Financing and per capita expenditure on selected health benefit schemes, 1999

Schemes	Private contributions (million baht)	Government budget (million baht)	Expenditure per capita (baht)	Dis-crepancy index*
Public welfare, low income, elderly (1999)	0	4,143.1	244	1.0
Primary school (1995)	0	161.1	>30	0.1
Fringe benefit, CSMBS (1994)	0	9,954.0	~2,000	8.2
Compulsory insurance, SSS (1993)	5,553.5	3,803.7	1,060	4.3
WCS (1993)	921.4	0	96.1	0.4
Voluntary insurance, Health Card (1994)	807.4	400	446	1.8

Note: * ratio between expenditure per capita of each scheme and the low income scheme.

Sources: adapted from Supachutikul (1996) and Office of Health Insurance, Ministry of Public Health (1999)

Table 15.7 shows varied levels of inequality in terms of health expenditure per capita among selected health benefit schemes. The low income scheme is financed by an annual global budget with no co-payment at the point of delivery; in 1995, it was estimated that the expenditure for the low income scheme was at least 225 baht per capita. The SSS is financed by tripartite contributions to the Social Security Fund for other benefits including health. The expenditure per capita for health in 1993 was approximately 712 baht (or three times higher than the expenditure of the low income scheme even though different years were compared). The most privileged group in terms of expenditure per capita was the CSMBS because the discrepancy index was a factor of 8 (Supachutikul 1996) (see Table 15.7).

Unequal benefits set by different insurers produce inequality in healthcare utilisation; in particular, the 'not covered group' has only half the hospitalisation rates of other health benefit groups in a study of a large urban area (Pannarunothai and Mills 1997a). Health benefit schemes as a whole served as an invaluable tool in influencing self-reported health status and the probability of hospitalisation of an individual. Furthermore, the 'not covered group' tended to be poorer, paid for healthcare out-of-pocket and at a higher percentage of household income than the covered groups (Pannarunothai and Mills 1997a). Recent studies confirm that the Thai healthcare system is not an equitable one: in terms of the Kakwani index, it is suggested that the financing system for healthcare is regressive to income (Rehnberg and Pannarunothai 1998), and in terms of the concentration index, the health delivery system clearly favours the rich.

Such evidence has raised more awareness among policy-makers and the Budget Bureau of the inequalities that exist within the Thai healthcare system. One way of dealing with this problem and with the long term in view, is to move towards a universally accessible healthcare system and the restructuring of existing mechanisms for payment. The larger question, however, is should the system be financed by general taxation or by the amalgamation of existing insurance systems?

POLICY ON UNIVERSAL COVERAGE

Since Thailand has already achieved a certain level of coverage of healthcare for the majority of the population, a policy aiming for universal coverage has been greatly welcomed and is currently under consideration to formulate an explicit strategy for implementation. One approach, learned from international experiences, is to provide legal backing. The National Health Insurance Act has been drafted and is being scrutinised by many parties, including political and government bodies as well as NGOs.

The timetable for implementing universal coverage   The time-frame for achieving universal coverage of healthcare was stated as policy by the present government. The initial plan had acknowledged that this could happen by the end of 2001. Since the economic crisis is used as the opportunity to upgrade the Thai healthcare system, the policy on universal coverage is combined with the objective of achieving equity, despite constraints on resources by improving the efficiency of the system.

Single or multiple organisations   There are two options for expanding health coverage to all: the first is to set up a National Health Security Fund as a single agency to manage the universal coverage policy; the second is to set up a National Commission on Health Security to coordinate the policy of universal coverage through multiple health insurance organisations (Pannarunothai and Tangcharoensathien 1993; Nitayarumphong 1996).

Setting up the National Health Security Fund requires radical reforms of all health benefit schemes, to be managed under a single agency. Funds from existing schemes would be pooled; in addition to new tax-

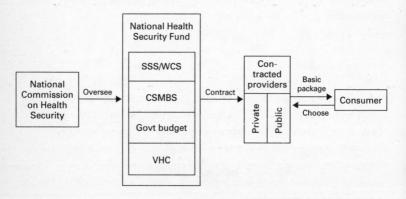

SSS = Social Security Scheme   WCS = Workmen's Compensation Scheme
CSMBS = Civil Servant Medical Benefit Scheme   VHC = Voluntary Health Card Scheme

FIGURE 15.1 National Health Security Fund, Thailand

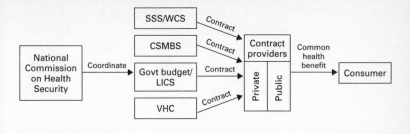

SSS = Social Security Scheme
CSMBS = Civil Servant Medical Benefit Scheme

WCS = Workmen's Compensation Scheme
VHC = Voluntary Health Card Scheme

FIGURE 15.2 National Commission on Health Security, Thailand

raising schemes, e.g. general taxes, taxes earmarked for health from cigarettes, tobacco, etc. Under this option, all citizens would have a right to choose their contracted health facility which would be accessible and would provide the specified essential health package. If they required anything not included in the package, they would have to pay for the service themselves or through a private insurance scheme. This option could equalise benefits to all citizens (see Figure 15.1), and act progressively.

The alternative to the radical reform, the National Commission on Health Security, is proposed as a coordinating body to bridge the gaps between existing health benefit schemes. This national commission would advise the government on expanding health coverage to the unprotected groups. Management of each scheme would be maintained (see Figure 15.2).

FINANCING OF UNIVERSAL COVERAGE

There is no answer as yet on how the proposed universal coverage might be financed. It is most likely to be financed by insurance contributions from those who are above the poverty line, with exemptions for those who need public assistance such as elderly people, children under twelve years old, and people with disabilities. Co-payments would be an additional source of finance raised from certain kinds of services and from the bypassing of the referral line. Details on premium contributions and co-payments have to be carefully designed; several studies are being conducted to shed light on these areas. In principle, universal coverage should be accomplished through a mix of financing sources:

general taxation, compulsory insurance and co-payment at the point of delivery. This section discusses the main possible sources of finance based on studies and recent policy developments. The following section discusses the different potential sources of finance for a new, universally funded scheme.

Arguments for a tax-financed healthcare system The trend in health benefit coverage in Table 15.1 shows that only the low income and public welfare schemes have significantly expanded the coverage of the population. The CSMBS has been faced with cost containment problems and the number of civil servants has been kept constant for years as part of civil service reforms. The SSS is expected to decrease in size if the economy worsens because workers become unemployed. The Health Card scheme, a MoPH-run voluntary health insurance scheme, has increased its popularity in recent years because of strong publicity and public relations. However, it cannot reach high coverage in many provinces, and thus puts MoPH health personnel under pressure to sell the cards each year to voluntary subscribers. On the other hand, sound policy discussions between the MoPH and the Budget Bureau on public subsidy to support equity and efficiency objectives in healthcare financing have significantly increased the budget for the low income and public welfare schemes.

A study by Pannarunothai and Wongkanaratanakul (1997) estimated a burden on the government budget (if the 'not covered group' were put under the same benefit packages as the public welfare schemes with co-payment) of 5–20 per cent of total charges. This policy had cost the government between 44 and 79 billion baht in 1995, while the total government health budgets in all ministries for all activities were already 46 billion baht. However, all the estimates on healthcare financing have to be scrutinised because the latest study on national health accounts (by Laixuthai et al. 1997) has not approved the plans for the financing of health services in Thailand.

The previous projection by the National Economic and Social Development Board (NESDB) of 1991 national per capita expenditure was 40 per cent too high and the public share was higher than had been thought: the public share was 49 per cent, up from the previous estimate of 25 per cent (Laixuthai et al. 1997). Therefore, new estimates support the position that the government can be the major purchaser of healthcare for its population with only marginal investment, but through drastic health sector reforms.

Arguments for retaining the existing insurance schemes   As Thailand has had to comply with the 'bail-out' package of the International Monetary Fund (IMF) known as structural adjustment, a major condition of this is to control public spending at a level no higher than government income. However, many believe that existing sources of finance for healthcare, despite the conditions, should not be abandoned. Each year, at least 3 per cent of public health spending comes from the SSS. Moreover, the SSS is operating with a surplus: its fund has accumulated over 50 billion baht. Hence, its stability is maintained, as it is a compulsory scheme.

The government voluntary insurance scheme, the Health Card, on the other hand, is operating a negative balance and even though it has received a matching subsidy from general taxation for each card sold, the actual expenditure per card was almost double the income of the scheme (revenue plus subsidy). This may be the result of adverse selection of the card subscribers and the price not indexed to inflation. However, the revenue raised in 1997 of one billion baht (about 20 per cent of the low income budget in 1997) may be significant enough that the MoPH would not want to lose it.

Community-based funds for health insurance   A few community-based funds, operating at village level and making a surplus from giving loans to members, have moved to provide health benefits for their members. An example of a community-based fund in the south of Thailand has operated for over a decade: the accumulated fund is over 50 million baht. The fund started to provide health benefits three years ago for reimbursing a part of medical bills at public health facilities and the proportion of reimbursement to the total charges has increased each year. The community considers this community welfare scheme comparable to the welfare that the government provides to civil servants and can be one mechanism to raise premiums from people in the informal sector in rural areas. It is, however, very difficult to generalise this to other communities on a voluntary basis.

Introducing co-payment at an affordable level   Approximately 20 per cent of the expenditure of government hospitals is financed by user fees at the point of delivery (Pannarunothai et al. 1994; Pannarunothai and Mills 1998). Many health benefit schemes provide exemptions from user fees, so the 'not covered' group have to pay higher fees which are regressive to income (Rehnberg and Pannarunothai 1998). However, the universal coverage policy will change this pattern and will certainly face resistance. The CSMBS is introducing co-payment for fees on private room and board if stays in public hospitals are lengthy (Tangcharoensathien 1997), even though there are debates about this.

PROVISION OF SERVICES AND PAYMENT OF PROVIDERS

According to the National Health Insurance Act, a comprehensive healthcare package will be made available. Family physicians will be assigned to every family member to make healthcare accessible to all. Healthcare providers must include both public and private sectors, and the public sector should not be limited to the MoPH only. The SSS has been successful in cost containment because the SSS contracts with both public and private hospitals on a pre-paid capitation basis. In areas where there are many public and private hospitals, competition among them to get a higher number of contracted workers is claimed to ensure that hospitals provide high satisfaction to consumers.

As far as the cost of care is concerned, private ambulatory services appear to be less expensive than public facilities, especially in urban areas (Pannarunothai and Mills 1997b), and some diagnostic related groups (DRGs) are treated less expensively in private hospitals than in public hospitals in terms of total costs (Kunaratanapruk et al. 1996). Competition among private hospitals, especially in Bangkok, tends to drive costs up because of information asymmetry between consumers and providers and weak regulation by the MoPH (Bennett 1997), yet policy implications can be drawn that public and private hospitals should put less emphasis on providing ambulatory care; at the same time hospitalisation should be paid for on a case-mix basis, and where possible with a global budget cap, to regulate prices and contain costs. The package for medium-term reform of the CSMBS contains two strong components of paying for ambulatory care on a capitation basis and paying for hospital care on a case-mix basis with a budget cap. Consumers would have to co-pay for both ambulatory and hospital care (Tangcharoensathien 1997). However, the private sector will argue for different co-payment rates for different 'perceived' quality.

The relationship between purchasers and providers Under the new arrangements, the likely purchasers of healthcare are the Civil Servants' Health Fund, the Social Security Fund, the Fund for the Low Income, the Public Welfare Groups and the Budget Bureau. These purchasers would contract for comprehensive health services with public or/and private health networks according to consumers' choices. People would have the right to choose their family physicians, and family physicians from the network would provide comprehensive health services for their registered population. Family physicians would refer cases to hospitals (both public and private) if they could not handle those cases and would pay the hospitals on the patients' behalf.

Specifying and assuring benefits   Guaranteeing complete access to the specified benefit packages is not an easy task. Strong financing mechanisms have to be made to realign resources in Bangkok and urban centres to rural areas. The resource allocation mechanism will be used to ration limited resources to only cost-effective services by putting these services into the resource allocation formula to the provinces. However, people would have to face higher co-payment if the referral line is not followed.

Quality assurance is a vital mechanism to achieve the aspirations of good health at reasonable cost. The SSS has implemented a hospital accreditation process with the contracted hospitals and this activity has raised awareness among health providers because those who get certification of good quality may be exempted from the annual accreditation procedure while the borderline providers have to be accredited every year (Chayasrivong 1997). Ongoing developments in total quality management (TQM), hospital accreditation and clinical audit, both internal and external to hospitals, are intended to improve the quality of care in both public and private sectors. These developments support the provision of health security to citizens (Health Systems Research Institute 1996).

CONCLUSION

This chapter has reviewed the key issues facing the Thai government in its attempts to move towards universal coverage. However, legislation is only one approach to providing effective universal coverage. Key questions remain about how it is to be achieved and how much it will cost to finance this policy and whether it is feasible under the current economic crisis. The implementation of a law is a difficult task as the country has to decide on politically and economically sensitive issues: for example, why should all the non-poor use healthcare without any payment, or what should be included in the basic essential health pack-ages? Mixed sources of finance are possibly the most feasible solution with support from the public welfare scheme coupled with a small share of co-payments. But there needs to be a committee at the national level to put this policy into practice. It is envisaged that this committee would be the purchaser of healthcare for all citizens by making contracts with networks of healthcare providers. Family physicians and hospitals would thus act as providers winning different contracts (family physicians would win a capitation contract for providing comprehensive ambu-latory care) and hospitals would get contracts for referral cases or hospitalisations.

The Thai healthcare system has for some time faced equity problems that have meant that it cannot deliver satisfactory care to all citizens regardless of socio-economic status. About one-third of the population remains unprotected by any health benefit schemes and the share of the population without cover is higher in urban areas. Universal coverage, in this view, is both a means and an end to reduce inequalities in health and in access to the use of services.

REFERENCES

Bennett S. (1997) 'The nature of competition among private hospitals in Bangkok', in S. Bennett, B. McPake and A. Mills (eds), *Private Health Providers in Developing Countries. Serving the Public Interest?*, London: Zed Books.

Chayasrivong, S. (1997) 'Guidelines to oversee hospital accreditation activities of the Social Security Scheme. An interview', *Health Systems Research Journal*, 5 (1), 29–33.

Health Systems Research Institute (1996) *Hospital Standards. Guidelines for Patient-based Quality*, Nonthaburi: HSRI.

Kunaratanapruk, S., Pannarunothai, S., Wongkanaratanakul, P. et al. (1996) *Medical Care Price Schedule for Road Traffic Accidents. The Accident DRG*, Research report to the Health Systems Research Institute, Nonthaburi.

Laixuthai, A., Tangcharoensathien, V., Prachuabmoh-Ruffolo, W. et al. (1997) *National Health Account in Thailand* (2537BE), Nonthaburi: Health Systems Research Institute.

Nitayarumphong, S. (1996) *Health Care Reform*, Nonthaburi: Office of Health Care Reform, Ministry of Public Health.

Nitayarumphong, S. and Tangcharoensathien V. (1994) 'Thailand: private health-care out of control?', *Health Policy and Planning*, 9 (1): 31–40.

NSO (National Statistical Office) (1993) *Report of the Health and Welfare Survey 1991*, Bangkok: NSO.

— (1998) *Report of the Health and Welfare Survey 1996*, Bangkok: NSO.

Pannarunothai, S. (1996) 'Public and private mix in health care: case of Thailand', in R. Haas, S. Mahbob and S. Y. Tham (eds), *Health Care Planning & Development* (Conference Proceedings), Kuala Lumpur: Malaysian Institute of Economic Research.

Pannarunothai, S. and Mills, A. (1997a) 'The poor pay more: health-related inequity in Thailand', *Social Science and Medicine*, 44 (12), 1781–90.

— (1997b) 'Characteristics of public and private healthcare providers in a Thai urban setting', in S. Bennett, B. McPake and A. Mills (eds), *Private Health Providers in Developing Countries, Serving the Public Interest?*, London: Zed Books.

— (1998) 'Researching the public and private mix in healthcare in a Thai urban area: Methodological approaches', *Health Policy and Planning*, 13 (3), 234–48.

Pannarunothai, S. and Rehnberg, C. (1998) *Inequity of Healthcare Delivery in Thailand*, Research report to the Swedish–Thai Collaboration in Health System Development (unpublished).

Pannarunothai, S. and Tangcharoensathien, V. (1993) 'Health financing reforms in Thailand', Paper presented at the Workshop on Health Financing in Thailand, Petchaburi, Thailand, 12–13 November.

Pannarunothai, S. and Wongkanaratanakul, P. (1997) *Estimation of the cost of basic essential health package for Thailand by using current health expenditure for the low income and other underprivileged groups* (HSRI research report), Nonthaburi: Health Systems Research Institute.

Pannarunothai, S., Tangcharoensathien, V., Khongsawatt, S. and Tantigate, N. (1994) *Government Hospital Financing in Thailand*, Nonthaburi: Ministry of Public Health.

Rehnberg, C. and Pannarunothai, S. (1998) *Inequity of Healthcare Financing in Thailand*, Research report to the Swedish–Thai Collaboration in Health System Development, Nonthaburi.

Supachutikul, A. (1996) *Situation Analysis on Health Insurance and Future Development*, Bangkok: Thailand Health Research Institute.

Tangcharoensathien, V. (1997) *The Reform of Civil Servant Medical Benefit Scheme*, Nonthaburi: Health Systems Research Institute.

Tangcharoensathien, V. and Supachutikul, A. (1997) 'Compulsory Health Insurance Development in Thailand', a paper presented at International Conference on Economics of Health Insurance in Low and Middle-Income Countries, Antwerp, Belgium, 17–18 January 1997.

CHAPTER 16

The Role of the State in the Privatisation and Corporatisation of Medical Care in Andhra Pradesh, India

K. V. NARAYANA

The objective of this chapter is to explore the role of the state in the privatisation and corporatisation of medical care and assess its impact upon public hospitals in Andhra Pradesh (AP), one of the fifteen most populous states in India. The information in this chapter is based on primary data collected by the CESS team under the aegis of a European Commission grant during 1998–99. To begin with, the size and nature of private medical care is reviewed.

THE SIZE AND NATURE OF THE PRIVATE SECTOR

There is no reliable source of data on private medical care in India as there is no compulsory registration of healthcare institutions with any public or professional agency. However, periodic surveys, on the utilisation of medical care and on household expenditure on health, indicate the predominance of private provision in the healthcare system. The forty-second and fifty-second rounds (in 1986–87 and 1995–96 respectively) of the National Sample Surveys (NSS) provide state-wise estimates on the share of private and public sectors in the provision of medical care (see Table 16.1) (Government of India 1989, 1998). In 1995–96, the private sector accounted for about 55 per cent of inpatient care and 80 per cent of outpatient care in the country. The private sector had the highest percentage (77.5) of inpatient care in the rural areas of Andhra Pradesh. Similarly, the National Family Health Surveys (NFHS), 1992–93 and 1998–99, provide estimates on the type of medical attendance at the time of delivery (IIPS 1995, 2001). In 1998–99, the public and private hospitals had equal shares in institutional deliveries

TABLE 16.1 Share of private sector in medical care in India, by state, 1986–96

State	Rural		Urban	
	1986–87	1995–96	1986–87	1995–96
Inpatient				
AP	70.1	77.5	62.0	63.8
Assam	10.0	26.2	17.7	34.8
Bihar	50.1	75.3	54.3	65.4
Gujarat	51.0	67.9	40.8	63.1
Haryana	49.0	69.5	44.7	62.7
Karnataka	42.0	54.2	51.1	70.2
Kerala	56.6	59.9	44.4	61.6
MP	20.8	46.7	23.0	44.0
Maharashtra	56.4	68.8	53.8	68.2
Orissa	11.9	9.4	18.5	19.0
Punjab	52.5	60.6	51.2	72.4
Rajasthan	20.0	35.1	14.4	26.9
Tamilnadu	43.9	58.9	42.0	64.3
UP	44.6	52.9	40.8	60.2
W. Bengal	8.4	18.0	26.1	27.9
All India	40.3	54.7	39.7	56.9
Outpatient				
AP	80.0	76.7	78.0	88.5
Assam	47.0	55.0	70.4	65.1
Bihar	83.1	94.9	82.0	80.9
Gujarat	67.5	81.6	81.4	81.8
Haryana	83.1	86.6	78.3	89.9
Karnataka	63.6	68.4	68.7	81.4
Kerala	65.5	70.1	63.7	69.5
MP	67.2	74.2	68.0	80.0
Maharashtra	73.7	88.1	75.0	89.9
Orissa	47.3	62.2	52.1	67.6
Punjab	87.2	93.0	89.1	92.8
Rajasthan	43.9	59.3	42.5	59.1
Tamilnadu	63.0	69.9	64.9	75.7
UP	n.a.	95.3	83.8	89.7
W. Bengal	80.6	87.1	76.8	86.2
All India	74.4	81.8	72.9	82.6

Source: Government of India (1989, 1998)

at the national level. But in the case of AP, private hospitals accounted for about 70 per cent of institutionalised deliveries (see Table 16.2). The NSS and NFHS surveys also indicate a rapid growth of the private sector in healthcare. Between the two rounds of NSS, the share of the private sector at the national level increased by about 15 per cent in inpatient care and by 10 per cent in outpatient care. In AP, its share in inpatient care in rural areas, which was already around 70 per cent, increased to 77.5 per cent (see Table 16.1). The share of private hospitals in institutionalised deliveries in the state increased from about 58 per cent to 70 per cent.

The fiftieth round of the NSS (1993–94) provides state-wise estimates of household expenditure on healthcare (Government of India 1996). Similarly, the Reserve Bank of India (RBI) gives data on public expenditure on health services in different states. Together, these sources indicate that about 75 per cent of health expenditure in the country was financed by households (see Table 16.3) (Government of India 1996; Reserve Bank of India 1995–96).

Local surveys of medical facilities in AP also indicate the predominance of the private sector in the state. For example, a survey of private healthcare institutions in 1992–93 indicated that the private sector had 59 per cent of hospital beds in the state (Institute of Health Systems 1996). However, there are considerable regional variations and the growth of

TABLE 16.2 Share of public and private hospitals in institutional deliveries

	Private hospitals	Voluntary hospitals	Public hospitals	Total
AP				
1992–93	353	n.a.	252	605
(%)	(58.3)	n.a.	41.7	100
1998–99	396	25	141	562
(%)	(70.5)	(4.4)	(25.1)	100
India				
1992–93	5,381	n.a.	7,208	12,589
(%)	(42.7)	n.a.	(57.3)	100
1998–99	5,410	227	5,284	10,921
(%)	(49.5)	2.1	(48.4)	100

Source: IIPS (1995, 2001)

the private sector has been positively related to overall development at the district level. Another survey, undertaken by the Centre for Economic and Social Studies, confirms these trends in the size of the private sector (Narayana 1998). This survey was a comparative study of medical facilities in Eluru, Cuddapah and Mahbubnagar towns, the headquarters of West Godavari, Cuddapah and Mahbubnagar districts respectively, which are at various levels of socio-economic development. West Godavari is the most developed district and Mahbubnagar the least developed, while Cuddapah is in between.

About 75 per cent of doctors in Eluru and Cuddapah, and a little more than half (53 per cent) of them in least developed Mahbubnagar, were in the private sector (see Table 16.4). In terms of hospital beds, the government sector is still predominant in Mahbubnagar town (57 per cent) but its share was reduced to 45 per cent in Cuddapah and 40 per cent in most developed Eluru. Thus, privatisation of medical

TABLE 16.3 Per capita health expenditure and state domestic product, 1993 (Rupees)

State	House-holds	Govern-ment	Total	% of HHs in total	Health expend. as % of SDP	SDP per capita
AP	244	75	319	0.76	4.6	6,930
Assam	63	79	142	0.44	2.6	5,550
Bihar	103	51	154	0.67	4.6	3,365
Gujarat	173	83	256	0.68	2.8	9,103
Haryana	265	67	332	0.80	3.1	10,582
Karnataka	165	86	251	0.66	3.5	7,242
Kerala	266	99	365	0.73	5.6	6,547
MP	174	60	234	0.74	4.3	5,483
Maharashtra	249	87	336	0.74	2.9	11,719
Orissa	128	58	186	0.69	4.0	4,683
Punjab	370	111	481	0.77	3.7	13,112
Rajasthan	193	85	278	0.69	5.2	5,314
Tamilnadu	222	99	321	0.69	4.0	8,061
UP	228	67	295	0.77	6.1	4,808
W. Bengal	209	74	283	0.74	4.4	6,493
All India	201	79	280	0.72	3.8	7,358

Sources: Government of India (1996); Reserve Bank of India (1995–96); Government of India (1994)

care is increasing in parallel with a rises in the level of development. In all these towns, diagnostic facilities are largely concentrated in the private sector. For example, more than 80 per cent of the laboratory and X-ray technicians were in the private sector.

Although the origin of private medical care can be traced to pre-independence days, the real spurt in the growth of private hospitals has taken place mainly during the 1980s and 1990s. For instance, between 75 and 90 per cent of existing hospital beds in Eluru, Cuddapah and Mahbubnagar for example, were established during the last two decades (see Table 16.5). The growth of private diagnostic centres is an even more recent phenomenon; most of these were established only during the 1990s. The private sector accounted for a higher percentage of medical facilities in the state, but the average bed strength of private hospitals was only fifteen. About 90 per cent of the hospitals in these towns are family owned and headed by a single doctor or by doctor-couples.

TABLE 16.4 Public and private mix in medical care (%)

Item	Eluru			Cuddapah			Mahbubnagar		
	Govt	Priv.	Total	Govt	Priv.	Total	Govt	Priv.	Total
Doctors									
MBBS	22.6	77.4	100	23.9	76.1	100	47.1	52.9	100
MS	34.6	65.4	100	26.1	73.9	100	41.7	58.3	100
MD	17.2	82.8	100	29.4	70.6	100	50.0	50.0	100
Total	23.6	76.4	100	25.2	74.8	100	46.6	53.4	100
Staff									
Nurses									
Trained	45.9	54.1	100	43.9	56.1	100	71.4	28.6	100
Untrained		100.0	100		100.0	100		100.0	100
Lab. technicians	18.2	81.8	100	4.5	95.5	100	10.3	89.7	100
X-ray technicians	14.7	85.3	100	17.6	82.4	100	16.7	83.3	100
Beds	40.0	60.0	100	44.8	55.2	100	56.6	43.4	100
Inpatients	49.4	50.6	100	50.4	49.6	100	55.3	44.7	100
Outpatients per day	39.7	60.3	100	31.7	68.3	100	46.7	53.3	100

Source: Narayana (1998)

TABLE 16.5 Establishment of private medical facilities

Period	Hospitals						Diagnostic Centres		
	Eluru		Cuddapah		Mahbubnagar		Eluru	Cuddaph	Mahbub-nagar
	Hospitals	Beds	Hospitals	Beds	Hospitals	Beds			
1950s	4	65	1	4				1	
1960s	3	72	1	50					
1970s			5	86	1	25		1	2
Sub total	7	137	7	140	1	25		2	2
1980s	12	215	7	103	6	101	7	8	2
1990s	15	157	15	191	3	39	17	41	11
Total	34	509	29	434	10	165	24	51	15
Percentages									
1950s	11.8	12.8	3.4	0.9				2.0	
1960s	8.8	14.1	3.4	11.5					
1970s			17.2	19.8	10.0	15.2		2.0	13.3
Sub total	20.6	26.9	24.0	32.2	10.0	15.2		4.0	13.3
1980s	35.3	42.2	24.1	23.7	60.0	61.2	29.2	15.7	13.3
1990s	44.1	30.8	51.7	44.0	30.0	23.6	70.8	80.4	73.3
Total	100	100	100	100	100	100	100	100	100

Source: Narayana (1998)

THE CORPORATISATION OF MEDICAL CARE

The growing capital intensity of medical technology, which requires substantial investments, is encouraging the growth of corporate hospitals. Private nursing homes run by individual doctors are not in a position to generate such huge investments. The corporate hospitals, therefore, are mobilising resources through promoters' share capital, borrowing from financial institutions and the share market. The state has also played a crucial role by offering various incentives to these entities.

The corporate phenomenon in Andhra Pradesh state began with the establishment of the Apollo Hospital in 1981, which was set up by non-resident Indian (NRI) doctors from the USA. The state government played an active role by providing government land at a highly subsidised rate. The corporate hospitals are usually established by NRI or local doctors and business families. The management of all these hospitals is in the hands of the respective families. There are no studies yet on the precise size and nature of the corporate sector in healthcare in the state. In 2001 there were six major corporate hospitals in Hyderabad City, the state capital. However, in recent years the corporate phenomenon has been spreading fast through acquisition of small private hospitals. For instance, the Apollo hospital has acquired four private hospitals located in different parts of Hyderabad. This is basically intended to widen the catchment area and to ensure a steady flow of patients for its main super-speciality hospital. The corporate hospitals are spreading their network by also providing franchises to small diagnostic centres, special clinics and pharmaceutical stores, thereby filling a clear vacuum in health service provision. Corporate hospitals have also sprung up in agriculturally prosperous towns such as Vijayawada and in the port city of Vishakapatnam.

In addition, there is also a trend towards trans-nationalisation of corporate hospitals. For example, the Apollo hospital has been negotiating with Parkway Health Group from Singapore to set up a joint-venture company in order to undertake management of hospitals in the region (Kai Lit 2001). While Parkway Health Group would undertake responsibility for securing the contracts, Apollo would supply doctors, nurses, engineers and so on to staff these hospitals. The basic objective is to take advantage of the value of India's human capital at the expense of providing the majority access to health services.

FACTORS BEHIND THE RAPID GROWTH OF THE PRIVATE SECTOR

In India there have been no explicit policies regarding the private sector in healthcare. However, the central as well as some state governments have created the necessary conditions and extended various financial incentives for its development and expansion. As a consequence, throughout the country the growth of private medical care has been haphazard and unregulated. In no way is it an integral component of the healthcare system. However, there appears to have been a marked shift in government health policy during the 1980s. By this time the state had absolved itself from meeting the health sector targets on its own and begun emphasising the role of the private sector and non-government organisations as service providers (Government of India 1983). The role of the state in promoting the rapid privatisation and corporatisation of health services is identified in the following sections.

Stagnation in the expansion of public hospitals The expansion of facilities in the public sector has not kept pace with the increase in population, and the excess strain on the public healthcare system has led to a decline in quality. The availability of hospital beds in the public sector in Andhra Pradesh declined from 6.2 beds per 10,000 population in 1961 to 4.8 beds during the 1970s and 1980s (Government of AP [various years]). It improved slightly to 5.1 beds per 10,000 population in the 1990s, but remains below the Planning Commission norm of 6.7 beds per 10,000 population (Government of India 1985).

The scarcity of resources in the public sector has been worsened by the lopsided distribution of medical facilities and public expenditure between the primary, secondary and tertiary hospitals. Keeping in view the inpatient load at different levels, the Planning Commission had (in the seventh Five-year Plan 1985–1990) recommended that 70 per cent of the total hospital beds in the public sector should be located at the secondary level and 15 per cent each at the primary and the tertiary hospitals (Government of India 1985). However, currently, secondary level hospitals have only 30 per cent.

A shift in internal allocations during the 1980s in favour of primary care was held responsible for the scarcity of resources at the secondary level. The share of primary health centres in the health budget increased from 15 per cent in the fifth Five-year Plan to nearly 30 per cent in the 1990s (Narayana and Nagi Reddy 1993). Moreover, there was a continuous increase in the share of salaries in the hospital budgets, from about 52 per cent in 1974 to 80 per cent in the 1990s (Narayana and Reddy 1993), leaving only meagre resources for the supply of materials. A decline in allocations to medical supplies also contributed to faster degeneration in the quality of treatment in the public hospitals.

A relatively low percentage of hospital beds at the secondary hospitals, along with overall decline in the per capita availability of hospital beds in the public sector, facilitated the growth of small private hospitals in the urban centres in the state. The shortfall in the quantity as well as quality of public health services provided tremendous opportunities for the growth of the private sector.

Impact of structural adjustment programmes The implementation of structural adjustment programmes (SAPs) during the 1990s has further worsened the scarcity of resources in the health sector. At constant (1993–94) prices, the per capita public expenditure on healthcare was about Rs. 58 during the fifth Five-year Plan (1974–78), and it reached Rs. 88 in the seventh Five-year Plan (1985–90) (see Table 16.6). However, with the initiation of SAPs in India (1991), it declined to Rs. 78 under the eighth Five-year Plan. When contrasted with economic services, social sector expenditure experienced a steep fall in public expenditure

TABLE 16.6 Per capita and public expenditure in AP (1993–94 prices) (Rupees)

Year	Health	Social	Eco-nomic	Total	SDP	% of health in SDP
	1	2	3	4	5	1/5
5th Plan (1974–78)	58	308	386	899	5,341	1.09
1979–80	67	405	484	1,135	5,545	1.20
6th Plan (1980–84)	77	502	468	1,243	6,038	1.28
7th Plan (1985–89)	88	575	581	1,516	6,569	1.34
1990–91	77	491	510	1,359	7,097	1.09
1991–92	79	462	490	1,313	7,135	1.11
8th Plan (1992–96)	78	510	556	1,485	7,786	1.00
1997–98	83	533	499	1,500	8,246	1.00
1998–99	85	603	479	1,611	9,118	0.93

Source: Government of AP, Budget Estimates, Detailed Demands of Grants; Bureau of Economics and Statistics (AP), estimates of SDP

throughout the states. Within social expenditure, the decline was highest in the case of healthcare. The share of the health sector in the SDP (Table 16.6) increased from 1.1 per cent in the fifth plan to 1.3 per cent in the seventh plan. But with the beginning of the SAPs in the 1990s it declined to 1 per cent in the eighth Five-year Plan.

The structural adjustment policy has also had an adverse impact upon internal priorities in the health sector. There was a decline in the allocations for the prevention and control of communicable diseases, financed mostly by the central government. Since the SAPs were promoted by the centre, the initial adverse impact has been on public health services as a whole.

Government doctors in private practice In many towns the origins of private medical care may be traced to the private practice of government doctors. Most of the doctors in the government (public) hospitals tended to be from the local community and it was quite common for them to resign or take long leave and continue their private practice if they were transferred to other places. In the late 1990s, about 65 per cent of doctors at the government hospital in Mahbubnagar were from the local community (Narayana and ISI 2000). Hence, to a large extent, the establishment of public hospitals appears to have actively encouraged the growth of private medical care.

The role of public hospitals in the origin and growth of private medical care can be better understood by the fact that one-half of the private hospitals in Mahbubnagar town belonged to doctors who were or continued to work in government service. The first private hospital in the town was started in 1979 by a doctor while still in government service. While four private hospitals were being run by doctors who had resigned from government service and one by a retired government doctor, three other private hospitals were run by the doctors who continued working in the government district hospital. Altogether, there were thirty-five doctors in the district government hospital and thirty-three of them had private practices in different forms, despite a government ban on private practice. While four of them had their own hospitals, all others had private clinics. In addition, some of them, including the hospital superintendent, served as consultants in the private hospitals. The government doctors had a major share in two advanced diagnostic centres, which accounted for a high proportion of the overall diagnostic tests in the town.

In Eluru town, too, government doctors played a crucial role in the development of the private sector. The origin of the private sector in Eluru goes back to the 1940s when there were three private hospitals with twenty-one beds. One of these, with a bed strength of fifteen, was owned by a government doctor who was working as a district medical officer. In 2001 there were forty-two private hospitals in Eluru, nine of which were started by doctors who resigned from government service and two by doctors after retirement from the government hospitals. The government doctors accounted for about 15 per cent of private clinics and outpatients in Eluru and about 35 per cent of private clinics and outpatients in Mahbubnagar.

Public investment in medical education Public investment in free medical education has created a vast network of medical professionals, who have provided a basis for the expansion of the private sector. According to private doctors in Eluru and Mahbubnagar, one of the main reasons for the growth of the private sector in their towns was lack of employment opportunities for local medical graduates in the government hospitals.

Lack of regulation The absence of government or any other regulations on quality and pricing has turned medical care into a lucrative business, as well as a very attractive outlet for private investment. About 75 per cent of expenditure on medical care in the state is financed from out-of-pocket expenditure by households under the fee-for-service system in the private sector. In view of this and in the absence of any regulation, supplier-induced demand and profit maximisation have become dominant aspects of private medical care. This is amply illustrated by the use of excessive diagnostic tests and unnecessary surgical procedures. More than 50 per cent of deliveries in the private hospitals, for example, are performed through Caesarean section. These rates are very high in comparison to international ones, even in those countries at similar levels of development.

Senior doctors in Eluru and Mahbubnagar towns reported as widespread the practice of doctors receiving commissions from the diagnostic centres and of hospitals paying commissions to quacks (unqualified local practitioners) for mobilising patients for hysterectomy, appendicitis and other surgeries. The problem of commissions has become so widespread that, at a recent press conference, the state unit of the Indian Medical Association warned doctors against such practices. The State Legislative Assembly's House Committee on Corporate Hospitals also recognised this problem and suggested the preparation of clinical manuals to curb the practice of unnecessary investigations and excess treatment in the private sector (APLA 1996).

FINANCIAL INCENTIVES FOR THE PRIVATE SECTOR

The privatisation and corporatisation of medical care has been further encouraged by the central and state governments by offering tax exemptions, subsidies and liberal lending from public financial institutions. As part of the liberalisation programme which began in the 1980s, customs duties on imports of medical equipment were reduced by the central government from more than 100 per cent to 40 per cent. In addition, customs duties were exempted if hospitals were willing to provide free treatment to at least 40 per cent of outpatients and reserve 10 per cent of beds for free treatment for the poor, as well as providing services to the general public at 'reasonable' rates (APLA 1996). The state governments also extended special benefits, such as the allotment of government land for free or at subsidised rates. For instance, a corporate hospital in Hyderabad was given 30 acres of valuable government land at a high subsidised rate on condition it reserved an additional 15 per cent of beds for the poor.

Another major incentive was to attribute 'industry status' to the provision of medical care, thus making it possible for the private sector to obtain easy loans from public financial institutions. In addition, the private corporate hospitals received substantial amounts of public funds in the form of reimbursements from public sector undertakings, the state and the central government for treating the families of employees, members of legislative bodies, freedom fighters and so on. Another major source of revenue of growing interest is inflated and fraudulent claims from the public insurance companies under various medical insurance schemes.

In 1995 the Andhra Pradesh Legislative Assembly (APLA) appointed a House Committee to find out whether or not the corporate hospitals and other such beneficiaries in the state honoured the conditions imposed for granting tax concessions, exemptions and other benefits. The study also covered experiences with corporate hospitals in Bangalore, Chennai, Mumbai and New Delhi. The committee found that most of the corporate hospitals which had obtained customs duty exemption were not treating any poor patients free of cost (APLA 1996). It was also observed that these hospitals were not maintaining any records for inspection by the government. The state government was negligent about implementing the aforementioned conditions upon the private hospitals. The committee observed:

> there was no check as to whether the Apollo Hospital was adhering to the condition of 15 percent of the beds to be reserved to the poor for free treatment. All these years there was no check and no one was made responsible. The Committee was at a loss to understand the failure of the State Government in implementing the conditions. (APLA 1996: 3)

It seemed neither the private hospitals nor the government were serious about the provision of free services to the poor. One may only conclude that this was an excuse to provide benefits to the private sector, as a form of public subsidy.

As a result of popular pressure, the Union Government withdrew exemption from customs duty and introduced a flat rate of 15 per cent on all imported hospital equipment (APLA 1996). However, there are still proposals by the state government to reintroduce total exemption from customs duty for corporate hospitals and private medical colleges, if they adopt two primary health centres (PHCs) each and provide hi-tech treatment free of charge. In return, the state government would recommend them to the centre for exemption from customs duty on medical equipment. Such a proposal illustrates a total disregard at the state level for past experience and evidence of abuse within the incentive system, and continues to neglect the findings of the APLA. Thus, public sector economic support to private sector entities continues in accordance with reforms of the health sector in India, as advocated by the World Bank.

The World Bank and privatisation in Andhra Pradesh   Andhra Pradesh is the first state in India where the World Bank introduced its reform-based lending to the health sector in 1996. Two major reform projects are being implemented, at the secondary (First Referral Project) and primary healthcare levels with a total lending of US $195 million. The objective is to develop a replicative state model that would subsequently be used to reorient the health systems in other states in India (World Bank 1994). The main reason for selecting AP was the existence of an autonomous public organisation (Andhra Pradesh Vaidya Vignyana Parishad – APVVP) to manage secondary-level hospitals in the state. 'This type of organisation … is innovative in the health sector. And it is believed that a corporate vehicle provides significant potential for improved efficiency in contracting, as well as in providing non-govern-mental participation in the health sector' (World Bank 1994: 71).

Further encouragement for expansion of the private sector seems to be the main motivation of the project. It assumes that reforms at the secondary level 'would encourage a greater participation of the private sector in healthcare through improved functioning of referral mechanisms' (World Bank 1994). The project proposes incentives, financial schemes and training to private providers in order to encourage them in case-finding, referral treatment and the monitoring of public health problems. To safeguard the interests of private hospitals the project insists on restricting the range of services to be provided by the public sector. For instance, in deciding the range and level of services at the secondary-level hospitals, the 'availability and accessibility of alternate sources of equivalent services' is to be taken into account (World Bank 1994: 111).

Similarly, at the primary healthcare level, the project criticises the existing population norm for locating primary health centres (PHCs) and proposes to take into account the availability of private services. The project discourages upgrading of PHCs in places where private healthcare facilities exist. It aims at upgrading 500 PHCs to provide enhanced service packages, and removing the doctors from the re-maining 835 PHCs and running them with the help of paramedical personnel. This would widen the scope for the private market at the primary care level. At the tertiary level also, the World Bank advocates a key role for the private sector. Instead of increasing the size of the health budget to meet the norms at the secondary level, it imposes the condition of transferring resources from tertiary to secondary hospitals in order to change the existing ratio in budgetary allocations from 51:49 to 67:33 (World Bank 1994). This can only act as further encouragement to the expansion of private capacity, without clear evidence of need.

Apart from encouraging the private sector, the World Bank projects in India introduce market mechanisms to improve the quality of care in the public sector, through the introduction of user charges and con-tracting out of support services in the secondary hospitals. While this has been implemented throughout the world, there is little evidence of positive results or of improvement of quality in any region (Sen and Koivusalo 1998).

Transfer of facilities to the private sector The entry of the World Bank is also associated with other measures aimed at encouraging the private sector in the state. For instance, the state government has initiated a pilot project to promote public–private partnership, by transferring a government primary health centre (PHC) to Messrs Masons and Messrs Access Associates (*Indian Express*, 3 February 2000). It is envisaged that the private partner would provide medical care in return for payment by the public partner. Similarly, a project on tele-medicine has been launched through provision of a loan to a private agency to set up a 200-bed hospital. Using a sophisticated information network, the hospital would be linked to about 150 PHCs. If the project is successful, it will be extended to the rest of the state.

The state government has launched a tele-medicine project at the secondary level also, linking the district hospital at Mahbubnagar with Care Hospital, a corporate hospital in Hyderabad. The Care Foundation developed the project in collaboration with some other private companies and the state government. The tele-medicine project was undertaken on the grounds that secondary-level hospitals are not able to attract specialists. The assumption is that tele-medicine will extend coverage. Its efficacy in a largely poor and low literacy population is questionable.

IMPACT OF THE PRIVATE SECTOR ON PUBLIC HOSPITALS

Sometimes state patronage of the private sector is justified on the grounds that it will reduce pressure on government hospitals. In reality, private hospitals are replacing, rather than complementing public hospitals, by attracting resources and specialists away from the government hospitals.

Increase in inequalities   The reimbursement policies of the government have resulted in the shifting of the political and bureaucratic elite from public to corporate hospitals. Overcrowding and lack of personal attention in the government hospitals have driven out the middle classes to the small private hospitals. Government doctors also encourage the diversion of well-to-do patients to the private hospitals with which they have consultancy arrangements. As a result, the government hospitals are used mostly by the poor and are often deprived of critical skills during times of need. The fact that public hospitals are used by the majority of the (poor) population is clearly manifested by the lack of demand for paying wards in the public hospitals (Narayana and ISI 2000). The occupancy in the paying wards of government tertiary hospitals has been much reduced in Hyderabad following the arrival of the corporate hospitals (Prasad 1995). It is evident that the arrival of the private sector has created a social dichotomy in medical care and further widened the inequalities in access to healthcare.

Lack of patronage for public hospitals   The social dichotomy in utilisation of public and private hospitals leads to further neglect of the former and encouragement to the latter. Public hospitals are facing unfair competition in mobilising resources since the policy-makers (politicians and bureaucrats) are more interested in extending state patronage to the private, mainly corporate, hospitals. The government hospitals are neglected in resource allocation and day-to-day maintenance.

Lure of specialists   The popularity and use of private hospitals depend mainly on the reputation of individual doctors (Prasad 1995). As a result, there is severe competition between the corporate hospitals to attract reputable specialists with offers of higher salaries and better service conditions. Increasingly, specialists are being lured away from government teaching hospitals. The shortage of specialists has a further adverse impact on the functioning of government hospitals.

While corporate hospitals offer attractive service conditions to the senior specialists, the junior doctors, nurses and other staff have low salaries, long working hours and no job security. Hence, the junior doctors prefer government service. Once they have enough experience, the private hospitals lure them with better service conditions. The government sector has thus become a cheap source of well-trained specialists for corporate hospitals.

Transfer of critical cases   Public hospitals are used by the private sector hospitals for dumping unwanted cases. The serious cases are transferred to government hospitals to avoid medico-legal problems and to save their reputation. Government doctors in Eluru and Mahbubnagar complained about the shifting of complicated cases by the private hospitals. The private doctors justified such transfers of critical cases on the grounds that the government hospitals do not come under the Consumer Protection Act (CPA), 1986. As a consequence, the public hospitals have an adverse case mix, which puts extra strain on their meagre resources.

Growing capital intensity   Duty-free imports of medical equipment and liberal loans have reinforced the capital intensity and added to the cost escalation in the medical sector. The growing competition within the private sector also encourages excess investments in diagnostic and other equipment to attract patients. An unregulated market has thus resulted in an over-supply of medical facilities and excess treatment in the urban centres.

CONCLUSION

Although there is no reliable source of data on the private sector in medical care anywhere in India, the household surveys at national level and local surveys on medical facilities indicate an increasing predomin-ance of the private sector in medical care. The state is encouraging privatisation and corporatisation of medical care, directly by offering various financial incentives, and indirectly by neglecting public hospitals. The growth of private medical care has had an adverse impact on public hospitals and created social segregation and dichotomy in access to medical care.

REFERENCES

APLA (Andhra Pradesh Legislative Assembly) (1996) *Report of House Committee on Corporate Hospitals*, Hyderabad: Andhra Pradesh Legislature Secretariat.

Government of Andhra Pradesh (various years) *Statistical Abstract of Andhra Pradesh*, Hyderabad: State of Andhra Pradesh.

Government of India (1983) *Health Policy Statement*, New Delhi: Ministry of Health and Family Welfare.

— (1985) *Seventh Five-Year Plan*, New Delhi: Planning Commission.

— (1989) 'Morbidity and utilisation of medical services', 42nd round, *National Sample Survey No. 364*, New Delhi: Central Statistical Organisation.

— (1994) *Estimates of State Domestic Product*, New Delhi: Central Statistical Organisation.

— (1996) 'Estimates of household expenditure', 50th round, *National Sample Survey*, New Delhi: Central Statistical Organisation.

— (1998) 'Morbidity and utilisation of medical services', 52nd Round, *National Sample Survey*, New Delhi: Central Statistical Organisation.

IIPS (International Institute of Population Studies) (1995) *National Family and Health Surveys, 1992–1993*, Mumbai: IIPS.

— (2001) *National Family and Health Surveys, 1998–1999*, Mumbai: IIPS.

Institute of Health Systems (1996) *AP Health Institutions Database: Private and Public, Technical Note* (Working Paper No. XI, 1–27), Hyderabad: Institute of Health Systems.

Kai Lit, P. (2001) 'Corporate healthcare, Singapore: making house calls', *Far Eastern Economic Review*, 15 February.

Narayana, K. V. (1998) *Public and Private Mix in the Medical Care in AP* (Report), Hyderabad: Centre for Economic and Social Studies.

Narayana, K. V. and ISI (Indian Statistical Institute) (2000) *Impact of Health Sector Reforms on Hospital Services in AP*, Report submitted by Centre for Economic and Social Studies, Hyderabad, to Indian Statistical Institute, Calcutta, as part of European Commission project on Health Sector Reforms: Impact on Vulnerable Groups in Three Indian States.

Narayana, K. V. and Nagi Reddy, C. P. (1993) *Public Expenditure on Health in Andhra Pradesh* (Report), Hyderabad: Centre for Economic and Social Studies.

Prasad, S. (1995) *Urban Health Care*, Delhi: Delta Publishing House.

Reserve Bank of India (1995–96) *Finances of the State Governments*, Mumbai: Reserve Bank of India.

Sen, K. and Koivusalo, M. (1998) 'Health care reforms and developing countries – a critical overview', *International Journal of Health Planning and Management*, 13, 199–215.

World Bank (1994) *Staff Appraisal Report, India, AP First Referral Health Project* (Report No. 13402-IN), Washington, DC: World Bank.

About the Contributors

Hixinio Beiras Cal has been a cardiologist in the General Hospital in Vigo since 1981. He has been a member of FADSP since 1982 and is at present the president of the AGDSP, the Galician Regional Association member of FADSP. He has been the speaker at the Regional Parliament during the People's Legislation Initiative debate.

Chan Chee Khoon is an epidemiologist and health policy analyst based at University Sains Malaysia. He is a co-founder and coordinator of the Citizens' Health Initiative which drafted *A Citizens' Health Manifesto for Malaysia*. Elected to a two-year term on the executive board of the International Society for Equity in Health, his current research interests include emerging and re-emerging infectious disease, environment and development, and healthcare financing policy in Malaysia.

David Hall is director of the Public Services International Research Unit (PSIRU) at the University of Greenwich, managing PSIRU's extensive database on privatisation and the restructuring of public sevices worldwide. He writes and contributes to reports on a range of public service issues. He has been doing research for trade unions since 1975, on public services, public finances and privatisation, and has addressed many meeting and seminars around the world. He has written a book on labour law and another on public expenditure.

Meri Koivusalo is senior research fellow in the Globalisation and Social Policy Programme in the National Research and Development Council for Welfare and Health in Finland. She has a background of active involvement in social movements. Her area of work covers international health, environmental epidemiology, population and development issues.

Hans Maarse holds the Chair in Health Policy at the Faculty of Health Sciences at the University of Maastricht. He has a special interest in international comparative health systems analysis and is currently investigating health systems reform in Europe. He is also conducting an international and comparative research project on privatisation in health care, its dynamics and potential implications for equity, efficiency and freedom of choice.

K. V. Narayana After taking a Master's degree in economics Dr Narayana gained an MPhil at the Centre of Social Medicine and Community Health at Jawaharlal Nehru University in Delhi. He then went to the School of Public Health, Johns Hopkins University in the USA for post-doctoral training, his areas of focus including healthcare financing, medical health delivery and intersectoral linkages in health status. He has recently published a book entitled *Health and Development and Inter-sectoral Linkages in India* and is also preparing a co-authored book with Dr Sen, *The Corporatisation of Public Health: Transformations in Secondary Care in India.* He is currently an associate professor at the Centre for Economic and Social Studies (CESS) a public sector research institute at Begumpet, Hyderabad.

Sanguann Nitayarumphong is director of the Health Care Reform Project at the Ministry of Public Health in Thailand. After graduating in medicine from Mahidol University in 1976, he obtained a Master's in Public Health Development from the Prince Leopold Institute of Tropical Medicine in Antwerp, Belgium. Since 1987 he has been working on issues of health policy and planning. He has published several articles and books on health policy and research and was awarded the Outstanding Rural Doctor of the Year from the Faculty of Medicine at Mahidol in 1985. In 1996 he was awarded a fellowship of the Royal College of Physicians from the FRCP, University of Edinburgh. He is currently vice-chairman of the International Alliance for Health Policy/System Research and is involved in many functions at the Commission of European Community and USAID. His current interests are health insurance and healthcare reform.

Supasit Pannarunothai is associate professor in community medicine at the Faculty of Medicine of Naresuan University, Thailand. He had been working with the Ministry of Public Health, Thailand, for more than twenty years prior to joining the faculty. After completing his PhD from the London School of Hygiene and Tropical Medicine, his main research interest has focused on equity in health and diagnostic related groups in patient classification systems to achieve equity and efficiency in the delivery of healthcare. He heads the Centre for Health Equity Monitoring based in Bangkok.

Aggie Paulus was born in 1967 and studied economics at the University of Maastricht. From 1990 to 1996 she held different positions in the Faculty of Economics and Business Administration of the University of Maastricht, obtaining a PhD in economics in 1995. Since April 1996, she has worked in the Faculty of Health Sciences. Her main research interests are health economics, the economics of integrated care, the international comparison of health systems, and cross-border care.

Imrana Qadeer is Professor at the Centre for Social Medicine and Community Health, Jawaharlal Nehru University, New Delhi, India. A qualified doctor, she works on issues at the interface of medicine and society. Her areas of interest include the organisation of public services, the political economy of health, the health of workers and women in India, and research methodology. Currently Professor Qadeer is involved with the planning efforts of both governmental and grassroots organisations.

Marciano Sanchez Bayle has been a paediatric nephrologist since 1977 at the Niño Jesús Hospital, Madrid. He is also a recognised expert on Spanish health-care policies, having published numerous papers and several books on the subject. He is a member of the Advisory Council and executive board of the International Association of Health Policy, and was one of the founders, in 1981, of the Federación de Asociaciones para la Defensa de la Sanidad Pública (FADSP), of which he is currently the president.

Félix Sansó Soberats graduated in 1990 and later specialised in family medicine in Cuba. He is an assistant professor at the Havana Higher Institute of Medical Sciences. He practised medicine in Cuba's rural areas until 1994, since when he has been based in Havana. He is a member of the Cuban Society on Family Medicine, the Family Medicine National (Cuban) Group, the National School of Public Health (Family Medicine Division) and of the National Formulary Commission. He was a member of the Cuban Medical Emergency Brigade in El Salvador (Dengue epidemic), September to December 2000. He has recently contributed an essay on the medical and ethical challenges facing primary healthcare in Cuba to the book *Bioethics from a Cuban Perspective*.

Kasturi Sen is based at the Department of Public Health and Primary Care at the University of Cambridge. Trained as a social scientist, she has a background in demography economics and public health epidemiology. Her main interests are in the comparative analysis of health and welfare in the context of structural adjustment. For the past twenty years she has been involved in research on multidimensional studies into the functioning of health systems with a special interest in the finance and organisation of public provision. As part of an international team, she has recently completed a major population-based study on the potential health effects of economic reforms (SAPs) in three states in India (1997–2001). The focus of her research is linked to policy and practice in international health and development.

Sarah Sexton works with the Corner House, a UK-based research and solid-arity group focusing on social and environmental issues, areas in which she has worked as an editor and researcher for the last fifteen years. Her chapter draws upon her recent work linking international trade, health and the environment.

Jean Shaoul is a senior lecturer in the School of Accounting and Finance at Manchester University where she concentrates on public and business policy and finance. She uses financial information derived from company accounts and other grey literature to evaluate public policy decisions from a public interest perspective. She has written widely for both academic and more popular forums on privatisation, outsourcing and the facilities management industry, the corporatisation of public services, the NHS, the Private Finance Initiative in the NHS and in education, the Public Private Partnership for London Underground, public expenditure, the financial context of the BSE crisis and food safety regulation. She is also a regular contributor to the World Socialist Website www.wsws.org

Francesco Taroni is the director of the Agenzia Sanitaria Regionale in Bologna. The agency is responsible for monitoring health services in the Regione Emilia Romagna and assessing the extent to which equity, efficiency and effectiveness are achieved; developing accreditation criteria for health services; organising a programme for guidelines development and implementation; and defining essential levels of care which must be assured to its citizens. Dr Taroni has served as a member of the Italian National Health Council and was director of the Italian National Agency for Regional Health Care Services and later director of research in Epidemiology and Bio-statistics at Istituto Superiore di Sanita. He has been a visiting professor in statistical methods for quality care evaluation at the La Sapienza University, Rome, and in clinical epidemiology at the University of Bologna. He is also a visiting research scientist in medical education and healthcare at Jefferson Medical College, Thomas Jefferson University, PA. Dr Taroni graduated in medicine and surgery at the University of Bologna in 1975.

Claudia Maria de Rezende Travassos works at the Oswaldo Cruz Foundation, a health research institution which also provides postgraduate training in public health. Her main areas of interest are health information and healthcare service research, with an emphasis on quality of care (performance indicator, outcome research and risk adjustment); social inequalities in healthcare; and healthcare service information systems. Recently, she has co-authored critical reviews of the WHO's *World Health Report 2000*.

Steffie Woolhandler grew up in Shreveport, Louisana. She practises primary care internal medicine at Cambridge City Hospital and teaches at Harvard where she is an associate professor of Medicine. In 1986 she co-founded Physicians for National Health Program which advocates a single payer system of national health insurance for the USA. She lives with her family in Cambridge, Massachusetts.

Index